THE SYSTEM WORKED

THE SYSTEM
WORKED

*HOW THE WORLD STOPPED
ANOTHER GREAT DEPRESSION*

DANIEL W. DREZNER

OXFORD
UNIVERSITY PRESS

OXFORD
UNIVERSITY PRESS

Oxford University Press is a department of the University of Oxford.
It furthers the University's objective of excellence in research,
scholarship, and education by publishing worldwide.

Oxford   New York
Auckland   Cape Town   Dar es Salaam   Hong Kong   Karachi
Kuala Lumpur   Madrid   Melbourne   Mexico City   Nairobi
New Delhi   Shanghai   Taipei   Toronto

With offices in
Argentina   Austria   Brazil   Chile   Czech Republic   France   Greece
Guatemala   Hungary   Italy   Japan   Poland   Portugal   Singapore
South Korea   Switzerland   Thailand   Turkey   Ukraine   Vietnam

Oxford is a registered trademark of Oxford University Press
in the UK and certain other countries.

Published in the United States of America by
Oxford University Press
198 Madison Avenue, New York, NY 10016

© Oxford University Press 2014

Library of Congress Cataloging-in-Publication Data
Drezner, Daniel W.
The system worked : how the world stopped another great depression / Daniel W. Drezner.
pages cm
ISBN 978–0–19–537384–4 (hardback : alk. paper)   1. Global Financial Crisis,
2008–2009.   2. Financial crises—Government policy.   3. Finance—Government
policy.   4. Recessions—21st century.   5. Economic history—21st century.   I. Title.
HB3722.D74 2014
330.9'0511—dc23
2013044640

1 3 5 7 9 8 6 4 2
Printed in the United States of America
on acid-free paper

This book is dedicated to Stephen D. Krasner, the Graham H. Stuart Professor of Political Science at Stanford University, a giant in the study of global political economy and, some moons ago, my dissertation adviser. In my professional career, Steve pushed me to think more rigorously and systematically about power than any other colleague. It's payback time.

CONTENTS

———⟨⟩———

ACKNOWLEDGMENTS

This book has been an intellectual exercise in trying to figure out why I was so wrong six years ago and why so many other smart analysts have been so wrong since.

Back then, I had a pretty good idea for a book—it would be a clarion call about the sclerotic state of multilateral economic institutions. In it, I would sagely observe that the last major burst of international institutional creation had been in the late 1940s and point out that the distribution of power looked a wee bit different in the twenty-first century. If current mismatches between global governance structures and the distribution of power were allowed to fester, then those structures would rest upon very shaky foundations. The rise of the BRICs clearly mandated such reforms. I would warn that although reforming global governance was a thankless task, failure to take action would leave these institutions ill-equipped for a severe global shock. Proactive steps would be necessary to prevent the global economy from experiencing the 1930s all over again.

Before I could start writing in earnest, however, Lehman Brothers went bankrupt, the federal government bailed out AIG, and the Reserve Primary Fund broke the buck. My warning was overtaken by events; the severe global shock had happened.

It was impossible to write a book on global economic governance when the global economy seemed to be melting down in real time. So, I stepped away and wrote on some issues that were not changing at the speed of light. I paid attention to the 2008 financial crisis and, like most other commentators, took a jaundiced view of how the global political economy was performing. I also got distracted by zombies for a spell.

By the time I doubled back to re-examine the state of global economic governance, I noticed two odd trends. First, the closer I looked at the performance of "the system," the clearer it became that the meltdown I had expected had not come to pass. Second, most other observers nonetheless remained deeply pessimistic about the functioning of the global political economy. Indeed, book after book on the financial crisis was arguing the exact opposite thesis to my initial impressions. I could not blame these commentators for being so pessimistic because I had felt that way too when the crisis began. Nevertheless, I had come to believe that I was wrong then and that they are wrong now.

I have racked up numerous debts during the thinking and writing of *The System Worked*. I am particularly grateful to David McBride at Oxford University Press. He was supportive of my original book proposal and even more enthusiastic about what the book turned out to be. Most important, Dave displayed superhuman patience while I sorted out exactly what I wanted to write. Sarah Rosenthal, Molly Morrison, and Ginny Faber also made superhuman efforts to convert my scribblings into this attractive-looking text you're now reading.

I also thank the Fletcher School of Law and Diplomacy and the Michael and Andrea Leven Foundation for enabling me to take a sabbatical year to focus on this project. I am particularly grateful to Peter Uvin and Stephen Bosworth, who were, respectively, the academic dean and dean of the Fletcher School during the start of this project. They provided unstinting support. I will assume that it is simply a coincidence that both leaders left Fletcher before I finished my manuscript. Similarly, I thank Fletcher's current dean, James Stavridis, and academic dean, Ian Johnstone. My other colleagues at Fletcher—particularly Kelly Sims Gallagher, Nancy Hite, Zeynep Bulutgil, Jenny Aker, Jeswald Salacuse, Joel Trachtman, and Michael Klein—made working on this project more bearable. My staff assistants, Karen Mollung and

Paulette Folkins, made the trains run on time. My research assistants at Fletcher—Dahlia Shaham, Maggie Riden, and Rebecca Perlman—were also extremely helpful in chasing down answers to some of the more abstruse questions I asked them. Estefania Marchan and Aaron Melaas did outstanding jobs of poring over the manuscript with fresh pairs of eyes, offering valuable perspectives and some last-minute research assistance. Martin Weiss at the Congressional Research Service and Amare Bekele at UNCTAD provided enlightenment when it was needed on some very obscure questions involving IMF quotas and bilateral investment treaties.

During my sabbatical year, Beth Simmons was kind enough to lend me an office at Harvard University's Weatherhead Center for International Affairs. Thanks to her, Jeffry Frieden, Bob Ross, Prerna Singh, and Dustin Tingley for making me feel at home there.

As I've wrestled with these issues, I've been the beneficiary of a rolling conversation with international political economy and international relations scholars across an array of venues—coffee breaks, small conferences, large meetings, and invited talks. I thank Kate McNamara, Walter Mattli, Duncan Snidal, Henry Farrell, Layna Mosley, Christina Davis, Mark Blyth, Courtney Fung, Bruce Jones, Abe Newman, Leslie Johns, Miles Kahler, Jonathan Kirshner, Michael Mastanduno, Manjari Chatterjee Miller, G. John Ikenberry, A. Iain Johnston, Carla Norrlof, Zhu Feng, Robert Ross, Pan Rui, David Victor, Steven Bernstein, Brad Glosserman, Peter Gourevitch, Todd Hall, Alan Alexandroff, James Lindsay, John Mueller, Matthias Matthijs, Eric Rauchway, Kevin Gallagher, Kevin H. O'Rourke, Randall Schweller, David Andrew Singer, Alexander Thompson, Tom Wright, and Charli Carpenter for their thoughts and feedback.

Portions of this book were presented at the School of Advanced International Studies at Johns Hopkins University, CSIS Pacific Forum, University of Toronto, Nuffield College, The Ohio State University, Boston College, Chicago Council on Global Affairs, and Council on Foreign Relations. I thank the attendees at these talks for their hospitality and their critical feedback—not necessarily in that order. A much earlier version of chapter 2 appeared as a working paper in the Council on Foreign Relations' International Institutions and Global Governance series, and a still earlier but revised version appeared in the January 2014 issue of *World Politics*. At CFR, I thank Stewart Patrick, who provided invaluable feedback, and Trish Dorff, who was indispensable in getting the paper published. I am grateful to Ilene Cohen and the four anonymous referees of the paper at *World Politics*. The two anonymous referees for Oxford University Press also provided invaluable feedback at light speed. Thank you, whoever you are.

I've also been the beneficiary of an ongoing online conversation about these topics in the blogosphere and on Twitter. Even though I have not actually met many of my online interlocutors, their links, feedback, and snark benefited me tremendously during the drafting of this book. So thanks to Heidi Moore, Joe Weisenthal, Noah Smith, Justin Wolfers, Greg Ip, Jay Ulfelder, Ezra Klein, James Pethokoukis, Zack Beauchamp, Gady Epstein, Tony Fratto, Pascal-Emmanuel Gobry, and Will Winecoff.

Finally, I am very, very, very grateful to my family. This book took its toll on Erika, Sam, Lauren, and our dog Mimi. As the months passed and deadlines loomed, I spent more time locked away with piles of paper and less time engaging with my loved ones. They never complained or rebelled. The thesis of this book might very well be proven wrong in the coming years. But, after unintentionally stress testing my wife and kids, I am pretty secure in the knowledge that my family system works really well.

Daniel W. Drezner
Newton, Massachusetts
February 2014

THE SYSTEM WORKED

I

The Puzzle of Successful Global Governance

THE CONVENTIONAL WISDOM ABOUT global economic governance resembles an old Woody Allen joke: the quality is terrible—and yet such small portions. In other words, the view for quite some time has been that global governance has produced bad policy, and yet not enough of it. The punchline of this book is that the conventional wisdom is wrong. In response to the 2008 financial crisis—contrary to expectations—global economic governance responded in an effective and nimble fashion. In short, the system worked.

Many people who are paid a lot of money to write about the world believe that the system of global governance is broken. Ordinarily, such collective pessimism, accurate or not, is unproblematic. So long as the global economy hums along, whether or not there is faith in governance structures matters very little. Unfortunately, in recent years, the performance of the global economy has been anything but ordinary.

THE PROBLEM

The 2008 financial crisis posed the greatest threat to the global economy since the Great Depression of the 1930s.[1] During the first twelve months of what is now commonly called the Great Recession, economic output, global trade, and global equity values all plummeted lower than they did in the first year of the Depression, as figures 1.1–1.3 demonstrate. The International Monetary Fund (IMF) calculated that banks and other financial institutions lost more than $4 trillion in the

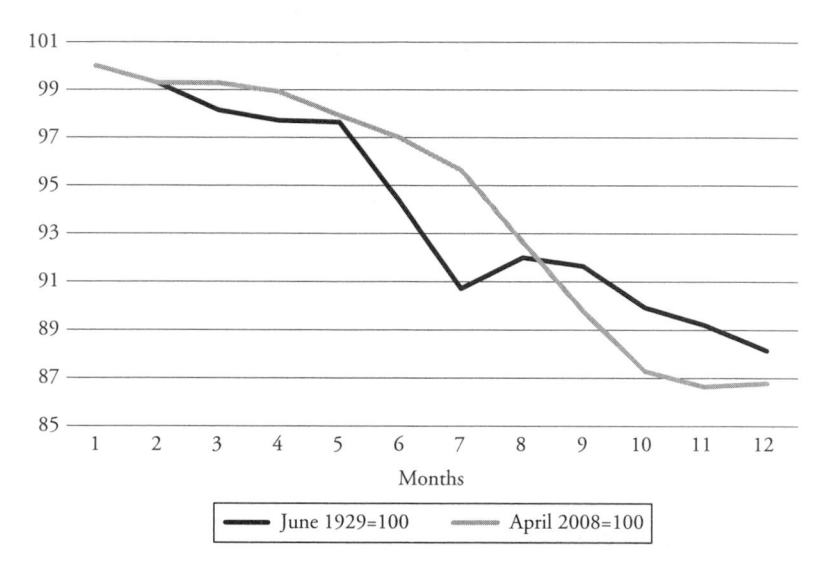

FIGURE 1.1 Global Industrial Output, 1929 versus 2008
Source: Eichengreen and O'Rourke 2010

value of their holdings as a result of the crisis.[2] The McKinsey Global Institute conservatively estimated that the global decline in asset values led to aggregate losses of $27 trillion in 2008, or roughly 50 percent of global economic output.[3] The International Labour Organization determined that global unemployment increased by 34 million people between 2007 and 2009.[4] Five years after the start of the subprime mortgage crisis, concerns about systemic risk were still elevated.[5]

The demand for effective global economic governance is at its greatest during severe crises. I define *global economic governance* as the set of formal and informal rules that regulate the global economy and the collection of authority relationships that promulgate, coordinate, monitor, or enforce said rules.[6] Even if national governments are the primary actors in world politics, they rely on a bevy of formal and informal institutions—the IMF, World Trade Organization (WTO), Bank of International Settlements (BIS), and Group of Twenty (G20) nations—to coordinate action on a global scale. These structures range from those with the ample resources, influential staff, and codified legal status of the IMF to the informal, resource-poor network of national officials of the G20. In the case of foreign direct investment (FDI), global governance is not even all that multilateral. Instead, a dense

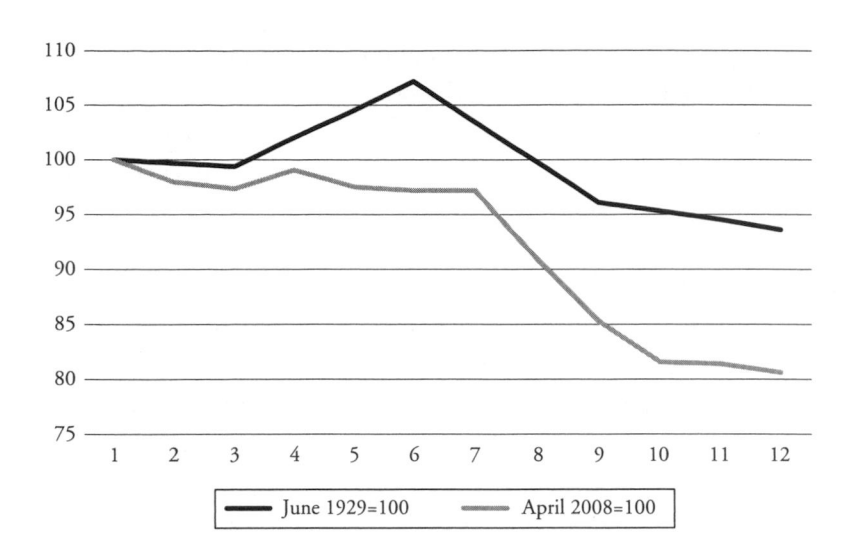

FIGURE 1.2 Global Trade Flows, 1929 versus 2008
Source: Eichengreen and O'Rourke 2010

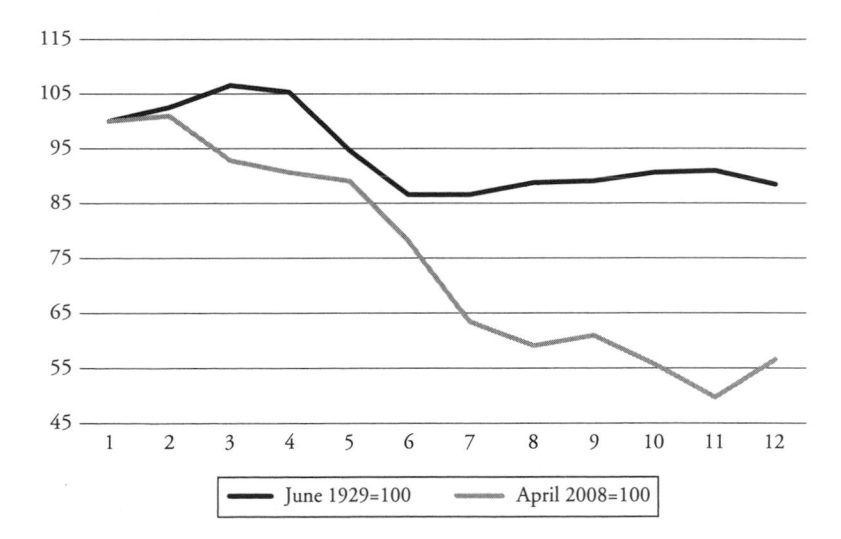

FIGURE 1.3 Global Stock-market Capitalizations, 1929 versus 2008
Source: Eichengreen and O'Rourke 2010

network of bilateral arrangements and private arbitration bodies governs investment.

Global governance structures can be the policymaker's pacifier. In an anarchic world, they provide a host of public goods and services, reducing uncertainty for all the participating actors.[7] When these structures function well, they facilitate communication and foster shared understandings among the policy principals, as well as reduce the transaction costs of policy coordination.[8] When they function poorly, a lack of trust and a surfeit of uncertainty among the actors stand in the way of cooperation. During normal economic times, global institutions articulate rules that advance the core principles animating the global economic order.[9] During abnormal times— such as the Great Depression, the collapse of Bretton Woods, or the Asian financial crisis—it is hoped that global economic governance structures will ensure sustained multilateral cooperation, even if it means that core principles will have to be reformed. Early in the 2008 crisis, Menzie Chinn and Jeffry Frieden noted, "The 1929 recession became a depression largely because of the collapse of international cooperation; the current crisis may head in that direction if international collaboration fails."[10] In the modern era, a primary aim of these structures during a crisis will be to keep barriers to cross-border exchange low. An open global economy lessens the stagnation that comes from a financial crisis, preventing a downturn from metastasizing into a depression.[11] The question in 2008 was, would the system do what was necessary?

THE CHALLENGES OF GLOBAL GOVERNANCE

There were excellent reasons to believe that global economic governance would fail in 2008. Even as the demand for global solutions rose, the supply seemed dodgy. Among both the public and elites, skepticism about the ability of global economic governance structures to ameliorate economic problems had increased in the decade before the crisis. In part, this reflected the waning reputation of governance more generally. World public-opinion polls show that a majority of citizens believe that their national government wastes more than half of its tax receipts on programs that do not benefit their countries.[12] Polling about global governance structures has been rarer, but prior to the financial crisis, public attitudes toward multilateral institutions like the United Nations were trending downward as well.[13]

That public skepticism about global governance has increased should not be surprising given the nature of the commentary about these institutions. The public may little note or long remember specific things said about the United Nations or the World Bank, but decades of disrespect eventually seep into the collective subconscious. Since their inception, global governance structures have invited scorn outside the United States because bodies like the IMF are viewed as puppets of America's hegemonic power. Inside the United States, partisans on both ends of the political specturm have spent decades bashing one international institution or another, degrading the reputations of all of them. Left-leaning critics decry international financial institutions for coercing developing economies into adopting "market fundamental-ism."[14] Neoconservatives loudly argue that international institutions, such as the United Nations, do nothing but constrain the United States into no-win scenarios.[15] These organizations have been roundly accused of preferring bloviation over action.

The problem is that international institutions all too often resem-ble caricatures, riddled with corrupt officials and sclerotic structures. The global governance of sports provides a high-profile example of the fecklessness of some international institutions. Corruption plagued the International Olympic Committee (IOC) for its first hundred years of existence.[16] By the end of the twentieth century, the IOC board mem-bers in charge of selecting the games' host cities were accustomed to accepting bribes, gifts, and favors from the various bidders. Eventually, the scandal over Salt Lake City's bid to host the 2002 Winter Olympics led to a scathing internal IOC report acknowledging decades of corrup-tion. Six board members were purged as a result. Yet, despite the scan-dals, IOC president Juan Antonio Samaranch was allowed to finish his term, with all its perquisites, including more than $200,000 in annual living expenses. Although the IOC did create an ethics commission to monitor the bidding process, the new commission reports to the IOC's executive board; it does not exercise any independent power.[17]

For an even more amusing example, consider the case of the Fédération Internationale de Football Association (FIFA), the world's governing soccer body. There have been long been allegations of cor-ruption within its executive committee; like the IOC board, FIFA's executive committee members routinely accepted bribes when choos-ing the World Cup host cities.[18] By early 2011, however, those alle-gations had mushroomed to a such a degree that FIFA's governance seemed to border on the farcical. FIFA announced that the 2022 World Cup would be held in Qatar, a country with an average temperature over 100 degrees Fahrenheit during the months the games would be played. The vote took place despite a *Guardian* investigation revealing that multiple members of the executive committee were alleged to be taking bribes.[19]

If FIFA had been a corporation or a government, some housecleaning would have been expected at that point to address the corruption problems. Instead, the Qatar vote-buying scandal managed to eliminate the sole challenger to the re-election bid of FIFA president Sepp Blatter, who had held the office since 1998. In summer 2011, he was re-elected without opposition. In response to the corruption allegations, Blatter allowed that FIFA's governance was "unstable" and proposed the creation of a "solutions committee" to address the question of ethics—to be chaired by Henry Kissinger. In response to skeptical questions at a post-election press conference, Blatter angrily told reporters: "I am the president of FIFA, you cannot question me."[20] Blatter's intransigence and buffoonery did lead to some pushback from FIFA's myriad stakeholders.[21] He responded by setting up an independent governance committee. But after the head of the committee acknowledged encountering resistance within FIFA to further reform, Blatter slapped him down in the press.[22] The anticorruption NGO Transparency International soon withdrew its support for the reform process.[23] Even Blatter's few defenders acknowledged the need for "greater transparency within FIFA's decision making and finances."[24] Blatter rejected further reforms, and today remains firmly ensconced as president despite ongoing controversies.[25] Even in the positive-sum case of regulating the world's most popular sport, international institutions find it hard to get things right.

Most international organizations are not as corrupt as FIFA, but they can be just as sclerotic. Global governance does not always respond to external change with the greatest alacrity. For example, at the start of the twenty-first century, it became clear that China and India were remaking the pattern of global energy usage. By consuming more energy, these behemoths were driving up oil prices, prompting concerns about "peak oil." A natural reaction was to bring these energy-importing giants into the salient global governance structures.

The International Energy Agency (IEA) was the organization of the world's leading energy consumers, set up following the first oil-price shock in the early 1970s. It made sense to have China and India in the organization. Outside experts concurred that the idea had a great deal of merit.[26] In early 2008, key US officials began making both public overtures and private diplomatic entreaties to China and India to join the IEA.[27]

A major roadblock quickly presented itself. To become a member of the IEA, a country must also be a member of the Organisation for Economic Co-operation and Development (OECD).[28] This was a "membership too far" for the advanced developing countries. The natural solution was to sever the legal relationship between the IEA and the OECD. The United States had in fact proposed five years earlier, to little avail. In March 2010, the executive director of the IEA publicly called for China to join the organization, noting, "Our relevance is under question because half of the energy consumption already is in non–Organization of Economic Cooperation and Development countries."[29] Nevertheless, the Chinese responded coolly to the proffer. Although policy coordination between India, China, and the IEA improved after 2008, those countries have yet to become members. Some IEA members feared a dilution of their influence. China and India feared being isolated among the advanced developed economies.[30] Regardless of the reasons, energy experts have been exasperated by the sclerosis.[31] The IEA is not that important a multilateral economic institution; if changing the institution's membership is this hard, then reforming the IMF or the WTO would be next to impossible.

THE CHALLENGES OF GLOBAL ECONOMIC GOVERNANCE BEFORE THE GREAT RECESSION

So even before the financial crisis fully bloomed, global governance structures were seen as little more than advertisements for dysfunction, corruption, and stagnation. As the subprime mortgage crisis escalated, it was justifiable to doubt the ability of global economic governance to act effectively in an emergency. Indeed, there were excellent reasons to believe that the failures of these governance structures abetted the crisis.

One cause of the subprime mortgage bubble in the United States was the surge in global macroeconomic imbalances to unprecedented levels, leading to greater amounts of capital sloshing around in US financial markets. These imbalances were partly the result of China's extensive efforts to keep the renminbi from appreciating in value, which included buying up dollar-denominated assets.[32] In theory, such actions violated IMF rules, requiring consultations at the fund. In practice, however, IMF management, fearful of China, blocked any serious discussion of exchange-rate issues.[33] According to the Fund's independent evaluation office, IMF staff failed to identify mounting financial risks in developed country because of "a high degree of groupthink." The IMF had been so dormant in the years leading up to the crisis that it was nicknamed the "Turkish Monetary Fund"—because its only sizable outstanding loan was to Turkey. By spring 2008, IMF leadership had opted to sell off some of the fund's gold reserves to shrink its operating deficit.[34]

The Basel Committee on Banking Supervision's primary function is to codify standards for banking regulation and supervision. The pre-crisis standards—called Basel II—had failed to prevent bank collapses across Europe. Indeed, multiple analysts have suggested that by permitting greater leverage in large financial institutions, the Basel II standards accelerated the banking crises.[35] The Doha Round of world trade talks had been stalemated for years, perpetuating a disturbing pattern in which each multilateral trade round takes longer to complete than its predecessor.[36]

In decades past, the Group of Seven (G7) countries had been sufficiently powerful to steer the global economy. In the 1980s, these economies controlled roughly two-thirds of all global output.[37] By 2008, the G7's share of global output had declined by roughly half, and it was clear that this grouping now lacked the economic muscle to act alone. To be fair, the G7 economies recognized the trend[38] and tried to ameliorate it. They reached out to the advanced developing economies, such as Mexico, Brazil, India, and China, and made efforts to include them in their summitry. The problem was that the efforts bordered on the insulting. One such initiative, called "Outreach-5," was launched at the 2007 Heiligendamm summit. Delegates from China, India, and other emerging markets were invited to the first-night dinner, and then dismissed for the rest of the summit meetings. In effect, this created a children's table at the summit, embarrassing even leaders sympathetic to the outreach idea.[39] This practice mercifully ended soon thereafter.

The final reason to doubt the efficacy of global economic governance at the time was that a breakdown of global cooperation was the proximate trigger of the Great Recession. The global financial crisis began in slow motion with BNP Paribas's announcement in August 2007 that it would suspend withdrawals from three of its investment funds that focused on US subprime mortgages. It was a signal that the market for those mortgage-backed securities had evaporated.[40] Over the next twelve months, the contagion of market panic spread rapidly, outpacing central bank and regulatory efforts to contain the fallout. Indeed, some of the great-power governments actively tried to spread panic in the markets. According to US Treasury secretary Henry Paulson, in summer 2008, Chinese interlocutors informed him of a Russian proposal to sell off holdings of Fannie Mae and Freddie Mac securities in the hopes that it would force the US government into action. Paulson described the effort in his memoirs as "deeply troubling." That qualifies as an understatement.[41]

By September 2008, it was clear that the US financial markets were seizing up, but non-American actors treated the news with more than a little schadenfreude. To Europeans, the subprime mortgage crisis was the fault of US market fundamentalism. In a March 2008 interview, French foreign minister Bernard Kouchner declared that "the magic is over" for the United States. Six months later, German finance minister Peer Steinbrück predicted that the United States would soon lose its status as a financial superpower.[42] Most European officials did not think the effects of the crisis would spread across the Atlantic.[43] To the BRIC economies (Brazil, Russia, India, and China), the problems of the developed world seemed increasingly remote. For much of 2007 and 2008, there was talk about how these markets were growing less dependent on exports to the advanced industrialized economies. Numerous analysts argued that the BRIC economies were "decoupling" from the West.[44] Kishore Mahbubani recommended that the United States and its Western allies simply get out of the way and let the developing world have its turn at global economic governance.[45] In other words, just about every other government on the globe assumed that the financial difficulties that were happening in the United States would stay in the United States.

The final straw was the failure of government efforts to prevent the Lehman bankruptcy. In a last-ditch effort to avert a collapse, US government officials had attempted to midwife a takeover of the bank by British-based Barclays Capital. The US Treasury Department and Federal Reserve Bank of New York coaxed a private consortium of financial institutions to assist in the sale. US-based firms were prepared to absorb some of Lehman's toxic assets as a way of sweetening the deal for Barclays. After a marathon weekend of negotiations, a deal appeared to be successfully completed. Great Britain's Financial Services Authority (FSA), however, needed to approve the deal before it could take place. The FSA was unwilling to relax capital adequacy requirements and unable to alter corporate governance protocols to permit the sale.[46] Consultations between US and UK finance officials during the crucial weekend were haphazard at best, leading to misunderstandings and mutual recriminations.[47] In a pivotal conversation between Paulson and Alistair Darling, Paulson's British counterpart, Darling made it clear that he was unwilling to coordinate regulatory actions with the United States, telling the secretary that he didn't want to import America's financial "cancer." The failure of cooperation between the world's two closest allies paved the way for the acute phase of the 2008 global financial crisis—a crisis that eventually ensnared the United Kingdom more deeply than the United States.

THE ASSESSMENT OF GLOBAL ECONOMIC GOVERNANCE AFTER THE GREAT RECESSION

By the time Lehman Brothers went bankrupt, global economic governance was stalemated, ineffectual, or being overtaken by events. Public confidence in multilateral institutions was in decline. Policy elites sounded alarms about a global governance crisis, to little avail.[48] Some modest steps had been taken to address these governance issues prior to the crisis, but they were feeble efforts in the face of the economic storm that started in fall 2007 and became a tsunami a year later.

Perceptions have not improved in the half decade since the onset of the Great Recession. Indeed, the very moniker "Great Recession" implies that the global economy has not performed well. Despite massive uncertainty about nearly every aspect of the global political economy, there is a strong consensus about the parlous state of multilateral economic institutions. Opinion polls reveal the public's frustration with the status quo and its desire for more-robust global governance structures. In early 2009, the overwhelming majority of respondents to a BBC World Service poll said that they supported "major reforms" of the international economic system. In July 2009, majorities in seventeen of nineteen countries polled wanted a more powerful global financial regulator.[49] Public pessimism about the global economy has persisted as well.[50]

Global public-policy elites were even more disdainful. In early 2011, Richard Samans, Klaus Schwab, and Mark Malloch-Brown concluded, "Nearly every major initiative to solve the new century's most pressing problems has ground to a standstill amid political gridlock, summit pageantry, and perfunctory news conferences."[51] The World Economic Forum similarly noted, "As the financial crisis unfolded in 2008 and 2009, the world lacked an appropriate and effective crisis response mechanism."[52] Ian Bremmer and Nouriel Roubini blasted the G20 grouping as being particularly toothless, proclaiming instead that we live in a "G-Zero" world: "The divergence of economic interests in the wake of the financial crisis has undermined global economic cooperation, throwing a monkey wrench into the gears of globalization."[53] Bremmer was particularly emphatic on this point. In January 2012, he concluded that "the effectiveness of many global institutions is under severe strain, as they remain largely unchanged from their postwar forms."[54] David Rothkopf, the CEO of *Foreign Policy* magazine, asserted that the, "current global economic leadership void [is] likely to be seen by history as worst since that preceding Great Depression." Stewart Patrick, the director of the International Institutions and Global Governance program at the Council on Foreign Relations, warned, "Demand for effective global governance continues to outstrip supply, and the gap is growing."[55]

Trashing global economic governance seemed to be a prerequisite for writing for the *Financial Times*. Alan Beattie epitomized the collective disdain in his book *Who's in Charge Here?* His thesis: "the collective response of the world's big economies since 2007 has been slow, disorganized, usually politically weak and frequently ideologically wrong-headed."[56] As time has passed, assessments have remained dour well beyond the salmon-pink pages of the *Financial Times*. At the end of 2012, Mark Leonard predicted that there would be "a single theme in 2013 . . . the idea of the unraveling of the global economy and the political integration that supported it." Contemporaneously, Martin Indyk and Robert Kagan warned that "the world's institutions—whether the United Nations, the Group of 20 or the European Union—are weakened and dysfunctional. The liberal world order established after World War II is fraying at the edges."[57]

The post-crisis skeptics include a broad array of social scientists.[58] Tom Hale, David Held, and Kevin Young noted that "in recent years the problem of addressing global policy challenges seems to have grown worse," attributing the problem to "gridlock" in global governance. In a joint report, Jeffry Frieden, Michael Pettis, Dani Rodrik, and Ernesto Zedillo observed that "on virtually every...important global economic issue, international cooperation is stalled, flawed, or non-existent." Historian Mark Mazower concluded, "With the WTO's Doha Round paralyzed and the World Bank chastened, [and] the IMF incapable of helping to rectify the global imbalances that threaten the world economy...the institutions of international governance stand in urgent need of renovation." David Zaring posited that international financial institutions had been "ineffective or, at best, marginally useful" since the start of the crisis. Naazneen Barma, Ely Ratner, and Steven Weber declared, "It's not particularly controversial to observe that global governance has gone missing."[59]

Commentators usually proffer two reasons for this pessimism. The first is that the distribution of power in the current era echoes the interwar period of 1919–1939 all too ominously.[60] Between the First and Second World Wars, Great Britain's relative power waned while America's rose. This power transition greatly complicated the ability to supply global public goods. The traditional theory of hegemonic stability requires the existance of a clear superpower to provide these goods; in the absence of a hegemon, buck-passing between waxing and waning powers becomes a possibility. As Charles Kindleberger famously observed in *The World in Depression*, "In 1929 the British couldn't and the United States wouldn't [stabilize the global economy]. When every country turned to protect its national private interest, the world public interest went down the drain, and with it the private interests of all."[61] Not surprisingly, during the 1930s, multilateral economic institutions were toothless in the face of the Great Depression. The last major effort to rewrite the global rules—the 1933 London Monetary and Economic Conference—ended in acrimony.[62]

The parallels between 1929 and 2008 seem strong. In 2008, it was easy to see the United States in Britain's fading role and China as taking over America's former rising status. During the depths of the crisis, financier Roger Altman lamented that "there could hardly be more constraining conditions for the United States and Europe" and that "[China's] economic and financial power have been strengthened relative to those of the West."[63] Altman's assessment encapsulated the elite consensus on this question. Before the crisis, Thomas Friedman wrote paeans to globalization; after the crisis, he coauthored a book titled *That Used to Be Us*, bemoaning American decline.[64] Similarly, Fareed Zakaria wrote about the "post-American" world.[65] Christopher Layne concluded that "in the Great Recession's aftermath...a financially strapped United States increasingly will be unable to be a big time provider of public goods to the international order."[66]

The question was whether the rising powers would support or spoil the US-created global economic order. Michael Mastanduno worried, "The collective action problem need[s] to be overcome to sustain effective cooperation is more formidable. And the United States will have to sit down not just with good friends but also with potential adversaries." Charles Kupchan warned that "emerging powers will want to revise, not consolidate, the international order erected during the West's watch."[67] China's rise provoked claims of an alternative to the discredited Washington Consensus, a "Beijing Consensus" that rested on principles of mercantilism and state capitalism, and was therefore antithetical to the liberal economic order.[68] China's economic revisionism ostensibly posed a serious challenge to the ossified state of multilateral economic institutions. As the US Congress flailed about in fall 2013, debating whether to increase the debt ceiling, a Xinhua op-ed blasted the United States for acting irresponsibly. The essay rocketed around US foreign-policy circles because of its ominous suggestion "to consider building a de-Americanized world." Two days later, a prominent Chinese economist penned a *Financial Times* op-ed urging China's government to stop purchasing US Treasuries.[69]

The second source of pessimism is the view that power itself has been diffusing so rapidly that no actor or concert of actors can credibly wield authority anymore. Even before the crisis, Richard Haass and Niall Ferguson had warned about the ebbing of power from governments to more-amorphous, networked actors.[70] In a world of WikiLeaks, anonymous transnational Occupy movements, and mass protests that can sprout up anywhere in the world, it does seem as though governments have lost their ability to shape events. Moisés Naím argues, "Today's panoply of international threats and crises…come as the hierarchy of nations is in flux and the very exercise of state power is no longer what it used to be." French foreign minister Laurent Fabius asserts that "today we live in a zero-polar, or a-polar world. No one power or group of powers can solve all the problems." Bruce Jentleson believes we are now in a "Copernican world" characterized by "power diffused and diluted more than realists portray, post–World War II norms and institutions more contested than liberal internationalists acknowledge." Randall Schweller goes even further, concluding that we are now living in "age of entropy" in which "world politics is being subsumed by the forces of randomness and enervation, wearing away its order, variety, and dynamism."[71] In such chaos, global governance efforts seem foolhardy.

To sum up: global governance had a bad reputation at the start of the twenty-first century, and it has only gotten worse since. The prevailing sentiment is that international institutions failed to prevent the Great Recession and might have abetted the crisis. Global economic governance has failed to repair the damage since 2008, and its structures are too sclerotic to repair themselves.

THE ARGUMENT

This book argues that almost every assertion in the previous section is wrong. I contend that a closer look at the global response to the financial crisis leads to a more optimistic assessment. Despite initial shocks that were more severe than those of the 1929 financial crisis, global economic governance responded in a nimble and robust fashion in 2008. Whether one looks at economic outcomes, policy outputs, or institutional operations, it is clear that global governance structures either reinforced or improved upon the pre-crisis status quo. The global economy bounced back from the 2008 crisis with relative alacrity. Compared to crises of this magnitude in the past, the world economy did not suffer as big an economic hit, and growth resumed more quickly than was expected. This is in no small part because global economic governance supplied the necessary public goods to prevent worst-case scenarios from being realized. In the key areas in which international institutions can help ameliorate a global economic crisis—keeping markets open to trade, supplying sufficient liquidity, coordinating macroeconomic policies, rewriting the most flawed rules of the game—both global governance and great power governments did their job. At the same time, many of the key global governance structures revamped their rules and memberships to better reflect the rise of the advanced developing countries in the international system. The Great Recession provided a severe "stress test" for global economic governance—and these structures passed.

To be sure, there remain areas in which governance has either faltered or failed. One can point to policy arenas, such as climate change, cybersecurity, and macroeconomic policy coordination, in which cooperation has been either illusory or ephemeral. The case that the system worked would be easier to make if the entire Doha Round had been completed, or if the G20 always spoke as one on macroeconomic policy. If one judges the success of global governance during this crisis by whether the optimal policies were enacted, then the system did fail, and fail spectacularly. But this is an absurd standard to apply. Looking for perfection in global governance is the enemy of finding the good in global governance.[72] The question is not whether global governance has been flawless but whether it has been good enough at supplying the necessary policies and public goods. And if the policy outcomes have been suboptimal, they have not been subpar. International institutions and frameworks performed better than expected. Simply put, the system worked.

Why, then, is the expert consensus just the opposite? One explanation has to do with where the pundits "live." Since 2008, there has been a disjuncture between where most of the people who write about the global economy are located and where many of the global economy's growth locomotives are found. The bulk of the actual economic growth has taken place in emerging markets—but emerging-market analysts have yet to affect the tenor of discourse on the global political economy. The bulk of intellectual output emanates from the countries of the developed world, places that have not exactly thrived since the start of the Great Recession. It is therefore natural that some analysts extrapolate from their downbeat local circumstances a downbeat assessment of global circumstances.

Analysts may also conflate the failings of national and regional governance with failures at the global level. Given the extent of political gridlock across the developed world, it is not surprising that analysts translate domestic policy deadlocks to global policy deadlocks. In an era of economic globalization, it is natural to conclude that the sources of significant policy solutions should also reside at the global level. Economist Dani Rodrik posits that the world has hit a governance "trilemma" in which it is increasingly difficult to reconcile the effects of global economic integration with democratic mass politics and national governance.[73] However, globalization has not upended the laws of politics. It remains the case that the most salient forms of governance for citizens are at the local and national levels. The best global governance structures in the world cannot compensate for dysfunctional national governments.

Nostalgia for past eras when the distribution of power seemed more certain also influences the view that today's global governance did not work. When analysts complain that global economic governance is fraying, they inevitably make comparisons with the Bretton Woods structures the United States crafted in the decade following the Second World War. But as we shall see, such nostalgia exaggerates the effectiveness of past global governance. In truth, the performance gap between the Bretton Woods structures at their acme and the post-2008-era global governance structures is not large. Furthermore, this nostalgia misses the key difference between the Great Recession and other postwar crises. The 2008 financial crisis hit the core global economies hardest. Yet, global economic governance structures have never imposed significant strictures on the great powers. The difference between the 2008 financial crisis and previous global crises isn't the relative strength of international institutions—it is that in 2008 the core economies faced the burden of adjustment.

It is easy to show that global economic governance has worked better than most people realize. It is easier still to dissect why misperceptions about global governance have taken such firm root. It is explaining why global economic governance has performed well that is hard.

The most commonly provided reason is that the shared sense of crisis in 2008 spurred the major economies to joint action. This is not a compelling argument, however, for two reasons. First, a crisis mentality did not necessarily lead to sustained cooperation in the past. Other significant twentieth-century economic crises, such as the Depression, collapse of Bretton Woods, the oil shocks of the 1970s, and the failure of the European Exchange Rate Mechanism in the early 1990s, also failed to spur meaningful cooperation among the great powers. It was far from obvious that powerful actors would think of the 2008 crisis as a "shared" one.

Second, the "crisis" argument assumes that cooperation ended as soon as the crisis abated. Eurasia Group founder Ian Bremmer, for example, argues that as the sense of collective crisis lifted, so did the impetus for policy coordination.[74] This assertion distorts what actually happened after Lehman Brothers collapsed. It is certainly true that macroeconomic policy coordination eroded after the G20 Toronto summit in May 2010. What had been a consensus about government spending making up the shortfall for private sector investment broke down over disagreements about the virtues of fiscal austerity. Beyond that issue area, however, international economic cooperation persisted. As this book will show, progress in negotiating and implementing new banking regulations continued unabated. Trade protectionism remained restrained, and free-trade agreements and bilateral investment treaties continued to be negotiated. Cooperation on antipiracy measures increased. Global governance reform efforts continued. What actually transpired is at odds with the narrative that there was only a brief burst of cooperation during the acute phase of the crisis.

Another argument is that global governance worked better in 2008 than in previous crises because policymakers had learned from past mistakes and created stronger multilateral institutions.[75] To be sure, the international institutional environment has never been thicker than it is today, and these institutions have learned from past mistakes. There are flaws in the argument, however. First, it does not explain why elites imbibed some lessons better than others. Policymakers avoided the mistakes of protectionism that plagued the Depression era; but, as we shall see, they also managed to repeat many of the macroeconomic policy errors of the 1930s. Second, to say that global economic governance worked because of strong institutions borders on tautology. In essence, one is arguing that the system worked because the system worked.[76] Institutionalists could counter that past institutional strength is what really matters, but there is no way to measure strength ex ante that would match up with the performance of the different institutions of global governance. The WTO, for example, is a formal, treaty-based organization with significant monitoring and enforcement capabilities. The G20, on the other hand, has no legal standing, no independent secretariat, and no real resources. Yet, despite these differences, one can persuasively argue that the latter was at least as significant as the former in affecting post-crisis global economic governance.

To understand why global economic governance performed the way it did, we need to look at the building blocks of international relations theory: interest, power, and ideas. As we shall see, commentators were not only wrong in assessing the state of international institutions, they also erred in assessing the shifts in the distribution of interest, power, and ideas. With respect to interest, the disaggregation of production has created powerful interests with a vested stake in maintaining openness. But this only tells part of the story. It also turns out that the crisis freed up international regimes to act with more policy autonomy than an argument solely grounded in sectoral interests would predict.

The conventional wisdom about post-crisis power and ideas is also due for a reassessment. Among the great powers, the United States retained far greater capabilities than is commonly appreciated. Across a range of issues, the United States was able to exercise leadership—or, at least, to maintain a status quo bias toward openness—in key arenas of global economic governance. It is true that, in recent decades, the BRIC economies have grown more rapidly than the economies of the developed world. Observers have been too quick, however, to project the future of the BRICs based on those past growth trajectories—and then to convert those extrapolations into inflated estimates of their current capabilities. The BRIC economies lack agenda-setting or convening power in the global economy. A dispassionate look at the distribution of capabilities reveals that the United States, the European Union, and China are the great powers in the post-crisis global economy. If they agree on what is to be done, then it is done. The 2008 financial crisis and Great Recession have led to a minor shift in the global distribution of power—but the key word is "minor."

Neither did the crisis seriously challenge the privileged set of economic ideas. Despite a lot of loose talk about its demise, the Washington

Consensus has endured. There are a variety of reasons for its resilience, but the two biggest are the deep intellectual roots of market-friendly policy ideas and the failure of challengers to articulate a compelling alternative. China could have been full-throated in its support of a Beijing Consensus. Instead, China acted like a supporter of the status quo far more frequently than it acted like a spoiler of the system. In 2005, US deputy secretary of state Robert Zoellick challenged China to act like a "responsible stakeholder" in the international system, by which he meant that China needed to "recognize that the international system sustains their peaceful prosperity, so they work to sustain that system."[77] In their post-crisis actions, China has acted like a fully responsible stakeholder of global economic governance.

WHAT DOES IT MEAN FOR THE SYSTEM TO WORK?

"The system" refers to the global economy and the rules of the game that govern it. It is theoretically possible for the global economy to function well without clear rules of the game. Usually, however, the global economy works when global economic governance works.

Empirical assessments about whether global governance "works" or is "effective" do not suffer from an abundance of analytical clarity.[78] To a great extent, the problem is normative. Normatively, any definition of global economic governance that shows it to be "working" is freighted with peril. Definitions of what "works" will automatically include—either implicitly or explicitly—preferences about what the rules for the global economy *should* look like. For example, suppose global economic governance were to effectively manage a regime based on the principle that all international trade should be executed through state trading companies and be in perfect bilateral balance. Ostensibly, such a system could work given its operating rules; but it would be based on principles most economists would categorize as horribly suboptimal. So, should global governance aim for a laissez faire system of unregulated cross-border exchange, for the "embedded liberalism" of the Bretton Woods era, or for the state-controlled aspirations of the New International Economic Order?[79] It is impossible to disentangle evaluations of the system from our preconceptions of what the system should do.

To be clear at the outset: my normative preferences for global economic governance rest on two underlying principles. First, a global economy more open to the exchange of goods, services, capital, people, and ideas generates the greatest expansion of welfare possible.[80] A global economy with high barriers to cross-border exchange will grow more sluggishly and suffer from more prolonged downturns than a global economy that is open to trade. Global governance should therefore focus on reducing cross-border barriers to exchange. This is particularly true for the largest markets. China's defection from the rules of the game has more impact on the global economic order than, say, Gabon's.

Second, paradoxically, global governance also must be prepared to cope with the vicissitudes of an open world economy. Charles Kindleberger called financial crises the "hardy perennials" of the global economy; the subsequent literature suggests that over the past century such crises have been more common than great-power wars.[81] Capitalist systems are inherently prone to crisis, which means that open global economies are inherently prone to global crises. In theory, the best forms of global economic governance forestall such crises. In practice, no global economic order to date permits the comprehensive management of key policy variables.[82] Pragmatically, global economic governance helps to contain and repair the damage as quickly as possible after such crises. These repairs can include reforming the rules of cross-border exchange, ameliorating macroeconomic downturns, and establishing guidelines for national regulations.

My set of first principles is different from those of some other observers. Advocates of laissez faire policies will decry my approval of the revisions to the Basel Committee on Banking Supervision's standards, seeing them as an example of excessive intervention into the marketplace. Harsher critics of globalized finance will decry my approval of those standards because they failed to adequately address the "too big to fail" problem in global finance. These criticisms are valid from their points of view—I would simply note that my preferences on how global governance should regulate the global economy reflect public attitudes on these questions.[83]

WHAT THIS BOOK IS AND WHAT IT IS NOT

This is not a standard work of political science. I do not rigorously test competing hypotheses, nor do I develop a formal theory of governance. Instead, I make an empirical assertion that is heavily contested in the public sphere. It would therefore be problematic to simply assert that global economic governance worked after 2008 and proceed from there. I thus seek to demonstrate that fact and explain why the conventional wisdom on this topic has been so wrong. To use the language of social science, the first half of the book is far more about descriptive inference than causal inference.[84]

Furthermore, I am not creating a generalizable theory about global governance in a crisis. Rather, the purpose of this book is to explain what happened to the global political economy and global governance after the Lehman Brothers collapse. My primary concern is thus explaining this case rather than apportioning causal weights to different theories. To be sure, this is a Big Important Case and therefore merits scrutiny. Nevertheless, it remains a single case study. There are vigorous methodological debates within political science about the salience of big cases, but I choose not to engage those debates here. The causal inferences that I discuss in the second part of the book are not necessarily generalizable. As political scientists will observe, I eschew a strictly paradigmatic approach for a more analytically eclectic treatment—with all the epistemological trade-offs that entails.[85]

WHY THIS MATTERS—AND WHAT COMES NEXT

Setting the record straight on global economic governance is important for three reasons. First, in the global political economy, the narrative matters. Stylized facts that have calcified into accepted wisdom among policymakers and public intellectuals become harder to challenge. Clearly, the emerging post-2008 consensus is that global economic governance has been an abject failure. If this becomes the accepted wisdom, then policymakers could waste valuable political capital trying to mend something that does not necessarily need fixing. The intrinsic need to understand the inner workings of global economic governance could not be clearer.

Second, the relative robustness of global economic governance represents a challenge to international relations theory. In 2008, it was far from obvious that the G20, BIS, WTO, and IMF would be able to do what they did. The major internatonal relations approaches—realist, liberal, and constructivist—shared a pessimistic outlook after Lehman Bothers collapsed. How agents and structures behave during crisis moments can reveal the deep, tectonic forces operating in world politics. The 2008 financial crisis stress-tested international relations paradigms as much as it tested global governance structures. An increasing amount of global political economy research is situated within a single paradigm called "open economy politics." This paradigm assumes that outcomes in the global economy can be derived from building models up from the microfoundations of domestic preferences and institutions. As we shall see in chapter 4, on its own, open economy politics lacks a convincing explanation for post-2008 events.[86] If alternative approaches can better explain what happened after the Lehman collapse, they merit a closer look.

Third, questions about global economic governance are no longer the exclusive province of global political economy scholars and policymakers who are far removed from the public. For much of the twentieth century, international relations commentators thought of the security realm as the place of "high politics." Economic cooperation was viewed as the more mundane realm of "low politics." No longer. War has become rarer and economic conflicts have become more common.[87] As two analysts at the US National Intelligence Council observed at the start of the Great Recession, "Artificial divisions between 'economic' and 'foreign policy' present a false dichotomy. To whom one extends swap lines and how the IMF is recapitalized are as much foreign policy as economic decisions. . . . Finance and markets are now high politics."[88] If the Great Game in the nineteenth century was about carving out spheres of territorial influence in Central Asia, the twenty-first-century equivalent is about carving out spheres of economic influence in the global marketplace. Global economic governance has become a pivotal arena for great-power politics.

The rest of this book is organized as follows. Chapter 2 looks at the policy outcomes, outputs, and operations of global economic governance to demonstrate that the system worked better than is commonly believed. Despite an initial shock worse than that of the Great Depression, the global economy managed to bounce back after the 2008 crisis. This was in no small part because global economic governance functioned properly to maintain economic openness and build resiliency into the international system. Chapter 3 dissects why the conventional wisdom about the value of global governance is so at odds with what global economic governance has actually accomplished. There are a number of reasons, including an exaggeration of its failures and misplaced nostalgia for past eras of global economic governance. Chapter 4 examines the role that material interests played in supporting global economic governance. To be sure, the complex interdependencies of globalization condition powerful interests to strongly prefer an open global economy. That said, a look at the Basel III banking accord negotiations also reveals the limits of a monocausal, interest-based explanation. Chapter 5 explores whether power-based arguments can explain these events. A net assessment shows that the great powers in the post-crisis economy are the United States, the European Union, and China. It also suggests that global economic governance functioned as well as it did because the United States retained economic primacy and exercised leadership; more surprisingly, however, the evidence also shows that China acted like a supporter rather than a spoiler in global economic governance. Chapter 6 examines the distribution of ideas in the post-crisis global economy. As it turns out, many of the economic ideas supposedly discredited during the 2008 financial crisis have demonstrated surprising resiliency—for good and ill. The final chapter considers where the system goes from here.

2

Yes, the System Worked

THERE IS A BROAD and deep consensus that global governance failed the world in the aftermath of the 2008 financial crisis. This gives rise to two important questions, however: How can we know whether or not global economic governance "works"? Are there any observable metrics to use in assessing global governance besides pundit perceptions? These, in turn, give rise to questions about first principles. How is global governance supposed to work? What exactly do global governance structures do to facilitate the functioning of the global economy? In this chapter, we answer these questions in reverse order.

How Can Global Economic Governance Work?

In theory, global governance structures can provide a welter of services to facilitate economic growth and international cooperation. International relations scholars have articulated multiple causal mechanisms through which global governance can facilitate cooperation. Even skeptics, for example, acknowledge that international institutions can serve as *focal points* in coordinating the global rules of the game.[1] Institutions inherently create a common set of rules or norms for all participants. They foster the convergent expectations that define cooperative behavior and the conditions under which revisionist actors are labeled as defectors.

The importance of institutions as focal points is a recurring theme in international relations. Indeed, the concept is intrinsic to political scientist Stephen Krasner's original definition of international regimes: "implicit or explicit principles, norms, rules and decision-making procedures around which actors' expectations converge in a given area of international relations."[2] More than a decade later, Robert Keohane and Lisa Martin reaffirmed Krasner's notion: "In complex situations involving many states, international institutions can step in to provide 'constructed focal points' that make particular cooperative outcomes prominent."[3]

International relations theorists have posited a number of additional roles for global governance structures. Another mechanism through which global governance can work is *reassurance*.[4] Even after actors in world politics agree on the rules of the game, uncertainty is inherent because no one can know whether the agreements will hold up over time. If there is even a small possibility that others will defect from a previously agreed-upon regime, then each actor has to prepare its own contingencies for what it will do if someone else defects. That kind of worst-case scenario planning can in and of itself sow doubts among other actors, eroding the probability of sustained policy coordination. One of the simpler virtues of any global governance structure is that it allows key actors to periodically reassure each other that there has been no change in the status quo. For example, even though the initial fall 2008 G20 summit in Washington, DC, accomplished little beyond leaders' pledges to maintain open markets, it reassured the major economies that they were on roughly the same page about how to respond to the crisis.[5] This kind of reassurance prevents participants from backsliding on their commitments. This, in turn, bolsters the credibility and reputation of the international regime.

The most prominent argument made by institutionalists is that global governance structures facilitate the *monitoring* and *enforcement* of cooperative agreements, rules, and norms.[6] This view recognizes that the opportunities for cooperation in world politics are plentiful—but so are the temptations to defect. International regimes can tamp down the incentive to cheat through monitoring and enforcement. At the same time, by pledging to abide by clearly defined rules, actors also make it easier for others to monitor and detect their own noncooperative behavior. Even without enforcement, actors will incur reputation costs if they choose to defect. If the regime is codified, the additional legal obligations to comply raise the costs of defection even more.[7] In the case of the WTO, for example, the codification of trade law has made it harder for governments to, even temporarily, waive their commitments to openness.[8] If global governance structures have the capacity to punish (as in the case of the IMF) or authorize punishment by others (as in the case of the WTO), then their ability to sustain policy coordination increases dramatically.

Constructivist scholars posit a different causal mechanism through which global governance does its job. According to their logic, membership in international regimes enhances the *normative desire to comply* with the promulgated rules and regulations through the socialization of its membership group. Whereas rationalist explanations for compliance focus on the material costs and benefits, the constructivist approach centers on group size and socialization as promoting the internalization of norms and principles.[9] International regimes can foster the acceptance of norms in several ways. Small, club-based structures can inculcate a desire to comply by conferring the privilege of membership and fostering the formation of close personal networks among participants. This is how the G7 and the Basel Committee on Banking Supervision have traditionally functioned.[10] Norms can also derive power from the number of actors that accept them.[11] The greater the number of actors accepting a given rule, the greater the social pressure on recalcitrant actors not to change position.[12] If the representativeness of a global governance structure increases, its perceived "democratic" mandate concomitantly increases, thereby enhancing its legitimating power. On this dimension, United Nations–type, universal-membership organizations provide powerful compliance-inducing pressures as well.[13]

Global governance can also matter through the *provision of expertise*. Economists, scientists, lawyers, and other professionals based at international institutions have an independent legitimacy, conferred through their mastery of abstruse subject areas of global public policy. Given the arcane nature of most arenas of global governance, the influence of international governmental organization secretariats with reservoirs of such expertise is enhanced. In the case of environmental policy, for example, the United Nations Environmental Programme had a profound effect on how international actors viewed such policy problems as ozone degradation and climate change.[14] To be sure, powerful actors often possess far greater resources than do global governance structures. Nevertheless, the research staffs and secretariats of international institutions can provide valuable independent expertise in the crafting of global rules and norms. Indeed, the prestige that their imprimatur, or stamp of approval, carries with weaker actors is one of global governance's greatest strengths. International institutions can command the agenda and set the tenor of the debate over the promulgation and enforcement of new rules. This is particularly true during emergencies. In a crisis, actors start to question established ideologies, standard operating procedures, and rules of thumb. Paradoxically, it is precisely during such moments of uncertainty, when actors begin to question the status quo, that they often seek out experts to help them gauge possible courses of reform. This is true even if these experts were partly or wholly responsible for the policies that precipitated the crisis in the first place!

Finally, global governance can be useful to national leaders trying to *ameliorate domestic political pressures*. Even when global policy coordination leads to welfare gains for all actors, there are domestic political and economic costs associated with any international agreement. Within jurisdictions, any policy change can upset the status quo and trigger a significant redistribution of costs and benefits among national actors. Because politicians must cater to powerful domestic constituencies, leaders always have an incentive to act unilaterally to bolster their domestic coalitions—even if such actions are contrary to maximizing the national interest. International institutions can function as external constraints on such unilateral actions. Global governance can allow national leaders to implement or adhere to politically contentious policies and to displace some of the political blame to international institutions.[15] Legally binding regimes, or those that activate powerful domestic norms, can help cement sustained cooperation even in the presence of powerful interest groups wishing to defect.[16] Alternatively, international institutions allow leaders to signal their commitment to a set of policies to key interest groups. For example, leaders who are suspected of being hostile to trade liberalization can assuage skeptics by signing free-trade agreements.[17]

Clearly, there are multiple possible pathways through which global economic governance can work. It should be stressed that these causal mechanisms are additive rather than mutually exclusive. A regime that can function as a focal point, engage in reassurance, actively monitor and enforce agreements, provide expertise, and blunt domestic pressures is far more likely to work than a governance structure that only utilizes one of these causal mechanisms. Because my focus is on how global economic governance functioned after the start of the 2008 financial crisis, I am less concerned with which mechanisms matter more than whether they collectively mattered.[18]

How Does Global Governance Work?

Assessing the performance of global economic governance presents an empirical challenge because of the difficulty of identifying the counterfactual. For example, one can argue that the joint G20 statements in late 2008 and early 2009 on fiscal and monetary expansion were an example of effective global governance. After these communiqués, the G20 economies did boost fiscal spending and pursue expansionary monetary policies, in what seemed to be policy coordination. Another possibility, however, is that each G20 actor simply pursued the policies it would have pursued anyway, rendering the G20 superfluous. In other words, rather than coordination, this could have been a case of harmony. Even the best counterfactual analysis cannot completely eliminate this type of uncertainty.

Critics of the current system of global governance tend to rely on a few stylized facts that are meant to suggest that it is dysfunctional. The following are some of the most commonly cited failures in recent years:[19]

- *The collapse of the Doha Round and the rise of protectionism.* Just as the global economy began to implode in the summer of 2008, last-gasp efforts to reach an agreement on the Doha Round of the WTO negotiations stalled. Subsequent G20 pledges to abstain from protectionism and complete the Doha Round of world trade talks did not appear to have much effect on policy. Within the first six months of the crisis, seventeen of the twenty countries had violated their pledge, implementing a combined forty-seven measures to restrict trade at the expense of other countries.[20] Six years after the financial crisis, most of the Doha Round remains unfinished. Indeed, the status of the round has been so moribund at times that one former US trade representative suggested abandoning the effort.[21] At the same time, the United States, the European Union, and China became embroiled in high-profile trade disputes on tires, steel, and solar panels, testing the limits of the WTO's dispute-settlement mechanism.

- *The breakdown of macroeconomic policy consensus.* For the first few years of the crisis, the governments of the great powers agreed on the need for expansionary monetary and fiscal policy to bolster growth in the fragile global economy. By the beginning of 2010, however, that consensus had frayed. The United States went to the June 2010 Toronto G20 summit committed to pushing for sustained Keynesian policies. What happened instead was a complete breakdown in the global macroeconomic policy consensus. Soon afterward, the European Union members of the G20 embraced austerity. In the subsequent eighteen months, numerous G20 members accused each other of starting "currency wars" with respect to unorthodox monetary policies.[22]

- *The escalation of Europe's sovereign debt crisis.* As the full impact of the Great Recession was felt, an increasing number of eurozone economies found their fiscal fortunes collapsing. European institutions were extremely sluggish in responding. As the Greek government's finances started to implode, the European Central Bank had only one economist monitoring the situation part-time.[23] In the end, neither the European Union nor the European Central Bank moved quickly enough to stop the spread of financial contagion. The result was a double-dip recession across most of Europe, unemployment rates of more than 25 percent in Greece and Spain, and protests and riots in the most-affected countries. If the European Union, the most-powerful supranational institution in existence, could not cope with the Great Recession, why would anyone expect less powerful global governance structures to do better with bigger problems?

- *The failure of climate-change negotiations.* There were high hopes going into the Copenhagen climate-change summit in December 2009. Heads of governments attended; numerous great powers had made presummit pledges; and for the first time in years, the United States appeared seriously committed to negotiations. Nevertheless, the summit ended with only a weak, ad hoc agreement among the major economies that pleased no one. European Commission president José Manuel Barroso decried the accord as a "commitment to the lowest common denominator." The summit also raised tensions between China, the United States, and the European Union.[24] In the aftermath, China was blamed for obduracy; the United States, for poor leadership; and the European Union, for poor logistics. Not surprisingly, climate-change talks stagnated after the summit.

These facts, though true, are not the whole truth. To assess the effectiveness of global economic governance after the 2008 financial crisis, I follow Tamar Gutner and Alexander Thompson's framework of using three different levels of analysis to assess the performance of global economic governance.[25] First, what do the *policy outcomes* look like? How have global output, trade, and other capital flows responded since the start of the Great Recession particularly compared to similar crises in the past? Second, what do the *policy outputs* look like? Did the key international institutions provide policies that, based on settled theory and prior experiences, can be considered significant and useful responses to a global financial crisis? Would these policies have been implemented in the absence of these global governance structures? Third, have these structures demonstrated *improved policy operations*? A common complaint prior to 2008 was that international institutions had not adapted to shifts in the world distribution of power and preferences. Did they maintain their relevance and authority? Did they ensure that rising actors have the incentives to view participation and compliance with existing arrangements as valuable?

This approach is best suited to counter the standard counterargument that global economic governance is either irrelevant or ineffective. It is frequently posited that successful episodes of global governance are merely the low-hanging fruit of the global political economy, because they only happen when a harmony of preferences makes governance easy to achieve.[26] If true, this critique renders international institutions epiphenomenal. The approach used here addresses this challenge by paying special attention to instances in which countries agreed to take actions that contravened powerful domestic interests. If countries adhere to a global policy that imposes costs on entrenched interests, it is a sign that genuine coordination, rather than harmony, is occurring. Examining the operations level will also refute the claim that global governance is epiphenomenal. Within these structures, the post-2008 goal at the operations level was to reallocate influence among the states. But governance reforms are intrinsically difficult to execute because such steps go against the interests of the actors whose power will be diluted. If process reforms nevertheless went through, we can infer that here, too, there was genuine policy coordination rather than a simple harmony of preferences.

Outcomes

How well has the global economy recovered from the 2008 crisis? The key question to ask is, compared to what?

The burgeoning literature on economic downturns suggests two factors that imposed significant barriers to a strong recovery from the Great Recession: it was triggered by a financial crisis, and it was global in scope. By any measure, financial crashes trigger economic downturns that last longer and have far weaker recoveries than do standard business-cycle recessions.[27] The global nature of a financial crash makes it extremely difficult for individual nation-states to simply "export their way" out of the problem. Countries that have experienced severe national financial crises since World War II have usually done so when the rest of the global economy was unaffected.[28] This was not the case for the Great Recession, which affected wide swaths of the global economy. The proper baseline for comparison is therefore the last severe global financial crisis—the Great Depression.

By any metric, the global economy rebounded much more robustly post-2008 than it did during the Great Depression. Economists Barry Eichengreen and Kevin O'Rourke compiled data comparing global economic performance from the start of the crises (see figures 2.1–2.3).[29]

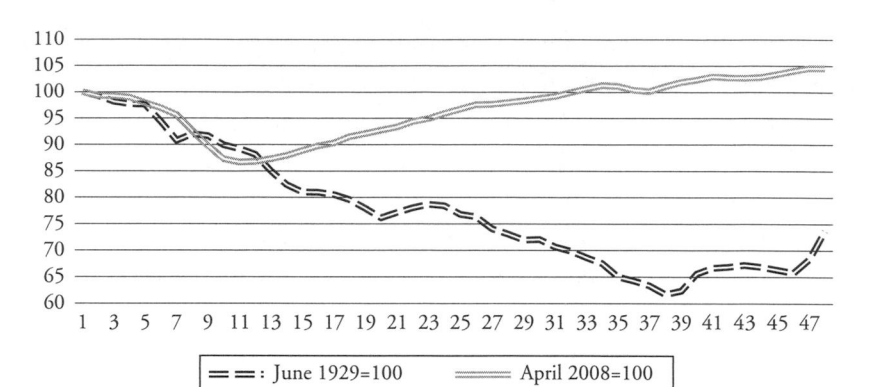

FIGURE 2.1 Global Industrial Production: Great Depression versus
Great Recession
Source: Eichengreen and O'Rourke 2010

Two facts stand out in their comparisons. First, the initial drop in
global industrial output and world trade levels at the start of the 2008
financial crisis was more precipitous than what followed the October
1929 stock-market crash. One year into the 2008 crisis, the falloff in
industrial output was greater than it had been eighty years earlier during the same period; the drop in trade flows was more than twice as
large. Second, the post-2008 rebound has been far more robust. Four
years after the onset of the Great Recession, global industrial output
was close to 10 percent higher than when the recession began. In contrast, four years after the 1929 stock-market crash, industrial output was
at only two-thirds of pre-crisis levels. Global equity markets after 2008
also outperformed their 1929 counterparts.

A similar story can be told about aggregate economic growth. Global
economic output shrank by approximately 3 percent in 1930, and then
contracted at annual rates of approximately 4 percent for the next two
years.[30] In contrast, according to the IMF's World Economic Outlook
series, global economic output shrank by 0.59 percent in 2009, but was
followed by growth in 2010 of 5.22 percent and of 3.95 percent in 2011.
Indeed, the average growth in global output between 2010 and 2012
was on par with the average growth rate in the decade that preceded the
financial crisis. More intriguingly, the growth continued to be poverty
reducing. Despite the 2008 financial crisis, extreme poverty continued

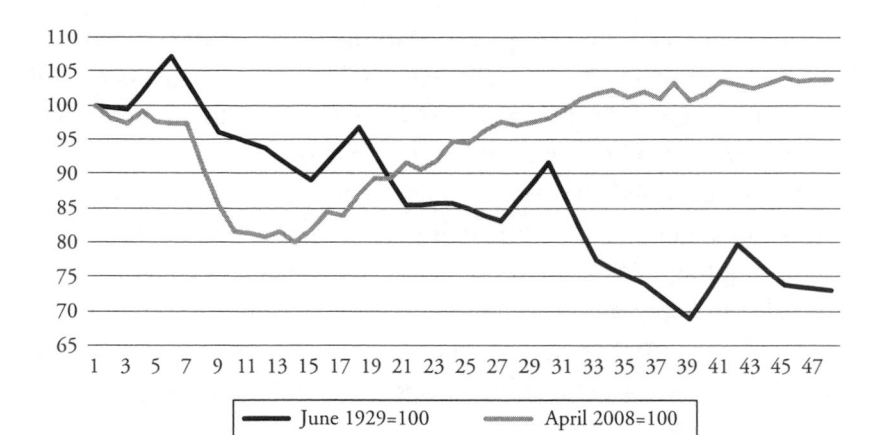

FIGURE 2.2 Global Trade Volumes: Great Depression versus Great Recession

Source: Eichengreen and O'Rourke, 2012

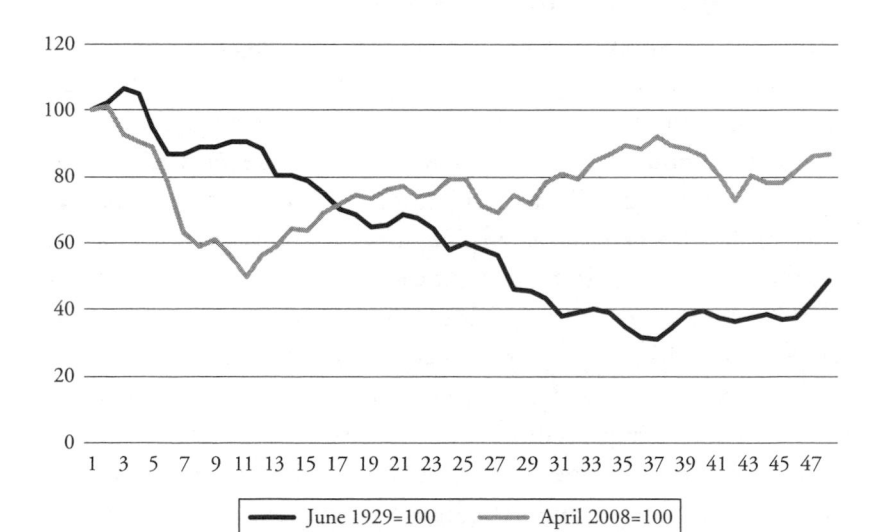

FIGURE 2.3 Global Equity Markets: Great Depression versus Great Recession

Source: Eichengreen and O'Rourke, 2012

to decline across all the major regions of the globe. In the teeth of the Great Recession, the World Bank reported that the first Millennium Development goal of halving the 1990 levels of extreme poverty had been achieved ahead of schedule.[31] The United Nations Development Programme reported that despite the 2008 financial crisis, there has been a more rapid improvement in human development since 2001 than during the 1990s—in no small part because poorer countries were better able to access global markets.[32] Consistent with this finding, the Legatum Prosperity Index, developed in 2009, has demonstrated small but persistent increases in global prosperity levels in the five years since the start of the Great Recession.

An important reason for the quick return to positive economic growth is that cross-border flows did not dry up after the 2008 crisis. The Swiss Economic Institute (KOF) constructs the KOF Index of Globalization, which covers a variety of cross-border exchanges, including trade, capital flows, remittances, tourism, and other metrics.[33] The mean scores for all countries and G20 members can be seen in figure 2.4. The Great Recession clearly caused globalization to plateau. But, at the same time, KOF's aggregate data for all countries showed no reduction in their globalization indices. Indeed, there was a very small increase.[34] Looking at the G20 economies in particular, we find that the mean national scores on both overall levels of globalization and economic globalization show the same pattern: a slight dip from the 2007 peak, and then a slight recovery by 2010.[35] For the G20, the 2010 average index score was the second highest in history, behind the 2007 peak.

This finding holds when one examines the components of cross-border exchange. Compared with the Great Depression, for example, post-2008 trade flows rebounded robustly. As Eichengreen and O'Rourke observe, and as figure 2.2 shows, four years after the 1929 stock-market crash, trade flows were down by 25 percent compared to pre-crisis levels. Four years after the start of the Great Recession, trade flows were more than 5 percent higher than their pre-crisis levels. Even compared with other postwar recessions, the post-2008 period witnessed a more vigorous bounce back in trade flows. Indeed, the growth in world trade since 2008 has been even more robust than in other postwar recoveries.[36] *The Economist* estimates that global exports as a percentage of global economic output have been higher on average

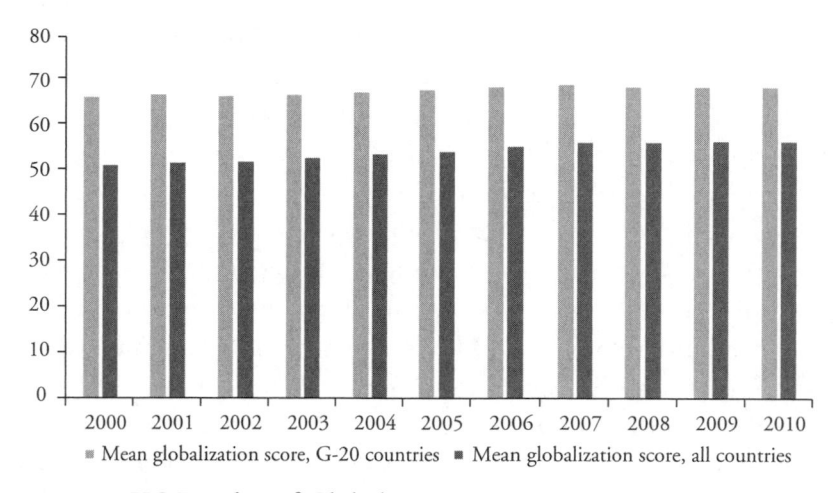

FIGURE 2.4 KOF Index of Globalization, 2000–2010
Sources: Swiss Economic Institute

between 2011 and 2013 than during the three years prior to 2008.[37] The Great Recession had only modest effects on aggregate trade flows.

Other cross-border flows have also rebounded from Great Recession lows. Multiple private-sector analyses conclude that global foreign investment assets have fully recovered from the financial crisis and are now valued between 10 and 15 percent higher than their pre-crisis highs.[38] Cross-border capital flows have also recovered from early 2009 lows, though they are still well below 2007 highs. Nevertheless, even the fiercest proponents of financial globalization allow that this slowdown might be a good thing. The McKinsey Global Institute characterized it as "a healthy correction" because some of the spikes in pre-crisis flows had been the result of unsustainable and unproductive trends. Many corporations, for example, had devoted more of their energies to financial engineering, leading to excessive leverage and investments in the carry trade and repo markets.[39] Indeed, in the run-up to the 2008 financial crisis cross-border lending was far more procyclical than domestic lending was.[40] *The Economist*'s Greg Ip has acknowledged that "a few constraints on global finance are not necessarily a bad thing," and said that "in retrospect, much of the rise in cross-border lending was foolish."[41] Returning to pre-crisis levels on these dimensions would not necessarily be viewed as boosting sustainable economic growth.

The more resilient components of cross-border capital flows rebounded well, however. Global FDI returned to robust levels. According to the United Nations Conference on Trade and Development (UNCTAD) *2013 World Investment Report*, the pre-crisis average of FDI inflows between 2005 and 2007 was $1.49 trillion. Between 2010 and 2012, the post-crisis, three-year FDI inflow average was $1.47 trillion—a negligible difference.[42] Furthermore, as with economic growth trends, an increasing proportion of FDI went to the developing world. Remittances from migrant workers have also become an increasingly important revenue stream to the developing world. The 2008 crisis barely dented that income stream. Cross-border remittances to developing countries quickly rebounded to pre-crisis levels and then rose to an estimated all-time high of $389 billion in 2012. Total cross-border remittances were more than $519 billion in 2012 and are estimated to exceed $700 billion by 2016.[43] Excluding intra-European bank lending, other cross-border capital flows also approximate pre-crisis levels. With FDI and remittances now occupying a greater share of cross-border capital flows, they are far more resilient to financial shocks than in pre-crisis capital markets.

Finally, the Great Recession did not lead to a deterioration in international security. Because political instability and violence can impinge on cross-border flows, increases in international conflict can dampen cross-border trade and exchange. During the initial stages of the crisis, multiple analysts asserted that the Great Recession would lead states to increase the use of political violence as a tool to stay in power.[44] They voiced genuine concerns that the global economic downturn would lead to an increase in conflict—whether through greater internal repression, diversionary wars, arms races, or a ratcheting up of great-power rivalries. Violence in the Middle East, piracy on the high seas, border disputes in the South China Sea, riots in European cities, and even the disruptions of the Occupy movement fueled impressions of a global surge in public disorder. As fiscal austerity in the developed economies curtailed social spending, economists predicted an explosion of unrest.[45]

Initially, there was some evidence of deterioration. Following the 2008 financial crisis, there was a spike in global piracy, particularly off the Horn of Africa. The International Maritime Bureau reported that in 2009 alone, there was a 40 percent surge in piracy attacks, with attacks near Somalia quadrupling during the same period. The Institute for Economics and Peace, which has constructed the Global Peace Index annually since 2007, reported in 2013 that there had been a 5 percent deterioration in global peace since 2008.[46]

A closer look at the numbers, however, reveals more encouraging findings. What seemed to be an inexorable increase in piracy, for example, turned out to be a blip. By September 2013, the total numbers of piracy attacks had fallen to their lowest levels in seven years. Attacks near Somalia, in particular, declined substantially; the total number of attacks fell by 70 percent in 2012 and an additional 86 percent in the first nine months of 2013. Actual hijackings were down 43 percent compared to 2008/9 levels.[47] The US Navy's figures reveal similar declines in the number and success rate of pirate attacks.[48] Security concerns have not dented the opening of the global economy.

As for the effect of the Great Recession on political conflict, the aggregate effects were surprisingly modest. A key conclusion of the Institute for Economics and Peace in its 2012 report was that "the average level of peacefulness in 2012 is approximately the same as it was in 2007."[49] The institute's concern in its 2013 report about a decline in peace was grounded primarily in the increase in homicide rates—a source of concern, to be sure, but not exactly the province of global governance. Both interstate violence and global military expenditures have declined since the start of the financial crisis. Other studies confirm that the Great Recession has not triggered any increase in violent conflict. Looking at the post-crisis years, Lotta Themnér and Peter Wallensteen conclude, "The pattern is one of relative stability when we consider the trend for the past five years."[50] The decline in secular violence that started with the end of the Cold War has not been reversed. Rogers Brubaker observes that "the crisis has not to date generated the surge in protectionist nationalism or ethnic exclusion that might have been expected."[51]

None of these data suggest that the global economy has operated swimmingly since the start of the Great Recession. Inequality continued to rise, and unemployment persisted at a high level in many parts of the developed world. Compared to the aftermath of other postwar recessions, growth in output, investment, and employment in the developed world all lagged behind. But the Great Recession was not like other postwar recessions in either scope or kind; expecting a standard V-shaped recovery was unreasonable. Given the severity, reach, and depth of the 2008 crisis, the proper comparison is with the Great Depression. And by that standard, the outcome variables look impressive. As Carmen Reinhart and Kenneth Rogoff conclude, "That its macroeconomic outcome has been only the most severe global recession since World War II—and not even worse—must be regarded as fortunate."[52]

One of the reasons for the relatively unscathed world economy has been the persistence of global economic openness. The salient data on cross-border flows suggests that globalization remains unbowed. Global trade flows bounced back after the dip during the acute phase of the crisis. FDI has returned to pre-crisis levels. The Great Recession failed to dent the growth in cross-border remittances. As a result, transnational capital flows rest on a more resilient foundation. Overall levels of cross-border finance remained lower compared to pre-crisis levels—but that was primarily due to the drying up of procyclical cross-border lending, particularly in Europe. International violence and insecurity also decreased during this period. The worst one can say about economic globalization in the post-2008 period is that it plateaued. Contrary to expectations and perceptions, the open global economy persisted.

Outputs

It could be that the global economy experienced a moderate bounceback in spite of rather than because of the global policy response. At the dawn of the twentieth century, for example, cross-border flows grew dramatically despite efforts by governments to raise barriers to exchange.[53] Economists like Paul Krugman and Joseph Stiglitz have been particularly scornful of both policymakers and central bankers.[54] In assessing policy outputs, Charles Kindleberger provided the standard definition of what should be done to stabilize the global economy during a severe financial crisis: he recommended "maintaining a relatively open market for distress goods," and providing liquidity to the global financial system through "countercyclical long-term lending" and "discounting."[55] Serious concerns were voiced in late 2008 and early 2009 about the inability of anyone to provide these kinds of global public goods, threatening a repeat of the beggar-thy-neighbor policies of the 1930s.[56] On the surface, the open market for distressed goods did seem under threat. The near-moribund status of the Doha Round, the rise of G20 protectionism after the fall 2008 summit, and the explosion in antidumping cases at the onset of the financial crisis suggested that markets were drifting toward closure. The WTO found that anti-dumping initiations surged by 30 percent in 2008 alone. In its June 2013 assessment, the free-trade group Global Trade Alert warned of a massive spike in protectionist measures leading to "a quiet, wide-ranging assault on the commercial level playing field."[57] *The Economist*'s Greg Ip lamented the rise of "gated globalization" because of rising trade protectionism.[58]

By Kindleberger's criteria, however, public goods provision has been quite robust since 2008. Warnings about an increase in protectionism have been vastly overstated. Figure 2.5 shows the way three different indices gauge shifts in trade protectionism from 2007. One component of the KOF Index of Globalization measures legal restrictions on cross-border flows of goods, services, and capital: tariffs, nontariff

FIGURE 2.5 Indices of Trade Freedom
Sources: Swiss Economic Institute, Heritage Foundation, Simon Fraser University
Note: KOF data ends in 2010; Simon Fraser data ends in 2011.

barriers, and capital controls. This component showed a modest decline after its 2007 acme—but the key word is "modest." Between 2007 and 2010, the drop-off among the G20 economies was 3.6 percent; among all the countries measured, however, the drop-off was only 1.3 percent. Other indices that measure trade restrictions suggest that the KOF index might be overly pessimistic. Simon Fraser University's Economic Freedom of the World report shows that the average freedom to trade internationally increased slightly between 2007 and 2011.[59] The Heritage Foundation's Index of Economic Freedom provides an even more optimistic picture. Its global index of trade freedom increased by 3.5 percent between 2008 and 2013.

The nonexplosion in protectionism is mostly attributable to minimal increases in tariffs. The average tariff levels of the G20 economies continued to decline after the 2008 crisis,[60] and the surge in WTO-recognized nontariff barriers quickly receded. As figure 2.6 shows, the surge never came close to the peak levels of these cases. By 2011, antidumping initiations had declined to their lowest levels since the WTO's founding in 1995. Both countervailing duty complaints and safeguard initiations also fell to pre-crisis levels. The combined effect of protectionist actions

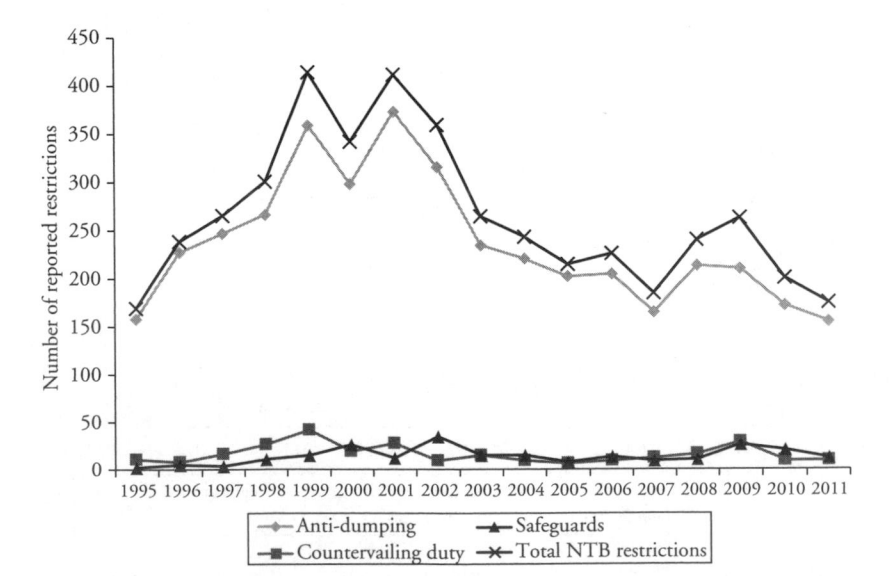

FIGURE 2.6 Trade Restrictions, 1955–2011
Source: World Trade Organization

for the first year after the peak of the crisis affected less than 0.8 percent of global trade.[61] Furthermore, the use of these protectionist measures declined further in 2010 to cover only 0.2 percent of global trade. Five years after the start of the Great Recession, the combined effect of these measures remains modest, affecting less than 4 percent of global trade flows.

Some post-2008 measures—such as those taken to bail out national banks, which can have a strong home bias—are not captured in these traditional metrics of nontariff barriers. It is therefore possible that such "murky protectionism" was on the rise as more traditional nontariff barriers were on the wane. The data suggests otherwise, however. The Global Trade Alert data—which casts the widest net in terms of measuring trade restrictions—shows a protectionist surge at the beginning of the crisis, followed by a relative decline in the ratio of trade-restricting to trade-liberalizing measures. Furthermore, 60 percent of the G20 temporary trade barriers imposed since 2009 were from countries that were responsible for less than 15 percent of all G20 imports.[62] Even if the number of trade-restricting measures increased, their aggregate effect on trade was minimal. The WTO's June 2013 estimate was that the combined effect of all post-crisis protectionist measures by the G20 had reduced trade flows by a total of 0.2 percent.[63] The WTO estimate jibes with academic estimates that "the Great Recession of 2009 does not coincide with any obvious increase in protectionism."[64] This is a striking contrast to the Great Depression. Economists estimate that increases in tariffs and nontariff barriers in the 1930s were responsible for more than 40 percent of the reduction in global trade.[65] Today's quick turnaround and the growth in trade levels further show that these measures have not seriously impeded market access.[66] What is particularly striking is that pre-crisis trade models predicted an increase in protection five to seven times greater than what actually transpired.[67]

Global governance played a significant role in this outcome. The G20 acted as a useful forum for reassuring participants not to raise their trade barriers, particularly toward the countries most affected by the Great Recession.[68] This is consistent with research showing that membership in the WTO and related organizations acted as a significant brake on increases in tariffs and nontariff barriers.[69] The major trading jurisdictions—the United States, the European Union, and

China—adhered most closely to their WTO obligations.[70] Peripheral countries have reversed course on specific protectionist actions in response to WTO warnings.[71] The WTO's dispute settlement mechanism helped to contain the spread of protectionist measures triggered by the Great Recession; compliance with these rulings did not wane after 2008.[72] As Alan Beattie acknowledged, "The 'Doha Round' of trade talks may be dead, but the WTO's dispute settlement arm is still playing a valuable role."[73] The WTO's Government Procurement Agreement (GPA) helped to blunt the most blatant parts of the "buy American" provisions of the 2009 fiscal stimulus in the United States, thereby preventing a cascade of "fiscal protectionism."

Policy advocates of trade liberalization embrace the bicycle theory— the belief that unless multilateral trade liberalization moves forward, the entire global trade regime will collapse because of a lack of forward momentum.[74] The last four years suggest that there are limits to that rule of thumb. The *Financial Times*/Economist Intelligence Unit surveys of global business leaders reveal that concerns about protectionism stayed at a low level.[75] Figure 2.7 shows that corporate officers were far less concerned about protectionism and currency volatility than they were about economic uncertainty. Reviewing the state of world trade, Carnegie Endowment for International Peace's Uri Dadush and his colleagues conclude, "The limited resort to protectionism was a remarkable aspect of the Great Recession."[76] Former US trade representative Susan Schwab concurs, noting, "Although countries took protectionist measures in the wake of the crisis, the international community avoided a quick deterioration into a spiral of beggar-thy-neighbor actions to block imports."[77] At a minimum, the bicycle of world trade is still coasting forward.

From the earliest stages of the financial crisis, central banks took concerted and coordinated action to ensure both discounting and countercyclical lending. Indeed, even most skeptics of post-2008 global economic governance acknowledge this point.[78] The central banks of the major economies slowly cut interest rates in the fall of 2007. A few months later, the central banks of the United States, Canada, the United Kingdom, Switzerland, and the eurozone announced currency swaps to ensure liquidity.[79] By fall 2008, they were cutting rates ruthlessly and in a coordinated fashion, "the first globally coordinated monetary easing in history," as one assessment put it.[80] Global real

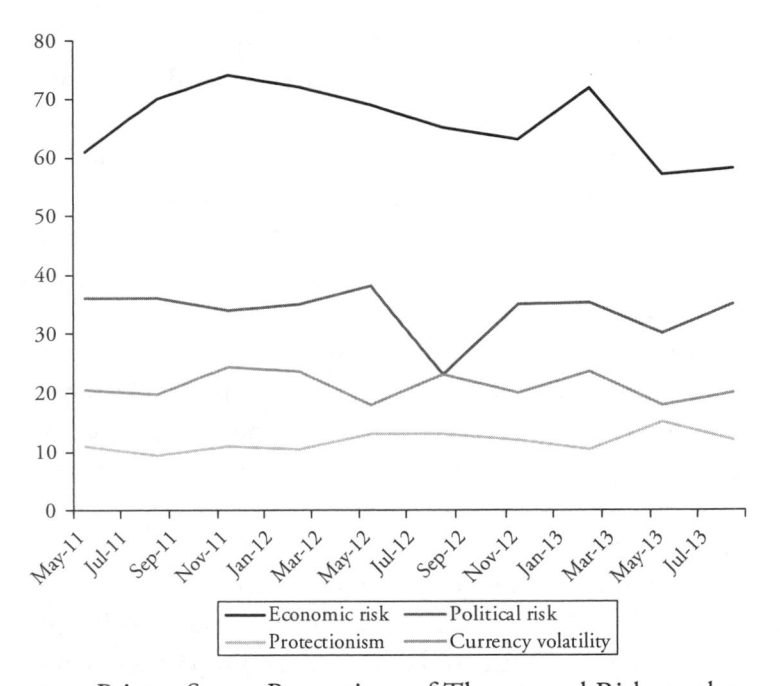

FIGURE 2.7 Private Sector Perceptions of Threats and Risks to the
Global Economy
Source: *Financial Times*/Economist Intelligence Unit

interest rates fell from an average of 3 percent before the crisis to zero
in 2012. In the advanced industrialized economies the real interest rate
was effectively negative.[81] Not content to just lower interest rates, most
of the major central banks also expanded emergency credit facilities
and engaged in more creative forms of quantitative easing. Between
2007 and 2012, the balance sheets of the central banks in the advanced
industrialized economies more than doubled. The BIS—which has
been unsympathetic to loose monetary policy—acknowledged in its
2012 annual report that "decisive action by central banks during the
global financial crisis was probably crucial in preventing a repeat of the
experiences of the Great Depression."[82]

Central banks and finance ministries also took coordinated action
during the fall of 2008 to ensure that cross-border lending would continue, so as to avert currency and solvency crises. That October, the G7
economies plus Switzerland agreed to unlimited currency swaps in order

to ensure liquidity would be maintained in the system. The United States then extended its currency-swap facility to Brazil, Singapore, Mexico, and South Korea. The European Central Bank expanded its euro-swap arrangements with Hungary, Denmark, and Poland. China, Japan, and South Korea, and the Association of Southeast Asian Nations (ASEAN) economies broadened the Chang Mai Initiative into an $80 billion swap arrangement to ensure liquidity. The IMF created the Short-Term Liquidity Facility, designed to "establish quick-disbursing financing for countries with strong economic policies that are facing temporary liquidity problems."[83] The IMF also negotiated emergency financing for Hungary, Pakistan, Iceland, and Ukraine. In the ten months after September 2008, the IMF executed more than $140 billion in standby arrangements to seventeen countries.[84]

Over the longer term, the great powers bulked up the international financial institutions' resources so they could provide for further countercyclical lending. In 2009, the G20 agreed to triple the IMF's reserves to $750 billion. In response to the worsening European sovereign debt crisis, G20 countries combined to pledge more than $430 billion in additional resources in 2012. The fund created multiple new credit facilities for its least-developed members, and established a flexible credit line that enabled members to sign up for precautionary arrangements without triggering market panic. Outside reviews of the fund's performance concluded that the IMF's response to the Great Recession "was larger in magnitude, was more rapid, and carried fewer conditions" than in prior crises.[85] The World Bank's International Development Association (IDA), which offers up the most concessionary form of lending, also increased its resources. The sixteenth IDA replenishment in December 2010 was a record $49.3 billion, an 18 percent increase of IDA resources over 2007 levels. The seventeenth IDA replenishment in December 2013 was $52 billion, a 5.5 percent increase from 2010 levels. Based on Kindleberger's criteria, it is clear that global economic governance responded rather well to the 2008 financial crisis.

To be sure, there are global public goods that go beyond Kindleberger's original criteria. Kindleberger himself later recognized the need for "coordination of monetary and fiscal policies among major nations."[86] Other international political economy scholars have stressed the need to coordinate, clarify, and reform cross-border-exchange regulations after a crisis. Again, the international system was active in these areas after 2008. Between the popping of the subprime mortgage bubble and the June 2010 G20 Toronto summit, the major economies were agreed on the need for aggressive and expansionary fiscal and monetary policies. The combined G20 stimulus in 2008 and 2009 amounted to approximately $2 trillion—or 1.4 percent of global economic output.[87] The estimated effect of fiscal and monetary policy coordination was to boost global economic growth by approximately 2 percent.[88] As discussed in greater detail in chapter 6, even reluctant contributors like Germany eventually bowed to pressure from economists and G20 peers. Indeed, in 2009, Germany enacted the third-largest fiscal stimulus in the world.[89] Germany's acting against its initial set of preferences is an example of global economic governance leading to greater policy coordination, rather than flowing from a simple harmony of preferences.

Progress was also made in the regulatory coordination of finance and investment rules. There were developments in two particular areas: investor protectionism and banking regulation. The rise of sovereign wealth funds before 2008 had ratcheted up restrictions to cross-border investment by state-owned enterprises and funds. The OECD articulated its own guidelines for recipient countries but warned that unless the funds demonstrated greater transparency, barriers to investment would likely rise even further.[90] In September 2008, an IMF-brokered working group approved a set of "generally accepted principles and practices" for sovereign wealth funds. These voluntary guidelines—also called the Santiago Principles—consisted of twenty-four recommendations addressing the legal and institutional frameworks, governance issues, and risk management of sovereign wealth funds.

The expert consensus among financial analysts, regulators, and academics was that these principles—if fully implemented—would address most recipient-country concerns. One newspaper characterized the new rules as "a rare triumph for IMF financial diplomacy."[91] And indeed, after the IMF approved the Santiago Principles, sovereign wealth funds began displaying significantly greater transparency.[92] Not coincidentally, national security exceptions to FDI have waned. Overall, investor protectionism has declined.[93] In their 2013 report to the G20 on the state of cross-border investment, the OECD and

UNCTAD concluded, "On the whole, G20 members have contin-ued to honor their pledge not to introduce new restrictive policies for international investment. Almost all new investment policy measures that G20 members adopted during the reporting period tended to eliminate investment restrictions, and to facilitate inward or outward investment."[94]

International regulators also significantly revised the Basel core banking principles. At the November 2010 Seoul summit, the G20 approved the Basel III banking standards. Basel III took only two years to negotiate—markedly less time than the six years it took to hammer out Basel II. The new rules, scheduled to be phased in over the rest of this decade, increase the amount of reserve capital banks must keep on hand and add new countercyclical capital buffers to prevent financial institutions from engaging in procyclical lending.

Financial-sector analysts and scholars have debated whether Basel III is a sufficient upgrade in regulatory stringency, and whether it will be implemented too slowly or not at all (see chapter 4 for a more detailed discussion).[95] There is consensus, however, that Basel III upgrades the Basel II standards in terms of preventing bank failures.[96] Furthermore, Basel III standards were approved despite fierce resistance from the global banking industry. By November 2011, the Financial Stability Board (FSB) had designated the systemically important global banks that would be required to keep additional capital on hand. The FSB is working with the International Organization of Securities Commissions to identify systemically important nonbank financial entities.

The final and most obvious global public good that global gover-nance can provide is international security—protecting the global commons in the air, space, and sea from security threats. Here, global governance also performed rather well. For example, in response to the worsening piracy problem, the United Nations Security Council quickly passed two resolutions—nos. 1846 and 1851—authorizing the use of force against pirates off the Somali coast. An ad hoc coalition of more than twenty-five countries formed the Combined Task Force 151 (CTF 151) to patrol the Gulf of Aden. Other countries that were not formally part of the task force—including China and Iran—also sent patrol ships. Reviewing the myriad efforts, a RAND analyst concluded, "The international response represents an unprecedented level of inter-governmental cooperation that has been achieved in a remarkably short period of time."[97] These efforts made a substantial contribution to the decline of piracy attacks.[98] CTF 151 and other activities off the coast of Somalia led to the arrests of nearly 1,200 pirates. Prosecutions have taken place in twenty countries, and top pirates have announced their "retirement" in response to more perilous conditions.[99] In September 2013 the ICC International Maritime Bureau concluded, "The pro-active responses by the [CTF 151] navies toward suspicious/ potential Somali pirates has ensured that the threat of piracy is continually addressed and removed from the water. As attacks continue to drop the presence of the navies cannot be underestimated."[100]

Operations

The degree of institutional resiliency and flexibility at the global level has been rather remarkable. Once the acute phase of the 2008 financial crisis began, the G20 quickly supplanted the G7/G8 as the focal point for global economic governance. At the September 2009 G20 summit in Pittsburgh, the member countries avowed that they had "designated the G20 to be the premier forum for our international economic cooperation."[101] This move addressed the worsening problem of the G8's waning power and relevancy—a problem of which G8 members were painfully aware.[102] The G20 grouping comprises 85 percent of global economic output, 80 percent of global trade, and 66 percent of global population. The G20 is not perfectly inclusive, and it has a somewhat idiosyncratic membership at the margins, but it is a far more legitimate and representative body than the G8. As Geoffrey Garrett puts it, "The G20 is globally representative yet small enough to make consensual decision-making feasible."[103] As a club of great powers, the G20 has the capability, when there is consensus within, to lead effective policy coordination across a wide range of issues.

Having the capacity to be an effective body and actually *being* one are two different things. Even skeptics of global economic governance acknowledge that the G20 successfully coordinated monetary and fiscal policies at the outset of the crisis.[104] The conventional wisdom, however, is that the G20's political momentum stalled out in 2010 after countries disagreed on macroeconomic imbalances and the virtues of austerity.[105] The reality is more complex. It is certainly true that consensus on macroeconomic policy broke down, but much of the rest of the G20's Framework for Strong, Sustainable and Balanced Growth agenda went forward.[106] According to the University of Toronto's G20 Information Centre, compliance with G20 commitments actually increased over time. The research group measured G20 adherence to "chosen priority commitments." Measured on a per country average, G20 members have steadily improved since the 61.5 percent compliance rate for the April 2009 London Summit commitments, rising all the way to 77 percent for the June 2012 Los Cabos Summit.[107]

An obvious rejoinder is that this kind of finding inflates compliance because the pledges made at these summits are so modest.[108] If the G20 has scaled back its ambitions—even in its "priority commitments"—compliance is easier. Nevertheless, the focal-point function of the G20 signaled European leaders to take more vigorous action on the eurozone crisis in the fall of 2011.[109] Great powers also used the G20 as a means of blunting domestic pressures for greater protectionism—at precisely the moments when the group was thought to be losing its political momentum.[110] For example, the G20 served as a useful mechanism to defuse rising domestic tensions in the United States concerning China's undervalued currency. In April 2010, in response to congressional pressure for more robust action, US Treasury secretary Timothy Geithner cited the G20 as "the best avenue for advancing US interests" on China's manipulation of its exchange rate.[111] This successfully deflected momentum in Congress to take unilateral action against China.

At the same time, Chinese central bank officials and advisers signaled a commitment to modify its posture on exchange rates.[112] Immediately prior to the June 2010 Toronto G20 summit, China announced that it would let the renminbi appreciate against the other major currencies. For the next three years, the renminbi nominally appreciated at a rate of 5 percent a year—more so if one factors in the differences in national inflation rates. Significant appreciations in the renminbi occurred in advance of G20 meetings, indicating China's desire to avoid clashes over the currency issue at those summits.[113] By late 2012, the renminbi hit record highs against the dollar, and China had dramatically curtailed its intervention into exchange-rate markets.[114] In the three years after China's pledge, the renminbi appreciated by 15 percent against the country's major trading partners. This contributed to a shrinking of global current account imbalances of more than 30 percent since the start of the crisis.[115] Assessing the state of current account imbalances in September 2013, *The Economist* concluded that "the world has rebalanced."[116]

Other key financial bodies also expanded their membership and authority as a response to the 2008 crisis. In March 2009, the Basel Committee on Banking Supervision enlarged its membership from thirteen advanced industrialized states to twenty-seven members by adding the developing-country members of the G20. The Financial Stability Forum was renamed the Financial Stability Board in April 2009 and given greater responsibilities for regulatory coordination; its membership expanded to include the developing-country members of the G20. During this period, the Committee of the Global Financial System also grew from thirteen countries to twenty-two members, adding Brazil, China, and India, among others. The Financial Action Task Force on Money Laundering added China, India, and South Korea to its grouping. Prior to 2008, the G7 countries dominated most of these financial standard-setting agencies.[117] That is no longer the case in terms of membership. Political scientist Miles Kahler described this expansion as "the most dramatic innovation in global governance in the wake of the global economic crisis—and one likely to be the longest lasting."[118]

In the future, this expansion might impair the efficacy of these groups—but their legitimacy has been enhanced since 2008. Indeed, the G20's assessment process has further enhanced the monitoring powers of many of these institutions. In requesting reports from the Financial Stability Board, as well as organizations ranging from the IMF to the WTO to UNCTAD, the G20 augmented the expertise and legitimacy of these governance structures. The pre-summit reports by these international organizations framed the discussions at the meetings.

The IMF and the World Bank also changed after the financial crisis, albeit in ways that may not be apparent on the surface. The implicit compact by which a European is given the IMF managing director slot, and an American is appointed to the World Bank presidency, for example, has continued. Despite the scandals that engulfed IMF managing director Dominique Strauss-Kahn in 2011 and World Bank president Paul Wolfowitz five years earlier, former French finance minister Christine Lagarde replaced Strauss-Kahn in 2011, and American Jim Yong Kim replaced Wolfowitz's successor Robert Zoellick as the new World Bank president in 2012.

Beneath the surface, however, the Bank and the Fund have witnessed significant evolution. Power within the IMF is based on quota size, calculated using a complex formula of economic variables. Prior to 2007, the allotment of quotas in the IMF bore little resemblance to the distribution of world economic power. This has changed. One important step has been two rounds of quota reform that the IMF implemented in 2011. An additional quota reform was proposed in 2010 that will further reallocate influence toward the advanced developing economies. Despite fierce resistance from European members, this reform will be implemented pending US congressional approval. The goal of all three reforms has been to expand the voting power of the advanced developing economies. Once the latest round of quota reform takes effect, China will possess the third-largest voting share in the Fund, and all four BRIC economies will be among the ten largest IMF shareholders. There is also a planned shift to an all-elected Executive Board at the IMF, a move designed to further reduce the number of European representatives on the board.

The World Bank Group underwent a parallel set of reforms. Between 2008 and 2010, the voting power of developing and transitioning economies within the main World Bank institution (the International Bank for Reconstruction and Development) was increased by 4.59 percentage points, and China became the third-largest voting member. The International Finance Corporation (IFC) approved an even larger shift of more than six percentage points. More important, the Bank's Development Committee agreed that Bank and IFC shareholding would be reviewed every five years beginning in 2015, routinizing the process of reallocating power within the committee.[119] At the same time, the Bank also took steps to improve its transparency. It is not surprising, then, that in the Council on Foreign Relations, April 2013 assessment of global governance structures, it was finance that received the highest mark among the different global issue areas.[120]

While the appointments of Lagarde and Kim might appear to be politically retrograde, they represent bargaining that reflected the greater influence of the advanced developing countries. In both cases, the nominee had to woo developing countries to secure political support in advance of voting. China, for example, was an early supporter of both Lagarde and Kim despite the presence of emerging-market candidates.[121] The appointment of Chinese national Min Zhu to be a deputy managing director of the IMF at the same time that Lagarde took over might have been one reason for this preference.

The content of bank and fund policies has also shifted to better reflect developing-country concerns. In the wake of the 2008 financial crisis, the IMF began to change its attitude about the wisdom of capital controls. In February 2010, an IMF staff paper concluded that under some circumstances, capital controls could be a legitimate and useful policy tool.[122] Dani Rodrik characterized the change in the IMF's tune as a "stunning reversal" of its previous orthodoxy.[123] By November 2012, the staff note had translated into the IMF's official position. The fund allowed that capital controls could be "useful" in some circumstances, and that "[there is] no presumption that full [capital account] liberalization is an appropriate goal for all countries at all times."[124] As for the Bank, Kim's appointment to the presidency in 2012 highlights the shift in priorities. Trained as a doctor and an anthropologist, Kim's entire pre-Bank career had focused on health policy. This suggests that the Bank will use a more capacious notion of development going forward, consistent with developing-country preferences.

The trade and investment regimes have displayed somewhat less vigor than global financial governance. But these regimes have not withered on the vine either. The multilateral trade regime would appear to have suffered the most from the Great Recession. The failure to complete the Doha Round negotiations in 2008 was a blow to the WTO. Nevertheless, the WTO as an institution has endured. In December 2013 in Bali, the WTO negotiated the trade facilitation part of the Doha Round, which outside analysts estimate will boost the global economy by $1 trillion over the next decade. Beyond Doha, the organization has expanded its reach in several ways. Geographically, the WTO finally secured the accession of the Russian Federation, the last G20 nonmember, after a slow-motion fifteen-year negotiation process. Since the start of 2007, the WTO has added seven members, including Ukraine and Vietnam.

The WTO also adapted to play a crucial role in constraining the rise in protectionism. The WTO enhanced its monitoring and acted as a focal point for additional plurilateral liberalization. Beginning in late 2008, the WTO's secretariat used the Trade Policy Review Mechanism to report to the G20 on a regular basis on increases in protectionism. After some initial reluctance, WTO members accepted the move as a useful increase in monitoring and transparency.[125] The WTO reports on trade restrictions became accepted as authoritative. A comparison of the WTO's monitoring reports with those of Global Trade Alert further shows some significant flaws with the latter. Global Trade Alert's monitoring has been based on less reliable metrics, exaggerating the increase in protectionism.[126]

WTO members also shifted their approach toward trade liberalization by expanding existing plurilateral agreements or starting new ones while still working on the Doha Round. China is negotiating to join the GPA, which requires that states not discriminate against foreign contractors for government contracts. The United States, the European Union, and eighteen other countries accelerated talks on a services liberalization agreement that would encompass most of the OECD economies as well as advanced developing countries.[127]

Enthusiasm for greater trade liberalization has found an additional outlet: the "open regionalism" of regional and bilateral free-trade agreements (FTAs). The traditional expectation that an economic downturn would dampen enthusiasm for greater openness has not been borne out by the data on FTAs. In the four years preceding the collapse of Lehman Brothers, fifty-one FTAs were reported to the WTO. In the four years since Lehman, fifty-eight FTAs have been registered.[128] The United States and ten other countries are currently negotiating a Trans-Pacific Partnership, with other countries preparing to join. The United States and European Union are negotiating a Transatlantic Trade and Investment Partnership as well.

To be sure, not all of these FTAs were created equal. Some have greater coverage of goods and services than others. Some might promote more trade diversion than trade creation. Nevertheless, their recent pattern of growth mirrors how FTAs spread in the late nineteenth century.[129] Even if the current FTAs do not include the most-favored nation provision that accelerated trade liberalization in the nineteenth century, the political economy of trade diversion still generates competitive incentives for a growth in FTAs, thereby leading to a similar outcome.[130] As the export sectors in states lagging behind in FTA creation lose out from trade diversion, they begin to lobby their national governments to join the crowd and sign more trade agreements. This kind of competitive liberalization can lead to reduced trade barriers. Through their own shared understandings and dispute-settlement mechanisms, FTAs also act as an additional brake on protectionist policies.[131]

There is no multilateral investment regime to display resiliency. No single institution has the authority of a WTO in trade or an IMF in finance. Instead, a network of bilateral investment treaties (BITs) makes up the principal governance mechanism for investment. Compared to the growth pattern in FTAs, it would appear that the pace of expansion of BITs has slowed since 2008. According to UNCTAD data, an annual average of seventy-eight BITs were completed in the three years prior to 2008; an average of only sixty-one per annum were negotiated in the three years after 2008. That indicates a slowdown.[132] A look at the longer time series, however, reveals that the Great Recession is not the cause of this slowdown. As figure 2.8 shows, the peak of BIT negotiations took place in the decade after the end of the Cold War. From 1992 to 2001, an annual average of 160 BITs were negotiated. After 2001, however, the number of negotiated BITs declined, following a standard diffusion pattern. Based on that kind of pattern of diffusion, the last three years have seen expected levels of BIT growth. Furthermore, in 2012 the United States introduced a new "model BIT" and started BIT negotiations with China, India, and other countriess, suggesting that there will be more significant liberalization going forward.[133]

Conclusion

When the subprime mortgage crisis began, there were rampant fears that global economic governance was dysfunctional and unprepared to cope with its severity. The Great Recession exacerbated those fears.

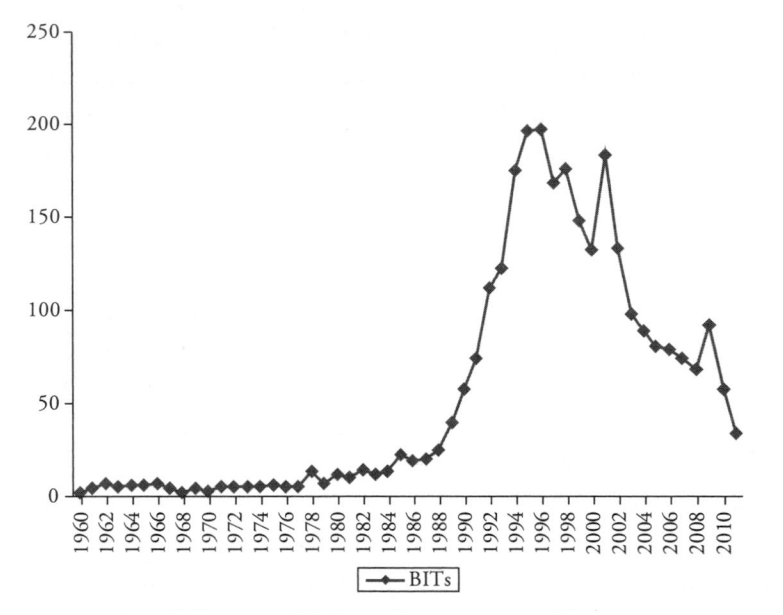

FIGURE 2.8 Annual Count of Bilateral Investment Treaties, 1960–2011

Source: UNCTAD

Yet, a review of policy outcomes, outputs, and operations shows a different picture. If we step back, we find considerable evidence that global economic governance responded adroitly to the 2008 financial crisis and Great Recession. Even though the initial drop in output and trade levels was more acute in 2008 than in 1929, by any measure the global economy has rebounded more robustly over the past five years than it did during the Depression. Global trade and investment levels recovered from their plunge in late 2008 and early 2009. In part this is because the great powers and global governance structures successfully coordinated policy outputs that alleviated the worst effects of the financial crisis. A mélange of international coordination mechanisms facilitated the provision of liquidity and served as bulwarks against protectionism. Multilateral economic institutions adapted and responded to the 2008 financial crisis in a surprisingly nimble fashion. Key international organizations expanded their policy competencies and adjusted their governance structures to better reflect the distribution of power in the world. Contrary to pre-crisis expectations, global economic

TABLE 2.1 The Functions of Global Economic Governance

IGO	Focal Point	Reassurance	Monitoring and Enforcement	Norms, Legal Obligation	Expertise	Containing Domestic Pressures
WTO		X	X	X	X	X
IMF	X	X	X	X	X	
World Bank		X		X	X	
BIS	X			X	X	
G20	X	X				X

governance performed the necessary tasks to prevent the 2008 financial crisis from metastasizing into a prolonged depression. In short, the system worked.

Table 2.1 compares the different ways in which international institutions can matter with what actually happened after 2008 based on the data in this chapter. Some of these results are unsurprising. The IMF, for example, with its considerable resources and expertise, mattered through a number of different mechanisms. Other results are more counterintuitive. Even with the trade facilitaton deal, the WTO did not really serve as a focal point for trade liberalization after 2008. But, on every other dimension, the organization was very relevant in containing protectionism. Similarly, the G20 has no independent staff or secretariat, but it served multiple roles. It was a useful focal point for great-power consultations on the global political economy, provided a forum for the great powers to consult with one another, and at crucial moments, usefully blunted domestic pressures. Although the G20 had no monitoring capabilities, it did empower other institutions to monitor commitments to economic openness. What is clear is that all of these regimes mattered in multiple ways. Monocausal explanations about why global governance is useful are clearly not satisfactory to explain their performance during the Great Recession.

The evidence presented in this chapter suggests that the liberal economic order proved to be more robust than expected. As John Ikenberry has observed, "The last decade has brought remarkable upheavals in the global system—the emergence of new powers, financial crises, a global recession, and bitter disputes among allies. . . . Despite these upheavals, liberal international order as an organizational logic of world politics has proven resilient. It is still in demand."[134] Despite uncertain times, the open global economic order that has been in operation since 1945 does not appear to be closing anytime soon. After the biggest stress test the world has seen in seventy years, the open global economy endured.

3

Why the Misperception?

RELATIVE TO PREVIOUS CRISES of similar severity, global economic governance responded in a surprisingly nimble fashion after 2008. Its ability to maintain the openness of cross-border flows played an important part in preventing a collapse of the global economy. Global governance structures supplied the necessary public goods and coordinating mechanisms to prevent the financial crisis from mushrooming into a full-blown global depression. The internal rules and memberships of key global economic governance structures were revamped to reflect shifts in the distribution of power. Whether one examines the outcomes, outputs, or operations of international institutions, the system worked—not perfectly, but "good enough."

As noted in chapter 1, few global policy elites and commentators agree with the points made in the previous paragraph.[1] Despite easily accessible data, the conventional wisdom among most analysts is that global economic governance is badly broken and in desperate need of repair. By any reasonable metric, global governance structures did what was necessary to preserve the open global economy. This remains a counterintuitive fact despite the abundance of supporting evidence.

Why is there such widespread misperception about the performance of global economic governance? Exploring the possible biases at work can be useful. Without a better understanding of why there is so much current confusion, it will be difficult to make any predictions for the future of global governance. In this chapter, I offer several reasons for this misperception: an exaggeration of the costs of perceived global governance failures, a misplaced nostalgia for prior eras of global economic governance, the distribution of benefits from current economic growth, and the conflation of national with global governance.

Exaggerating the Failures

There is an excellent reason commentators have been so skeptical about the state of global economic governance—there are numerous areas in which global economic governance did falter or fail. The Doha Round of world trade talks had stagnated for years. The breakdown of macroeconomic policy consensus between 2010 and 2012 acted as a genuine drag on global economic growth. No appreciable progress was made in climate change talks. Negotiations to update existing telecommunications protocols broke down in angry political posturing in late 2012.[2] In other issue areas, such as cybercrime, there is not even a whisper of an effective international regime.[3] On financial regulations, no reform has truly solved the "too big to fail" problem at the global level. There are prominent examples of dysfunctional outcomes in the security realm as well. It is safe to say that global governance since 2008 has been imperfect.

The problem comes when one tries to weigh the significance of these governance failures relative to the successes detailed in the last chapter. And here we run into a dirty little secret of world politics: many international relations or politics commentators do not know much about economics or international economic policy. In fact, very few of them have the requisite interest to opine in detail about the global economy. International affairs professionals frequently talk about "high politics" and "low politics." They usually relegate economic issues into the latter category and focus their energies on the former. Political pundits are even more disinterested in this topic.

This lack of interest matters when political commentators try to assess economic policy or global economic governance. They naturally rely on surface-level policy outputs as the most obvious metric. And as I just noted, many of the most obvious data points did suggest a breakdown in global governance. The snail's pace of the Doha Round, the failure of the Copenhagen climate change summit, and the deadlock of the G20 summits seemed like sufficient evidence to proclaim that global governance was imperiled—hence the fast-congealing consensus that the international system was broken. It is difficult to correct such misperceptions once they are cemented, particularly if the topic in question is outside a pundit's bailiwick.[4] If international relations commentators collectively overestimated the costs of governance breakdowns, then groupthink can prevent a reassessment despite falsifying evidence.

The best example from the Great Recession has been the repeated concern voiced about exchange-rate volatility and currency wars. Initially, there seemed to be valid reasons for such fears. Currency volatility spiked in fall 2008. Concerns escalated after developed economies began pursuing more unconventional forms of monetary policy. With interest rates set close to zero, central banks engaged in quantitative easing as a way of pumping more money into the economy. In 2010, the US Federal Reserve began hinting at a second round of quantitative easing, known colloquially as QE2. One of the policy externalities of quantitative easing was US dollar depreciation. A falling dollar boosts American exports and reduces American imports. It can also trigger an increase in capital outflows to countries that could offer appreciating assets or higher rates of return—in this case, the advanced developing countries.

Fearing domestic-asset bubbles from an inward rush of capital, many of these countries complained loudly and publicly about the prospect of QE2. In September 2010, Brazilian finance minister Guido Mantega labeled the phenomenon an "international currency war." A week later, IMF managing director Dominique Strauss-Kahn seemed to endorse this concern, warning in a *Financial Times* interview against using currency depreciation as a "policy weapon."[5] Analysts quickly adopted "currency wars" as a term of art; within a month it had made the cover of *The Economist* magazine. Despite this rhetoric, the Federal Reserve went ahead with its QE2 program, angering most of the other G20 members. Officials from Germany, Brazil, and China blasted Federal Reserve chairman Benjamin Bernanke in a private G20 meeting in South Korea in October 2010; those critiques went public a month later.[6] By the end of 2010, Brazil, South Korea, Taiwan, Thailand, Indonesia, and Chile had all imposed capital controls to slow down hot money inflows.[7] These few months of public skirmishing strongly fed perceptions that the G20's influence was fading and that exchange

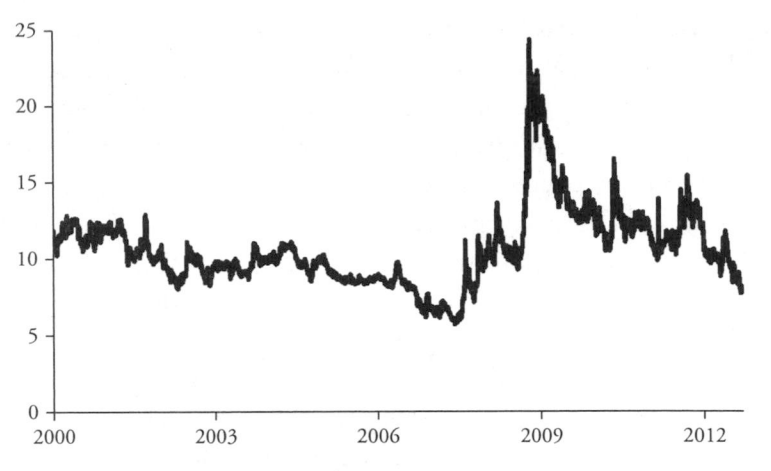

FIGURE 3.1 J. P. Morgan G7 Volatility Index, 2000–2012
Source: Hood 2012, chart 3

rates were gyrating wildly.[8] Foreign policy analysts joined the chorus of concern, warning about the global implications of a currency war.[9]

Lost in all the hype was the simple fact that neither markets nor experts were terribly perturbed about the possibility of excessive exchange-rate volatility or an actual currency war. After fall 2008, exchange-rate volatility receded to close to pre-crisis levels, as figure 3.1 demonstrates. Even including the acute phase of the crisis, exchange-rate volatility did not reach the levels that immediately preceded the collapses of the Bretton Woods system and the gold standard.[10] Assessing the performance of the international monetary system during the worst of the crisis, Uri Dadush and Vera Eidelman at the Carnegie Endowment for International Peace concluded: "Over the worst days of the crisis, from September 2008 to June 2009, the international monetary system remained orderly and flexible currencies provided a safety valve. Exchange rates adjusted quite smoothly and, while month-to-month volatility increased in 2009, changes in real exchange rates were modest. Those changes that did occur appeared justified by economic fundamentals…today's international monetary system is remarkably resilient."[11]

The gap between perceptions and reality about the currency wars continued to diverge as time passed. As figure 3.2 demonstrates, J. P. Morgan's G7 Volatility Index did spike briefly in fall 2010 but never came close to approaching its 2008 peak. By the end of the calendar year, the index had fallen back to pre-2008 levels—continuing a downward secular trend in exchange-rate volatility toward levels below the pre-crisis average.[12] Surveys of international business executives and financial analysts in the Bloomberg Global Poll conducted in September 2010 revealed minimal concerns about exchange rate volatility and relative comfort with US monetary policy.[13] By January 2011, investors were far more interested in taking risk in overseas investments, indicating muted fears about currency volatility.[14] Indeed, in its issue on currency wars, the *Economist*'s lead editorial concluded that "these skirmishes fall far short of a real currency war...The capital-inflow controls are modest....Nor is there much risk of an imminent descent into trade retaliation."[15] This matched the assessment of market analysts and economists as well.[16] By spring 2011, fears of exchange-rate volatility had died down in the popular press as well.

Despite the failure of a currency war to actually emerge, the meme never died out. A Google Trends analysis shows that "currency wars" repeatedly triggered elevated search levels despite continued declines in currency volatility.[17] The meme peaked again in December 2012—and this time the gap between perception and reality was even more pronounced. By that fall, the United States was engaged in a third round of quantitative easing, and the European Central Bank had also reversed course, moving from raising interest rates to making more aggressive purchases of eurozone sovereign debt. The Japanese central bank acted aggressively to lower interest rates on the yen. This triggered rumblings from other Pacific Rim central bankers about the need to prevent "negative spillover effects" and the creation of a "regional core currency."[18] Again, the use of the term "currency war" spiked. Bundesbank president Jens Weidmann gave a speech in which he cautioned against the "increased politicization of exchange rates" and a potential "devaluation competition." Other G20 central bank officials publicly warned that a currency war was brewing yet again.[19] So did notables such as Pimco's Mohammed El-Erian and Microsoft's Bill Gates.[20]

Again, both the hard data and expert analyses refuted the bubble of concern about a currency war. As figure 3.2 demonstrates, J. P. Morgan's G7 Volatility Index only increased modestly. Indeed, it failed to come close to its 2012 high, much less the 2010 levels.

Neither the Bloomberg Global Poll of investors nor the *Financial Times/Economist* poll of executives showed any elevated concern about currency volatility. Numerous experts pointed out that during this episode, as during the 2010 period, central banks were simply trying to stimulate their domestic economies through expansionary monetary policy. Former central banker Philipp Hildebrand explained in the *Financial Times*, "Central banks are simply doing what they are meant to do and what they have always done. They set monetary policy consistent with their domestic mandates."[21] Indeed, this sentiment was reflected in the G20 communiqué issued by finance ministers in February 2013: "Monetary policy should be directed toward domestic price stability and continuing to support economic recovery according to the respective mandates. We commit to monitor and minimize the negative spillovers on other countries of policies implemented for domestic purposes."[22]

By summer 2013, an interesting policy turnabout had taken place between the United States and the developing country members of the G20. The Federal Reserve had announced forward guidance suggesting a slow tapering of quantitative easing as the US economy picked up steam. In anticipation of higher interest rates, capital rushed out of the developing world and toward the United States. The movement in capital markets negatively affected India, Brazil, and other emerging markets. In response, the same countries that had accused the United States of launching a currency war three years earlier reversed their policy position. They complained that the United States was going to do exactly what these countries had advocated three years earlier—but now it was a bad thing.[23]

The gap between the rhetoric and the reality about currency wars remains wide. Barry Eichengreen noted, "'Currency war' is a meme that will not go away."[24] Why? One reason is that the term "currency wars" was catchy enough for even noneconomists to understand and repeat. Goldman Sachs's Jim O'Neill went so far as to blame social media for the idea catching on, labeling it as "another sign of the 'Facebook Times.'"[25] *Business Insider*'s Joe Weisenthal concurred, noting that "basically, 'currency wars' is a silly phrase with huge viral potential."[26] The currency wars meme demonstrates that when other perceptual biases cause observers to believe that global economic governance is faltering, those perceptions are hard to reverse.

Days of Global Economic Governance Past

The presumption in much of the commentary on the current global political economy is that past eras of hegemonic leadership or governance structures were better and stronger. For example, adroit management of the gold standard facilitated nineteenth-century globalization, boosting trade flows between 30 percent and 70 percent.[27] When commentators talk about reviving the gold standard, they reference this period as an example of why such a policy would succeed today.[28]

An even greater number of post-crisis analysts look back on the late 1940s as a halcyon time when global economic governance "worked" in any plain-sense definition of the word. That postwar era witnessed a major burst of growth in global governance structures. The creation of the Bretton Woods institutions, backstopped by the United States, ushered in a new era of global governance.[29] In 2012, former US national security advisor Brent Scowcroft encapsulated the post-crisis conventional wisdom on this subject.[30]

> The [2008] crisis demonstrated that we had a single worldwide financial system in which a crisis in one area could quickly spread throughout the world. But the world clearly had no single global way to deal with that crisis. This was far different even from the end of World War II.... The postwar leaders set up the International Monetary Fund, the World Bank, and the General Agreements on Tariffs and Trade to develop rules of the road. The new G20 is but a pale reflection of that once-brilliant institution building.

This narrative elides two inconvenient facts. The first is that past efforts at global economic governance have had more than their fair share of futility. For example, American hegemonic leadership did indeed achieve its acme in the late 1940s. According to the traditional narrative, this was a period of peak performance in global economic governance as well. Even during this peak, however, the United States failed to ratify the Havana Charter, which would have created an international trade organization far wider in scope than the current WTO. With the Marshall Plan, the US decided to act outside the purview of the Bretton Woods institutions, permanently weakening their influence.[31] The United States created the Coordinating Committee for Multilateral Export Controls (CoCom) to restrict trade with the Soviet bloc but encountered severe difficulties in getting its allies to expand the strategic embargo. After the late 1940s, American leadership and global financial governance experienced as many misses as hits. The logic of the Bretton Woods system rested on the economic contradiction that the United States continue to export dollars but also be able to redeem those dollars into gold—a paradox that became known as the Triffin dilemma. Extravagant macroeconomic policies in the United States, combined with the growing reluctance to accommodate the US position, eroded that global financial order. As the logical contradictions of the Bretton Woods regime became more evident, existing policy coordination mechanisms failed to correct the problem. The IMF found itself incapable of pressuring countries running surpluses.[32] By 1971, when the United States unilaterally decided to close the gold window, all the major economies had chosen to prioritize domestic interests over coordinating action at the global level.[33] In ending Bretton Woods, the United States also undercut the IMF's original reason for existence.

Post–Bretton Woods global economic governance was equally haphazard. While tariffs continued to fall, the developed world embraced a plethora of nontariff barriers designed to restrict imports. An increase in antidumping cases, countervailing duties, and quantitative restrictions on imports weakened the rules of the global trading system over the next two decades. Neither the United States nor any international institution was able to prevent the Organization of Petroleum Exporting Countries (OPEC) from raising energy prices from 1973 to 1986.[34] Exchange rates and macroeconomic policy coordination devolved from the IMF to the G7. A predictable cycle emerged: other G7 countries would pressure the United States to scale back its fiscal deficits. In turn, the United States would pressure Japan and West Germany to expand their domestic consumption in order to act as locomotives of growth. Not surprisingly, the most common outcome on the macroeconomic front was a stalemate.[35]

There is a second problem with the nostalgia for past eras of global governance: it understates the considerable policy errors that occurred when there actually was agreement. The history of efforts at exchange-rate and macroeconomic policy coordination illuminate this problem, as even perceived successes had perverse policy outcomes. The era of the classical gold standard, for example, was the heyday of international exchange-rate coordination. This period was also unusual for other reasons, however. The limited extent of the democratic franchise, combined with the low degree of political organization among the working classes, made it easier for governments to make the painful domestic adjustments necessary to keep the gold standard functioning. Economic historian Barry Eichengreen has observed that the pressure that twentieth- and twenty-first-century governments experienced to subordinate currency stability to other policy objectives was not a feature of the nineteenth-century world.[36] Adherence to the gold standard during periods when gold discoveries were small contributed to crushing depressions and deflations across Europe—often forcing countries to abandon the gold standard. Only after 1895, when a burst of gold discoveries allowed global liquidity to increase, did the domestic costs of adhering to the gold standard temporarily ease.[37]

Similarly, the "successes" in postwar macroeconomic policy coordination yielded mixed results at best. The most notable success was the aggressive US macroeconomic response to the Asian Financial Crisis in 1998. By cutting interest rates rapidly in order to serve as a market for distressed goods, the United States expedited the regional recovery. Yet, policy coordination during other eras was more problematic. The G7 economies were successfully managing the depreciation of the US dollar—and the US current account deficit—via the 1985 Plaza Accord and 1987 Louvre Accord. But while successful, these agreements allowed the value of the yen to skyrocket and triggered the beginning of an unsustainable asset bubble in Japan. In Europe, the creation of the euro in 1999 seemed to count as an example of successful monetary policy coordination. The European Union's Growth and Stability Pact that was attached to the creation of the common European currency, however, was less successful. Within a year of the euro's birth, five of the eleven member countries were not compliant; by 2005, the three largest countries in the eurozone were ignoring the pact.[38] Since the start of the 2008 financial crisis, the inherent flaws of the eurozone arrangement have become manifestly clear.

Regardless of the distribution of power or the robustness of international institutions, macroeconomic policy coordination does not have a distinguished history.[39] In comparison, the three years of successful macroeconomic policy coordination between mid-2007 and mid-2010 were downright remarkable. None of this is to deny that global economic governance was useful and stabilizing at various points after 1945. Rather, it is to observe that even during the heyday of American hegemony, the ability of global economic governance to solve ongoing global economic problems was limited.[40] The original point of Kindleberger's analysis of the Great Depression was to discuss what needed to be done during a global economic crisis. By that standard, the post-2008 performance of key institutions has been far better than extant commentary suggests.

Where You Stand on Global Economic Governance Depends on Where You Live

An old axiom of bureaucratic politics is that "where you stand depends on where you sit." The point of the aphorism is that one's attitudes toward a policy problem depend crucially on where one is located in the government bureaucracy. An official at the Federal Reserve, for example, might approve of the centralization of bank oversight if it were placed under the Fed—but not if it were placed under the Securities and Exchange Commission (SEC). It is possible to apply the same logic to attitudes about global economic governance. Relative optimism or pessimism could depend crucially on where one is situated. And what is interesting about the post-2008 global economy is the distribution of the rebound.

Two trends have marked most post-1945 global business cycles: economies recover as quickly as they drop, and the advanced industrialized states suffer less than the economic periphery. Neither of these trends has held during the Great Recession. As previously noted, recovery from a financial crisis is longer and slower than from a standard business-cycle recession.[41] But the deviation from the second trend is particularly pronounced. The core economies—the advanced

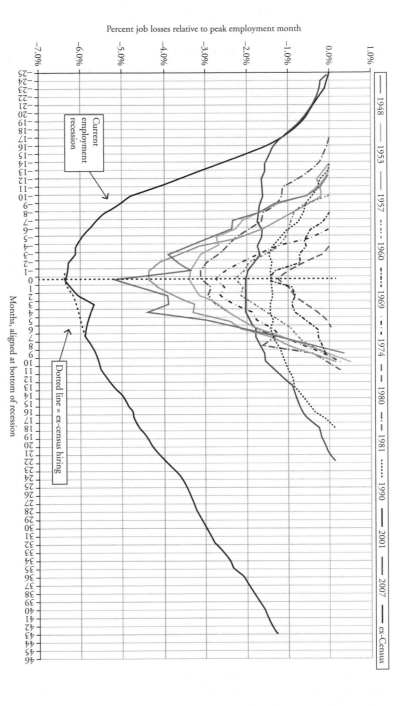

Percent job losses relative to peak employment month

Months, aligned at bottom of recession

FIGURE 3.2 Percent Job Losses in Post–WWII Recessions, Aligned at Maximum Job Losses

Source: Bill McBride, "Comments on the Disappointing Employment Report," *Calculated Risk* blog, January 10, 2014, http://www.calculatedriskblog.com/2014/01/comments-on-disappointing-employment.html

industrialized democracies—did not rebound as vigorously as they did in prior recessions. According to the Economist Intelligence Unit, the OECD economies averaged annual gross domestic product (GDP) growth of 0.5 percent between 2008 and 2012. The non-OECD economies averaged 5.2 percent during the same period. The US economy did better than both the European Union's and Japan's, but as figure 3.2 shows, the Great Recession led to deeper and longer job losses than the United States experienced in any other postwar recession.

The distribution of growth matters because it does not mirror the distribution of commentary about global economic governance. The overwhelming bulk of analysis about the global political economy in general—and global economic governance in particular—emanates from the advanced industrialized democracies. A quick survey of the top international relations and international political economy journals makes this clear. Since the start of 2009, the top five journals have published a combined total of more than a hundred articles on global economic governance. Authors based in the United States and Europe were responsible for approximately 93 percent of those articles.[42] The United Nations–sponsored journal *Global Governance* is ostensibly supposed to counteract this trend and offer up "a wide range of multidisciplinary and multicultural perspectives" in its pages, according to its own website. Yet, in the four years after the 2008 financial crisis, Western scholars and practitioners authored 88 percent of the articles published there. Similar biases would be found in the distribution of authors among prominent policy journals as well. The same story can be told in the distribution of analyses of the 2008 financial crisis and the Great Recession—they mostly emanated from the advanced industrialized states.[43] In other words, the overwhelming majority of subjective assessments about the state of the post-crisis global economy and global economic governance are based in the parts of the globe that did not rebound robustly.

The Western-centric nature of international political economy scholarship is hardly a recent complaint. Most Western assessments of how global governance structures handled the Asian financial crisis are disconnected from the assessments of analysts based in the region.[44] This is salient because experiencing a weak national economy can affect perceptions of the quality of governance. It is a general rule in public opinion research that a faltering economy causes greater distrust in institutions.[45] A weak economy feeds perceptions that the system is not working, institutions are breaking down, and those in authority are not to be trusted. Since economic growth has stagnated in the developed world but not in the developing world, we should see more skepticism about all levels of governance in the OECD economies.

Indeed, the 2012 Edelman Trust Barometer reflects this phenomenon. It shows that trust of elite institutions is significantly higher in developing countries than in the developed world.[46] This is a reversal of pre-crisis findings, which showed lower levels of trust in emerging markets.[47] We can also see this in the tenor of most articles and books produced about the financial crisis and global economic governance. As previously noted, the consensus in the West is that the system has failed. In contrast, authors like Kishore Mahbubani or Arvind Subramanian may be skeptical about the prospects of the advanced industrialized democracies, but they are bullish on the future of the global economy and global economic governance.[48] The study of global political economy and global economic governance has been anchored in the developed world. Given the weak nature of the post-crisis rebound in these parts of the globe, it should not be surprising that this literature suffers from a pessimism bias.

Conflating National and Global Governance

Pessimism about current economic conditions in the developed world might also be causing analysts to conflate poor domestic and regional governance with poor global governance. To be fair, this is a tricky issue to parse. On many dimensions, global governance is the sum of political decisions that are made at the domestic level. A decision to ratify a treaty, file a trade dispute with the WTO, or issue prudential regulation in conformity with Basel Committee rules are all domestic policy acts that are also part and parcel of global governance. However, there is a much larger category of economic policy decisions that are unrelated to global governance and have a more powerful impact on national economic performance. Large-market jurisdictions have far more domestic policy autonomy. This autonomy translates into a greater capacity for domestic policymaking institutions to make mistakes. The primary causes for domestic economic weakness in these countries are not global in origin—and neither are policies at the global level necessarily the best response.[49]

Consider the fates of the three largest markets in the developed world: Japan, the United States, and the eurozone. Japan's economic growth was lackluster long before the start of the subprime mortgage crisis. Ever since its property bubble popped in the early 1990s, Japan's financial sector has been in a zombie-like status.[50] Massive fiscal stimulus throughout the nineties did little to boost Japanese economic growth, though it did increase Japan's debt-to-GDP ratio. The problems with Japan's political economy required a much deeper fix. With interlocking institutions based on export-led growth, it has been difficult for successive Japanese governments to find ways to boost domestic consumption. Even "Abenomics," Prime Minister Shinzo Abe's radical efforts starting in late 2012 to boost the economy through massive fiscal and monetary expansions has yielded mixed results.[51]

By the time the 2008 financial crisis hit, demographic factors had sapped another possible driver of economic growth. A combination of low birth rates and a deep policy aversion to immigration guarantees that Japan's population will shrink for the rest of this century.[52] Political instability has played a role as well: between August 2008 and December 2012, Japan had six prime ministers—most of them politically incapacitated soon after taking office. Little wonder then, that Japanese public trust in government fell by 26 percentage points in the Edelman Trust survey in 2012 alone.[53] The aftereffects of the Fukushima nuclear disaster—estimated to cost a quarter of a trillion dollars—did not help matters. Japan's economy has struggled significantly since the start of the 2008 financial crisis. Its struggles, however, are not closely related to any failure at the global governance level. Most of Japan's policy problems reside in Tokyo, not elsewhere.

A similar story can be told about the United States. US economic misfortunes have little to do with either the global economy or global economic governance. Indeed, the United States benefited from the post-crisis global political economy through lower borrowing costs and higher exports. Domestic policy stalemates and political uncertainty, on the other hand, acted as a significant drag on the US recovery from the Great Recession. Political gridlock in the US Congress hampered policymakers throughout the post-crisis period. The average number of Senate filibusters, for example, was twice that of the post–Cold War era.[54] After the 2010 midterm elections, when Republicans regained control of the House of Representatives, legislative action ground to a halt. The 112th Congress passed substantially fewer laws than were passed in any session of Congress in the previous half-century. Partisanship also thwarted President Obama's efforts to appoint Nobel Prize–winning economist Peter Diamond to the Federal Reserve Board of Governors.[55]

Even when Washington acted on budgets, taxes, and debt, it did so in a way that maximized the economic trauma. The 2011 debt-ceiling negotiations had significant direct and indirect costs. The US federal government came close to being legally prohibited from borrowing money to finance its operations and pay off maturing debts. Measurements of policy uncertainty were considerably higher during the negotiations than during the 2008 financial crisis; this in turn created a net drag on economic growth.[56] The Bipartisan Policy Center estimated that the deadlocked negotiations increased US borrowing costs by more than $18 billion. During the protracted three-month negotiations, consumer confidence plummeted and job creation fell by 50 percent.[57] Standard & Poor's removed the AAA rating from US government debt. The downgrade decision had nothing to do with global market expectations, but rather, according to the agency's statement, "that the effectiveness, stability, and predictability of American policy-making and political institutions have weakened at a time of ongoing fiscal and economic challenges."[58]

One legacy of the 2011 budget deal was the "fiscal cliff"—a cluster of tax hikes and steep budget cuts that would have been implemented in January 2013 unless Congress acted to stop them. The slow-motion backing away from the fiscal cliff acted as a further drag on the American economy. Producers uncertain of whether tax cuts or government spending would be extended scaled back their business activities, curtailing private-sector investment.[59] Another legacy was the automatic sequester of budget cuts in 2013. The architects of the Budget Control Act of 2011 designed the sequester to be suboptimal, assuming that the specter of inefficient cuts would goad both parties into a grand bargain on fiscal policy. Despite consensus within Washington that the sequester was a stupid way of cutting the budget, no bargain ever materialized. Instead, partisan deadlock allowed the sequester to occur in March 2013.

Whatever lessons politicians learned from the 2011 debt showdown had been unlearned by fall 2013. The government was shut down for the first time in nearly twenty years, and the United States again came perilously close to defaulting on its obligations because of a failure to raise the debt ceiling. The final deal preserved the sequester as a mechanism for restraining government spending. Public- and private-sector analysts estimated that the shutdown shaved between 0.2 and 0.6 percent of growth off fourth-quarter GDP in the United States.[60]

The most optimistic assessment of the US macroeconomic policy response to the Great Recession is that it was better than that of other developed economies.[61] Other assessments have been somewhat more downcast. Macroeconomic Advisers estimates that the combined effect of fiscal drag and policy uncertainty between 2010 and 2013 slowed annual GDP growth by up to 1 percent and raised the unemployment rate by 0.8 percent, or approximately 1.2 million jobs.[62] Not surprisingly, the political paralysis over the debt ceiling and fiscal policy accelerated the decline in public trust in government. Both Gallup and Pew data showed a marked decrease in the trust in the federal government to do the right thing.[63] Norman Ornstein and Thomas Mann concluded, "We have been studying Washington politics and Congress for more than 40 years, and never have we seen them this dysfunctional."[64]

Europe's situation is more complex because of the sui generis nature of the eurozone. International relations scholars are often unsure about whether the European Union is an example of global governance or a proto-state. And to be sure, the Great Recession was the trigger for the eurozone's sovereign debt crisis. The international response to the crisis has been that of a modest supporting role. The IMF proffered both its technical expertise and financial support in excess of $100 billion to Greece, Portugal, and Ireland. The United States and other major economies reopened swap lines with the European Central Bank to ensure liquidity.[65] European and national policy responses to the crisis, however, badly exacerbated the economic situation. Greece's reckless pre-crisis government spending and borrowing made that economy a ripe target for market pessimism. European officials allowed Greece's sovereign debt crisis to fester, ratcheting up the costs of any intervention. As the crisis worsened, the initial proposal in conversations for a rescue fund among European officials was only 60 billion, woefully inadequate to address Greece's deteriorating debt dynamics.[66] As is discussed further in chapter 6, the austerity policies advocated in some quarters have not panned out as expected.[67] Austerity-related policies led to a double-dip recession in Great Britain, higher borrowing costs in Spain and Italy, and continued uncertainty about the euro's future. The European Central Bank's decision to raise interest rates prematurely in 2010 stalled any nascent recovery on the continent. Europe's fiscal and monetary policies were far less expansionary than those in the United States. This, in turn, prevented any appreciable private sector deleveraging in Europe, thereby guaranteeing a longer downturn before any sustained recovery was possible.[68]

The IMF came under criticism for failing to exert more influence over the eurozone crisis. One high-ranking staffer resigned in June 2012, blasting the fund for its "European bias" and consensus culture that keep it from criticizing countries in the middle of lending programs.[69] There are two counterpoints to this argument, however. First, the IMF *was* critical at various moments during the eurozone crisis. IMF staff issued warnings about the health of the European banks in August 2011, and Managing Director Christine Lagarde called for debt sharing among the eurozone countries in June 2012.[70] The first criticism received significant pushback from the European Central Bank and the eurozone governments, and Germany ignored the second criticism. This leads to the second point: it is highly unlikely that national governments would feel compelled to respond to IMF criticism in the absence of a market response.[71] The fund always walks a tightrope between transparent criticism and setting off market panic. This is hardly an ideal position from which to strong-arm governments with sizable IMF quotas.

The policy responses of Japan, the United States, and the eurozone economies were widely variable. Most of their macroeconomic policy errors, however, had little or nothing to do with foreign economic policy or adherence to global governance strictures. In each case, it was domestic institutions and beliefs that led to suboptimal responses—which in turn caused a decline in the public trust of national governments. This highlights a vicious cycle in Great Recession politics that makes cooperation at the international level even more remarkable. The financial crisis led to negative economic outcomes, which in turn triggered increased vulnerability and instability for incumbent governments.[72] Unpopular and short-term governments are far less likely to stress the need to cooperate at the global level. The perception of failed global governance might be a way of venting about national-level failures. Indeed, domestic-policy elites had an incentive to scapegoat global governance as a way to divert populist anger. In a world where elected officials in the United States, Europe, and Japan were politically weak and tempted to redirect anger at unelected multilateral institutions, it is extraordinary that global governance worked as well as it did.

No matter how globalized the economy becomes, the center of gravity for the provision of public goods will remain at the national and local levels. It is possible, however, for national and local governance to be impaired while global governance structures accomplish their tasks. This reflects a fundamental truth about the global political economy: international economic institutions have a greater capacity to do harm than good. If global economic governance does not disrupt the functioning of the global economy during boom times, and cushions the worst effect of busts, then it has "worked." On the whole, the great powers are sufficiently large for domestic policy to matter far more than global economic governance. Or, as Uri Dadush and Vera Eidelman phrased it: "The rules of the game do not need a big change; rather, the big players need to raise their game."[73]

Conclusion

Chapter 2 demonstrated that the system of global economic governance performed admirably in the wake of the 2008 financial crisis. Despite that fact, there is a powerful perception among both elites and the public that the system did *not* work. What explains this cognitive dissonance? This chapter has explored the origins and possible causes of this misperception. There are four possible explanations.

First, many commentators extrapolated from a few high-profile failures in global economic governance a conclusion that the entire system was dysfunctional. The kerfuffles over currency wars further revealed a gap in understanding between political commentators and global political economy scholars.

Second, many commentators made the default assumption that global economic governance was better in the past. In point of fact, such governance was haphazard at best. For much of the previous two centuries, the great powers failed to agree or to adhere to agreements on the open global economy. In some instances, there was an agreement to coordinate policy—but that agreement had catastrophic economic effects. Compared to the past, the post-2008 global economic governance has been plenty "good enough."

Third, the distribution of economic growth since the start of the Great Recession does not track the distribution of commentary about global economic governance. Global political and economic analysis remains anchored in the West; yet the biggest beneficiaries of post-2008 global economic growth are located elsewhere. Western analysts might extrapolate from their national circumstances an assessment that global governance perfomed poorly or not at all. Not surprisingly, the areas in which the global economy has done better also show more optimism about the current situation.

Similarly, commentators often conflate global governance and national governance. It would be hard to dispute that Japan, the United States, and the European Union have experienced high levels of political dysfunction since 2008. The weakening of political incumbents has undoubtedly contributed to a series of macroeconomic policy miscues, particularly after 2010. These miscues have, in turn, depressed aggregate economic output in these countries. With the partial exception of the eurozone, however, these mistakes are not a failure of global economic governance but rather of domestic institutions and beliefs.

The fourth reason so many commentators have bemoaned the state of global economic governance lies in international relations theory. It seemed logical to expect that the system would not work terribly well. As previously noted, global governance *was* dysfunctional in the run-up to the 2008 financial crisis. Furthermore, a divergence of interests, shift in the distribution of power, and breakdown of hegemonic ideas seemed to be taking place. All these factors suggested that in the face of a crisis, the system would not work. And yet, counterintuitively, it did. The next three chapters look at the role that interest, power, and ideas played in ensuring that outcome.

4

The Role of Interest

THE STORY SO FAR is simple: despite widespread ex ante fears and ex post perceptions to the contrary, the system worked after the 2008 financial crisis. Economic openness was maintained, providing the global public goods necessary to jump-start the economy. There had been, however, excellent reasons to believe that politicians would advocate a shift toward autarky once the crisis began. The pre-crisis observations about sclerotic international institutions and a looming power transition also did not seem too far off the mark. How did these institutions manage to produce the necessary policy outputs and reforms to stave off another worldwide depression? To answer the why, we need to look at causes. The meat and potatoes concepts of international relations are interest, power, and ideas. This chapter looks at the role played by interest groups to see if they were the reason the open global economy persisted, when, at first glance, one would have expected the opposite.

The Great Recession created "hard times" for almost every government in the world.[1] Such deep or prolonged economic downturns can undercut preferences for global economic openness in three ways. First, public support for trade protectionism and economic nationalism usually rises during significant recessions.[2] Even if functioning global governance yields positive outcomes, there may be an increase in the proportion of the public that fears the sovereignty loss brought about by continued openness. Historically, protectionism has increased in economies experiencing prolonged slowdowns.[3]

Second, the longer a downturn persists, the more all actors will focus on the distributional effects of any global bargain. The standard argument in favor of economic openness is that cooperation at the global level produces win-win outcomes. The longer a low-growth period lasts, the less positive-sum agreements will be seen through a strict lens of absolute gain. Actors will start to think that driving a harder distributional bargain is the best way to maximize their national welfare.

Third, hard times increase the barriers to exit for concentrated interests. As Albert Hirschman observed, actors can utilize market exit or political voice when confronted with unfavorable policy conditions, and they tend to specialize in one or the other over time.[4] Immobile factors or sectors—which cannot move easily across sectors or borders—will concentrate on the use of political voice, because for them, the barriers to exiting the market are higher.[5] During a downturn, however, it is difficult for even mobile factors of production to craft a viable exit option. When market exit is blocked, more actors turn to political voice as a means of getting what they want from national government. Voice options carry greater political and economic costs for governments trying to comply with global governance arrangements. The more actors exercise political voice, the greater the adjustment costs for any country attempting global policy coordination. Governments feel more political pressure to cater to the demands of entrenched interests.

Previous eras of hard times demonstrate the difficulty of sustaining viable international economic regimes during downturns. The global economic upheavals of the 1930s and 1970s, for example, also led to demands for global governance reform, but multilateral efforts foundered because of negative domestic political feedback. The volatility and uncertainty of the thirties and seventies triggered national-policy shifts that changed the global economic order. The onerous demands placed on domestic markets to adjust to the gold exchange standard in the interwar period led social movements in most of Europe to push back against it.[6] In the United States, stagflation in the 1970s led to strong popular support for more hawkish anti-inflationary policies, the political management of exchange rates, and the deregulation of financial markets.[7] These policy shifts were not embraced by other great powers, leading to clashes at the global level.

So there were excellent reasons to expect that, in response to the Great Recession, none of the great powers would be terribly interested in sustaining an open global economic order. And yet, the purpose behind most post-2008 great-power actions was to reinforce existing global economic governance structures. The result was a system of rules that kept a firm bias toward economic openness, while tweaking some aspects of regulation at the margins. What explains these policy preferences?

In looking at the role material interests played in the calculations of the great powers during the crisis, this chapter asks the question Did interest groups "capture" great-power governments and push them to make the system work—and if so, why? It briefly reviews how global political economy scholars think about interest-based explanations and discusses why those theories do in fact predict sustained levels of economic openness, particularly in the capital account. It then focuses on the negotiations surrounding the creation of the Basel III banking accord. This case provides an easy test of theories that predict the capture of national interests by powerful economic sectors. Basel III, however, suggests that there are hard limits to theories rooted in sectoral interests.

Material Interests and Global Political Economy 101

As previously noted, the resilience of a functioning, open global economy was a surprise to many after 2008. Politics 101 suggested that the downturn should have led to an upsurge in scapegoating the international economy, calls for protectionism, and a push toward more autarky in the name of "resilience." Punditry 101 also suggested a problem resulting from the perceived power transition taking place between the United States and China. The financial crisis was expected to accelerate this transition, amplifying uncertainty in the global economy.

Global Political Economy 101, however, offers a different take. The degree of interdependence among the key actors in the current era of globalization gave powerful interests a strong stake in maintaining a functioning, open global economy.[8] As John Ikenberry observes, "The complex interdependence that is unleashed in an open and loosely rule-based order generates expanding realms of exchange and investment that result in a growing array of firms, interest groups, and other sorts of political stakeholders who seek to preserve the stability and openness of the system."[9]

The dominant way of thinking about the global political economy for the past two decades has been the open economy politics (OEP) paradigm, which is a two-step model for determining interests and outcomes. The first step centers on how material interests and domestic institutions shape foreign economic policies. After mapping policy preferences from the position of powerful sectors in the domestic economy and looking at how domestic institutions aggregate those preferences, OEP moves to the next step, analyzing how the constellation of different foreign economic policies combines into global policy outcomes. David Lake accurately summarizes OEP as follows:[10]

> OEP begins with individuals, sectors, or factors of production as the units of analysis and derives their interests over economic policy from each unit's position within the international economy. It conceives of domestic political institutions as mechanisms that aggregate interests (with more or less bias) and structure the bargaining of competing societal groups. Finally, it introduces, when necessary, bargaining between states with different interests. Analysis within OEP proceeds from the most micro- to the most macro-level in a linear and orderly fashion, reflecting an implicit uni-directional conception of politics as flowing up from individuals to interstate bargaining.

In other words, OEP privileges domestic interests as the sources of preferences and constraints on national policies and essentially "brackets" everything else.[11] These interests inform, influence, and capture national and international policymaking structures.

OEP can offer a parsimonious narrative about why the system worked after the 2008 crisis. It argues that powerful interests across the major economies had a deep stake in the continued process of globalization. Production, trade, and finance in the twenty-first century are so globalized that they inculcate truly transnational interests. Developments like the global supply chain, "just in time" delivery systems in merchandise trade, repo markets, and the carry trade imbricate national economies into the international system. The interests that earn the most concentrated profits from these global production regimes then capture key policymaking institutions, causing them to take necessary actions at the national and global levels so as not to interfere with the global supply chain.

To understand the extent to which the global economy is truly integrated, consider the extent to which the manufacture of the Apple iPod and successive products enmesh different countries. Apple introduced the iPod in October 2001. Over the next decade, it triggered a wave of new gadgets and apps from Apple and other firms, including smartphones, tablet computers, and cloud computing. Since Apple is headquartered in the United States, it would be natural to presume that the iPod and iPhone represent an American success story. Gadget enthusiasts are no doubt aware that the answer is more complex. Although the iPhone was invented in America, it is assembled in China. According to economists Yuqing Xing and Neal Detert, the iPhone alone contributed $1.9 billion to the US trade deficit with China in 2009.[12]

But the globalization of twenty-first century production is even more complicated than that. If you break down who produces the component parts of the iPhone, the picture changes. While China plays a major role in the final assembly of the iPhone, it plays a minor role in the creation of its value added. The iPhone's flash drive comes from Toshiba—a Japanese firm. The South Korean firm Samsung provides the application processor. The German company Infineon provides the camera module. An American corporation provides the Bluetooth application. All of these parts are assembled by a Taiwanese firm, Foxconn, with operations in Shenzen, China. The People's Republic of China is responsible for less than 4 percent of the total value added of the iPhone.[13]

The OECD and WTO jointly produced a data set on "trade in value-added" in 2013 to clarify how the global supply chain affects cross-border exchange.[14] Their preliminary results demonstrate that the simple dichotomy of export interests and import interests has broken down in major sectors of the global economy. For example, in the transport goods market, between one-third and one-half of the total value added of national exports comes from intermediate-good imports. A similar amount emerges in the electronic goods sector.

Indeed, for most of the OECD economies, approximately one-third of all intermediate-goods imports are intended for finished goods that are then exported. This fraction of value-added imports rises to over 50 percent for Pacific Rim exporters. The global economy, as it is currently constituted, makes even the most prolific exporting countries dependent on imports from the same sector in order to maintain a functioning economy. Any individual national node in a global value chain needs access to efficient imports of goods and services in order to stay globally competitive.

One can tell a similar story in the financial realm. By 2008, the complex interdependencies of global finance were such that most significant financial institutions were engaged in extensive overseas operations. The "home bias" of institutional investors ebbed considerably in the ten years before the Great Recession.[15] Financial innovations accelerated the cross-border spread of capital. The "carry trade" allowed money-market-fund managers to take assets from one country and make overnight deposits into other countries with higher interest rates, turning places like Iceland into temporary financial hubs. Repurchase, or "repo," markets, permitted financial institutions to give each other massive short-term credit.[16] By 2006, gross cross-border flows in both the United States and the United Kingdom had expanded to more than five times GDP.[17] The reason the collapse of Lehman Brothers proved so disastrous is that it exposed the complex interdependencies and tight coupling within the financial sector.[18] One would therefore expect each national financial sector to fight vigorously against any move toward capital controls or regulatory stringency.

The political effect of global supply chains and imbricated capital markets is to harmonize the interests of the trading sectors of the major economies. While competition among individual suppliers may be powerful, the effect of global integration is even more powerful. Crude protectionism is therefore a useless gesture, even during hard times. Policy preferences over matters such as exchange rates wane as specialization increases.[19] And in the absence of powerful interest groups lobbying for greater closure, the OEP paradigm would predict minimal steps toward closure, even in response to the crisis.

OEP is not the only international political economy approach that arrives at this prediction. Whereas OEP starts with economic interests and then moves to the aggregation of those interests, historical institutionalism emphasizes the feedback mechanisms that build up between institutions and interest groups.[20] As Henry Farrell and Abraham Newman explain, historical institutionalism stresses "the propensity of state institutional reforms to create client groups that then have a strong incentive to push for their maintenance." In any temporal process of interest formation, policy feedback and path dependence shape the contours of future public policy.[21] The logic is as follows: at time t, a set of rules is codified for actors based in a particular economic sector. These rules help to shape and reinforce the preferences of the salient actors, weeding out firms and workers incompatible with those rules and bolstering actors who are compatible. At time $t + 1$, the cost of switching away from the status quo is somewhat higher for the remaining actors, so they lobby harder to make sure the status quo stays the same. With each interaction, the reinforcement between actor preferences and the rules of the game that bind them make it increasingly unlikely that the status quo will be changed endogenously. Political institutions shape the preferences of interest groups, and this in turn reinforces the stability of the original set of policy preferences.[22]

For this paradigm, the predominant fact of life in the pre-2008 global political economy was the twenty-year persistence of capital-account liberalization and deregulation.[23] Because these policies diffused widely and deeply, the market should have winnowed or weakened any financial actors that could not survive the openness of economic globalization. Furthermore, those remaining actors would have exerted even more pressure on government institutions to enforce status quo policies. This can be seen most clearly in the evolution of financial regulation in the United States. In the decades before the Great Recession, the financial sector resisted all efforts at regulation and pushed for deregulation at every opportunity. As a result, the 1933 Glass-Steagall Act was repealed in 1998, allowing investment banks to acquire commercial banks, and vice versa. Banks lobbied fiercely to switch capital-adequacy standards from a simple reserve ratio (Basel I) to more flexible standards (Basel II). Key sectors of the financial sector were left essentially unregulated. Despite efforts by the SEC to enact regulaton in these areas, for example, Congress expressly forbade the commission from regulating derivatives markets. Private-equity firms and hedge funds were also left untouched.

The complex revolving door between regulators and private-sector financial firms only reinforced this set of policy preferences.

Each of these policy moves caused the financial sector to grow wealthier and more powerful. Finance went from comprising 2.5 percent of US GDP in 1947 to being 7.7 percent of GDP in 2005.[24] And at the peak of the housing bubble in 2006, the financial sector comprised 40 percent of all the earnings of the Standard & Poor's 500. The incomes of the country's twenty-five top hedge-fund managers exceeded the total income of all the CEOs of firms in the S&P 500.[25] As Andrew Baker noted, "Regulatory capture was in part a natural outcome of the 'financialization' of Anglo-American society and the sheer size of the financial sector."[26] With the United States having this kind of clout, it is no wonder that former IMF chief economist Simon Johnson described it as akin to a kleptocratic third world state.[27] Furthermore, the growth of the financial sector in the United States was matched by similar rates of growth in Great Britain, Canada, Australia, and other Anglosphere economies.[28] It would not be surprising, then, if these other economies also developed finance-friendly institutions and regulations.

So, according to Global Political Economy 101, powerful and shared interests drove the functioning of global economic governance during the Great Recession. Despite the 2008 crisis, entrenched private-sector groups across powerful economies had a vested interest in maintaining the openness of the global economy. Whether one relies on OEP or historical institutionalism, the strength and homogeneity of the private sector's preference to maintain an open global economy were overwhelming. The rise of global supply chains meant that export sectors would lobby for lower levels of import protection at home as well as abroad. The concentration of global financial firms meant that the financial sector would lobby national and international actors, pushing strenuously for limiting financial regulation and promoting open capital accounts. These interests captured powerful state institutions, which, in turn, were able to motivate global economic governance into doing what was necessary to maintain economic openness.

There is prima facie evidence to support this argument, particularly in trade policy. One World Bank study examined trade restrictions since 2008 and found "vertical specialization" to be the most powerful economic factor determining post-crisis tariff rates. The more a country's economy was enmeshed in the global supply chain, the less likely it was to raise tariffs.[29] Other studies have demonstrated that the major trading states refrained from raising import barriers to stagnating trade partners, even when such actions were permissible under WTO rules.[30] This suggests that governments refrained from protectionist actions for reasons that go beyond international institutional constraints. Similarly, an examination of the relationship between a G20 member's exposure to the global economy and its compliance with G20 commitments supports this argument. Comparing pre-crisis country scores from the Swiss Economic Institute's the KOF globalization index with the University of Toronto's G20 monitor scores shows that greater ex ante exposure to globalization is positively correlated with compliance with global economic governance.[31] In other words, the economies most dependent on the global economy before the Great Recession were also the most cooperative after the financial crisis began.

The Ideal Test of Basel III

An excellent test of the power of material interests in the wake of the 2008 financial crisis comes from an examination of the Basel III banking accord. One of the big post-2008 questions was how global banking regulations should be reformed to prevent a crisis of its magnitude from occurring again. The existing international standard at the start of the subprime mortgage crisis, articulated by the Basel Committee on Banking Supervision (BCBS), was the Basel II accord. To be sure, the expert consensus was that Basel II was *not* one of the primary causes of the failures of the global financial system.[32] As the crisis unfolded, however, there was a growing appreciation that the Basel II accord had contributed to the procyclical nature of bank lending during the pre-crisis years.[33] Basel II gave banks the option of relying on internal models to assess their balance sheets. The 2008 crisis revealed those value-at-risk models to be badly flawed.[34] Banks overestimated the value of their assets because of their inflated value during the bubble years. This permitted banks to increase their loan portfolios and engage in even riskier investment practices. This cycle simultaneously fueled the subprime mortgage bubble and left financial institutions badly overextended when the crisis hit. European banks were woefully undercapitalized when Lehman Brothers went bankrupt, and the markets for some of their assets dried up completely. This, in turn, highlighted another flaw of Basel II: a failure to require banks to hold liquid forms of capital. Without higher liquidity levels, banks were unable to function properly during credit crunches. Even before the acute phase of the crisis, the Financial Stability Forum blasted the "significant weaknesses" of existing banking standards, concluding that "further improvements to Basel II and strengthened supervisory liquidity guidelines are needed."[35]

The reason Basel III is an ideal test for the power of material interests during the Great Recession is that the distribution of preferences reveals clear, cross-national preference divergence between the financial sector and governments.[36] The public pressure to re-regulate financial institutions following the 2008 crisis was powerful.[37] Hostility to large financial institutions spiked during the crash. Global public opinion polls showed strong, transnational demand for greater regulation of banks and other financial institutions. In July 2009, for example, majorities in seventeen of nineteen countries polled wanted a more powerful global financial regulator.[38] At the same time, financial sectors in almost every country were implacably opposed to more rigorous standards. In the short term, banks were concerned about being asked to comply with tougher standards for liquidity and solvency at the exact moment when their balance sheets were the most precarious. In the long term, financial institutions opposed any regulatory requirements that would reduce their profitability.[39] As the president of one US banking lobby characterized the financial sector's attitude toward new regulation, "The gut reaction of the entire industry was of course we have to oppose, oppose, oppose, because it's going to mean more regulatory burden on us all."[40] US Treasury secretary Timothy Geithner articulated governments' preference divergence on financial regulation quite clearly in a 2013 interview with the *Wall Street Journal,* "We were changing the economics of finance in a very significant way. We thought it in the interest of the country; they thought otherwise."[41]

If sectoral material interests really explain what happened, then the financial sector should have been able to push global economic governance to maintain openness on its terms: light regulatory standards at both the global and national level. Indeed, this represents an "easy test" of the power of interest groups on global governance. As

previously noted, both the OEP and historical institutionalism paradigms would predict the financial sector to exert an outsized influence
over global financial governance. The financial sector is one of the most
concentrated and well-organized interest groups in modern societies.[42]
According to Simon Johnson and James Kwak, this was particularly
true in the United States: "By March 2009, the Wall Street banks were
not just any interest group. Over the past thirty years, they had become
one of the wealthiest industries in the history of the American economy,
and one of the most powerful political forces in Washington."[43] In the
other great powers, such as the European Union and China, the role of
banks in the economy is even more outsized, and their strenuous lobbying efforts are not hard to identify. Furthermore, the revolving door
of individuals moving between government and the financial sector
has been well documented.[44] Even in the absence of outright corruption, the promise of a lucrative private-sector position gives the government's banking regulators an incentive to avoid offending the sector
they regulate. Multiple scholars have argued that the Basel Committee
on Banking Supervision was a regime that had long suffered from regulatory capture by the big banks.[45] One would therefore expect this
sector to capture the negotiation process and exercise significant sway
over any new financial regulation. If, on the other hand, Basel III con-
travenes the financial sector's policy preferences, it suggests that there
are hard constraints on the ability of even powerful sectoral interests to
alone explain how global economic governance functioned after 2008.

The Basel III Negotiations

Discussions on how to fix global banking standards began during the
depths of the 2008 crisis. As early as the November 2008 G20 summit
in Washington, leaders recognized that something needed to be done
to address financial-sector regulation. The summit communiqué noted
that "unsound risk management practices, increasingly complex and
opaque financial products, and consequent excessive leverage combined
to create vulnerabilities in the system. Policy makers, regulators and
supervisors, in some advanced countries, did not adequately appreciate
and address the risks building up in financial markets, keep pace with
financial innovation, or take into account the systemic ramifications

of domestic regulatory actions." The G20 call for action was equally clear: "We will implement reforms that will strengthen financial markets and regulatory regimes so as to avoid future crises." This included "intensified international cooperation among regulators and strengthening of international standards."[46] Every subsequent G20 communiqué included an explicit call to strengthen global financial standards.[47] Even officials and bankers who had resisted more stringent capital market regulation before 2008 recognized that something had to be done. As former Goldman Sachs chief executive and US Treasury secretary Henry Paulson acknowledged in his memoirs, "Virtually everyone agrees that we have had inadequate regulation of banks and capital markets."[48] The question was: what regulations would be imposed to address this deficit?

By July 2009, the Basel Committee had already proposed revisions to the Basel II framework to address post-crisis concerns about financial stability.[49] At the Pittsburgh summit in September 2009, the G20 leaders' communiqué called on the Basel Committee to augment the Basel II standard with additional provisions to ensure "internationally agreed rules to improve both the quantity and quality of bank capital and to discourage excessive leverage...with strengthened liquidity risk requirements and forward-looking provisioning." That same month, the Basel Committee issued a press release articulating the "comprehensive steps" the BCBS would take to set new standards for banking regulation and supervision. Beginning in December 2009, the BCBS began issuing draft documents and requesting feedback as negotiations took place among the regulators.[50]

The issues before the regulators were formidable. One question concerned how much additional capital banks would need to hold in reserve to guard against insolvency should another crisis unfold. In its initial press release, the Basel Committee stressed the need for a higher "quality, consistency and transparency" of the "Tier 1" capital held by banks. Tier 1 capital consists of retained earnings and funds raised from the issuance of equity. Under Basel II, banks were required to hold only 2 percent of their assets as Tier 1 capital. Regulators wanted to see enough of an increase in reserve requirements to prevent panic during another downturn. The larger a bank's capital adequacy, the less likely it would find itself under duress if another financial institution went bankrupt. The lower the likelihood of contagion, the lower the level of systemic risk. Regulators also wanted to create countercyclical buffers of additional capital during boom times, as a check against excessive lending. Not surprisingly, banks wanted as minimal an increase in capital adequacy as possible, so as to maximize profits. Capital held in reserve cannot be loaned out or invested; the more banks have in reserve, the smaller their profits. On capital adequacy, banks and regulators had diametrically opposing preferences.

A second issue concerned the relative liquidity of a financial institution's capital buffer. During the 2008 crisis, a lot of bank assets that were nominally part of the capital buffer—such as mortgage-backed securities—proved to be useless because the market for them had dried up completely. As the Basel Committee noted in its December 2009 draft document on liquidity coverage, "The crisis illustrated how quickly and severely liquidity risks can crystallize and certain sources of funding can evaporate, compounding concerns related to the valuation of assets and capital adequacy."[51] Regulators wanted to ensure that banks held more liquid forms of capital—such as cash and government bonds—to hedge against a crisis. Liquidity comes at a cost to the financial institutions, however. The more liquid an asset, the lower the rate of return. Financial institutions therefore preferred holding as much of their capital in higher-yield, if less liquid, assets.

By late 2009, the Basel Committee had crafted a basic framework for how to improve the regulatory framework. They proposed a strengthening of Tier 1 capital to be held by banks—although the draft document was silent on what the precise increase in capital adequacy should be. The BCBS also proposed additional countercyclical capital buffers during boom times to ward off procyclical lending. They further proposed two new standards. The first was a leverage ratio to "contain the build-up of excessive leverage in the banking system." The second new proposal was a global minimum-liquidity standard. This was designed to ensure that banks had enough liquid forms of capital to sell these assets and raise cash in markets even during a severe financial downturn.[52]

Both the leverage ratio and the liquidity standard were new innovations for the BCBS. In pushing for these new standards, as well as for countercyclical capital buffers, the Basel Committee signaled a philosophical shift in its approach to financial regulation. In Basel I and Basel II, the emphasis had been on "microprudential" regulation—the principle that if each individual bank took steps to ensure the soundness of its own balance sheets, the entire financial system would be secure. The 2008 crisis had revealed the flaws in this approach. It was possible for each financial institution to act prudently at the firm level while promoting the buildup of risk at the systemic level. The procyclicality of the Basel II accord suggested the need for macroprudential regulation. The proposals for liquidity standards and countercyclical capital buffers were significant steps in this direction.[53]

The evidence that the financial sector opposed Basel III en masse is straightforward. According to multiple surveys in the industry journal *The Banker*, the preferences of financial sector representatives shifted dramatically after the crisis. For the three years prior to October 2008, an average 44 percent of respondents held a negative attitude toward the expected output of financial regulations. In the four years after the collapse of Lehman Brothers, the bankers' negative attitudes jumped to 73 percent.[54] Five months after the BCBS first issued its proposed draft regulations, more than 270 comments had been received, and more than 95 percent of them came from financial institutions.[55] Prominent banks, including J. P. Morgan Chase, BNP Paribas, Deutsche Bank, and Standard Chartered, warned that the draft standards would impose crippling costs on their firms and on the economy writ large.[56] For example, Wells Fargo's chief financial officer warned that "the cumulative financial impact represents a level of conservatism so extreme that it will harm the banking sector, banking customers and national economies."[57]

After the Basel Committee issued its preliminary draft regulations, financial sectors across the developed world responded by lobbying fiercely to dilute every element of the proposal. BCBS officials held multiple meetings with private banking representatives, coordinated by the banks' principal lobbying group, the Institute for International Finance (IIF).[58] *The Economist* characterized the negotiations at Basel as "the most vicious and least public skirmish between banks and their regulators."[59] In her memoirs, Sheila Bair, former chairperson of the Federal Deposit Insurance Coorporation (FDIC), characterized it as "a major battle" between the BCBS and the banking industry.[60] Interviews with BCBS officials confirm that the banks devoted significant effort to influencing Basel III. In the United States alone, securities and investment firms spent a record $101.6 million on lobbying in 2010, attempting to water down the regulations in the proposed Dodd-Frank legislation as well as in Basel III.[61]

Beyond private lobbying, the IIF also tried to frame the public debate by being the first to estimate the expected economic costs of Basel III.[62] In June 2010, the institute issued an interim report, predicting that the macroeconomic impact of Basel III would reduce GDP by significantly raising interest rates. In the United States, Japan, and Europe, interest rates would rise by more than 130 basis points in the first five years after implementation. This spike in interest rates would create a deep drag on economic growth in the affected countries. The IIF estimated that annual growth in the first five years would be reduced by 0.6 percent, and that the cumulative impact over the first decade of implementation would equal a deadweight loss of 3 percent of the developed world's output over the decade. Total job losses were estimated at 9.7 million people. In other words, the IIF predicted a massive hit for economies that were already weakened by the 2008 financial crisis. Some national lobbying groups went even further than the IIF. The French banking association, for example, claimed Basel III would lead to a 6 percent drop in France's economic output.[63]

But contrary to the regulatory capture argument, it appears that bank lobbying had almost no effect on the Basel III negotiations. In July 2010, the BCBS staff submitted its list of recommendations for review by its oversight body, the central bank governors, and heads of financial supervision. Later that month, the supervisors approved the changes. In September 2010, the BCBS approved the higher capital adequacy standards. The G20 signed off on the new standards at its November 2010 Seoul leaders' summit, trumpeting the approval of Basel III as the summit's primary achievement. At that point, private-sector analysts acknowledged that the core principles of Basel III were "here to stay."[64]

Basel III requires banks to retain 4.5 percent of assets as Tier I capital by the year 2019—a 125 percent increase over Basel II. It also calls for an additional 2.5 percent as a capital conservation buffer. National banking authorities were further encouraged to suggest that large banks hold an additional 2.5 percent as a "discretionary" capital buffer during periods of significant credit expansion. Basel III also created a leverage ratio—the ratio of Tier 1 capital to a bank's total exposure—of more than 3 percent by 2018. Finally, the new standard created global liquidity standards designed to ensure that banks could function even when asset markets seized up. By 2019, banks would be expected to have a 100 percent "liquidity coverage ratio"—the proportion of "high-quality liquid assets" to the estimated net liquidity outflows over a thirty-day period of market stress. A net stable funding ratio proposed a similar 100 percent ratio of a bank's available stable funding to cover estimated outflows over a calendar year.[65]

On the whole, the approved Basel III accord does not jibe with a regulatory capture argument. To be sure, some national regulators wanted even higher capital adequacy levels than Basel III.[66] Other, more radical proposals—such as a tax on international financial transactions—also fell by the wayside.[67] Nevertheless, the final Basel III regulations approved by the G20 remained largely unchanged from the draft proposals of a year earlier, despite the intense bank lobbying. The IIF's analysis of the new rules came to the same conclusion.[68] One BCBS official told me about the IIF's lobbying: "In all honesty I can't point to any one area where they had any influence." The media coverage also reflected a narrative at odds with interest-group capture. In September 2010, Felix Salmon of Reuters blogged that Basel III would reduce systemic risk and strengthen the international banking system, noting that "the Basel committees did a masterful job of depoliticizing the process as much as possible."[69] By October 2011, the *Wall Street Journal* concluded, "The tug-of-war between banks and regulators over post-crisis financial rules has so far moved in the watchdogs' favor with banks largely failing to upend the tougher proposals in the U.S. and Europe."[70] Financial analysts concurred, noting that with the approval of Basel III, financial markets would punish banks that failed to boost their capital adequacy beyond the minimum standard.[71] Numerous scholars agreed, concluding that the new Basel III standards represented an improvement over the Basel II standards in terms of preventing bank failures.[72]

Market reactions to Basel III announcements also suggest that the financial sector did not get what it wanted during consultations with the Basel Committee. Meredith Wilf examined the stock market reaction at five major junctures in the formation of Basel III, from the initial announcement of new reforms in September 2009 to the issuance of the final set of rules in December 2010. She found statistically significant negative effects on the stock prices of the US banks that would be affected by Basel III. She concluded that "despite enormous lobbying pressure from the banking industry, this study suggests that banks were not able to capture the regulatory process in 2009 and 2010."[73] Given that US banks were better positioned to comply with Basel III than their European or Japanese counterparts, it would be safe to conclude that the transnational financial lobby lost on Basel III.

Why did the financial sector have such limited influence? Part of the reason is that global financial governance had significant reservoirs of expertise as well, which they were able to convert into greater authority.[74] While the Basel Committee needed the banks' proprietary data, they did not need the bankers' expertise for most dimensions of banking regulation. For example, in interviews, Basel Committee staffers were very dubious about the quality of the IIF's June 2010 impact study on Basel III. Other analysts report similar reactions from regulators, noting that American and European finance officials quickly discounted the IIF's impact study.[75] In contrast, when the Basel Committee's Macroeconomic Assessment Group subsequently came out with its own quantitative impact study, national regulators viewed it as more credible. The BCBS committee's study relied on more-sophisticated economic models and more-granular data than the IIF analysis, and had a larger staff. The conclusions of the Basel study also contrasted sharply with those of the IIF analysis. The BCBS estimated that the total cost of Basel III would be 0.34 percent in lost economic growth, a marginal amount compared to the estimated 2.5 percent gain in economic growth that would result from the financial sector's reduced exposure to another systemic crisis.[76] Independent public and think-tank analyses produced results that were much closer to the BCBS position than to the IIF position, further eroding the latter's credibility on the issue. One BCBS official was particularly blunt in comparing the IIF and Basel Committee analyses: "We creamed them."[77]

The crisis itself also expanded the audience of parties interested in Basel III. As a result, the affected global governance structures and national regulatory authorities met with sectoral representatives beyond finance.[78] For example, the Basel Committee met with International Chamber of Commerce officials for the very first time after the 2008 financial crisis. By interacting with a wider array of interests, regulators evinced less concern about banking preferences in particular.

Regulators and officials also reacted badly to overly aggressive lobbying. In a speech to IIF members, delivered immediately after the IIF had released its initial impact study, European Central Bank president Jean-Claude Trichet compared the financial crash to the Deepwater Horizon oil spill in the Gulf of Mexico.[79] He further argued that the 2008 crisis had "shattered" the idea that self-regulation would work in the financial sector. A year later, at a Financial Services Forum meeting, J. P. Morgan chief executive Jaime Dimon scolded incoming Financial Stability Board chairman Mark Carney about Basel III, calling the proposed rules "cockamamie nonsense."[80] Carney angrily left the room while Dimon was in mid-rant. Other bankers, including Goldman Sachs's Lloyd Blankfein, tried to smooth things over. This did not stop Carney from telling the IIF attendees, "If some institutions feel pressure today, it's because they have done too little for too long rather than being asked to do too much too soon."[81]

A final possibility is that the regulatory-capture theory was exaggerated even prior to the Basel III negotiations. As previously noted, much of the international political economy literature simply assumed interest-group dominance in financial regulation, particularly with respect to the Basel Committee. However, Kevin Young has examined the negotiations surrounding the creation of Basel II and found that the financial sector's influence was more circumscribed. Contrary to the conventional wisdom about Basel II, for example, BCBS regulators pushed back on efforts by the banks to rely solely on their internal risk-management systems to calculate the appropriate level of capital adequacy. He concludes, "There was more scope for public agencies, at least when organized transnationally, to resist and reject private sector demands than has been depicted in the existing IPE literature."[82]

This is not to say that sectoral interests did not affect the Basel Committee's bargaining. Rather, the effect was muted. There are two ways in which financial interests shaped the Basel III outcome. First, the relative health of a country's banking sector affected the way national regulators approached Basel III. As Sheila Bair noted in her memoirs, the distribution of preferences among the Basel Committee representatives was clear-cut: "The United States, United Kingdom, Canada, Switzerland, the Netherlands, Sweden, and most other Basel Committee members advocated, or at least were willing to support, higher standards; Germany, France, and Japan would resist."[83] Interviews with BCBS staffers, as well as the contemporaneous news coverage, confirms this basic cleavage.[84] When the advanced developing countries from the G20 joined the BCBS, they shared the preference for more-stringent standards. This was because market pressures had long ago forced banks in these countries to hold much higher levels of capital than those in the developed world.[85]

One could ascribe the preferences of national regulators from France, Germany, and Japan to push for less-stringent standards as evidence of interest-group capture in those countries. However, there are reasons to view these preferences as equally grounded in national interest. Because the continental European banks had gone the furthest in implementing Basel II, they were the least well capitalized of the globally systemic banks. Japan's banks had never fully recovered from the country's recession in the 1990s. As a result, the banks based in these countries were more vulnerable to increases in capital adequacy and liquidity requirements. Furthermore, as coordinated market economies, Germany, France, and Japan relied far more on bank financing than other forms of raising capital than the liberal market economies of the United States and Great Britain did.[86] As big as the American banks were, for example, in 2008 the six largest had assets approximately equal to 60 percent of US GDP. In contrast, the top three French banks had assets equal to more than 315 percent of French GDP; the top two German banks held assets equal to 114 percent of German GDP.[87] Any regulation that constrained bank lending would have a disproportionate macroeconomic impact on countries that relied more heavily on bank finance than equity markets for financing.

It should also be noted that lobbying during the Basel III negotiations was not strictly based on material interests either. If short-term interests really dictated national preferences on banking, for example, then US banks would have lobbied for more-stringent standards as a means of improving their competitive position vis-à-vis European banks. This would have been consistent with their behavior during previous rounds of Basel rule writing.[88] That did not happen during Basel III, however. The US financial sector continued to loudly resist any ratchet upward of regulatory stringency.[89] Indeed, J. P. Morgan Chase CEO Jaime Dimon epitomized the attitude of the US financial sector when he repeatedly blasted the Basel III accord as "blatantly anti-American."[90] Furthermore, the negative US stock market reaction to the Basel announcements suggests that financial markets did not view the shift in global economic governance as beneficial to the US banking sector.[91]

The second significant effect of sectoral interests on the Basel III process has been the lobbying to slow down the implementation phase. Any kind of governance reform takes place in three stages: agenda setting, policy formulation, and policy implementation. In the immediate aftermath of the 2008 crisis, the financial sector had minimal influence during the first two stages. As a result, it concentrated its firepower on the implementation stage. As Kevin Young observed, "Rather than arguing that new regulations already on the table should not be pursued, or that the particular details of regulation should be substantially adjusted, post-crisis arguments often take the form of arguing for the postponement of regulatory implementation."[92] Theoretically, interest groups would be expected to exercise more influence at this stage, particularly after the immediate crisis receded. As populist anger against the banks fades, any countervailing pressure against bank lobbying is likely to erode over time, leaving a "quiet politics" more amenable to interest-group capture.[93] Indeed, the primary bargaining cleavage during the Basel III negotiations was over the implementation dates. The British and Americans wanted Basel III fully implemented within five years, but a larger constellation of countries with weaker financial sectors preferred a slower process.[94] The latter group of countries succeeded in delaying the full implementation dates for Basel III until 2018 and in reducing capital adequacy levels to 7 percent.

The slowdown on implementation can be seen most clearly in the timetable and rule writing on the liquidity ratio. As the Basel Committee moved toward finalizing the rules and timetable for the liquidity coverage ratio (LCR) in January 2013, banks in the United States and Europe lobbied fiercely for looser standards and a longer timetable.[95] On this front, the banks were successful. The revised LCR rules made two significant changes to the draft rules the committee had issued in December 2010. First, they extended the timetable for implementation. Banks will only have to comply with 60 percent of the LCR by 2015; full compliance will not kick in until 2019. Second, the Basel Committee softened the requirements for what banks needed to hold to ensure liquidity. The 2010 draft implied that banks could only apply "Level 1" high-quality liquid assets—cash and government bonds—toward the ratio. In the 2013 revision, banks were permitted to hold up to 40 percent of liquid assets in the "Level 2" form—including commercial bonds, equities, and mortgage-backed securities.[96] Stock prices for the major banks rose after the announcement, reflecting the perception that this was a victory for the financial sector. One analyst described the outcome as "a fairly massive softening" of the Basel Committee's approach.[97]

One can argue that sectoral lobbying for slower implementation had an appreciable effect on global economic governance. Insiders like Sheila Bair blamed bank pressure on the dilution of the Basel III standards.[98] Outside observers cited the revision as an example of the banks taming the regulators yet again.[99] Simon Johnson noted in the *New York Times* that "these officials caved in, as they did so many times in the period leading to the crisis of 2007–8. As a result, our financial system took a major step toward becoming more dangerous."[100]

While this may appear to be a data point in favor of the regulatory-capture argument, the revisions were equally consistent with the model of regulatory autonomy. In contrast to the ratcheting up of capital adequacy, BCBS officials were far less confident in their calculations on an "appropriate" liquidity ratio. In moving into a new area of regulation, Basel Committee officials were understandably warier about their command of the data and therefore more willing to listen to bank complaints.[101] As the *Financial Times* noted, the LCR was "an experiment, with calculations based on estimated needs rather than solid experience."[102] This was publicly acknowledged by regulators as well. As British banking regulators explained, "The state of macro-prudential policy today has many similarities with the state of monetary policy just after the Second World War. Data is incomplete, theory patchy, policy experience negligible. Monetary policy then was conducted by trial and error. The same will be true of macro-prudential policy now."[103] This is consistent with the hypothesis that the Basel Committee listened to bankers in a discriminate manner, relying on them more when their own data and models rested on shakier ground.[104]

A related problem is that key assumptions made by bank regulators were challenged in the interregnum between the draft rules and the final rules. The poor performance of the eurozone made regulators skittish about exacerbating any downturn. In forcing banks to acquire more capital, Basel III encouraged a drying up of cross-border lending in Europe. As the liquidity rules were being debated, the BIS noted that at the end of 2011, quarterly global cross-border lending had dropped to its lowest levels since the Lehman collapse in fall 2008. The decline was "largely driven by banks headquartered in the euro area facing pressures to reduce their leverage," according to BIS officials.[105] Given the fragility in the eurozone economies as the final liquidity rules were being written, regulators were concerned that too onerous a liquidity ratio would worsen the downturn by drying up commercial bank lending.[106]

Another macroprudential concern was about how Basel III, combined with the sovereign debt crisis, would affect the market for safe assets. In theory, government bonds were supposed to be the principal means for banks to hold "Level 1," or high-quality, liquid assets. In practice, the worsening fiscal position of the advanced industrialized states caused a decline in the quality of their sovereign debt. The eurozone crisis and 2011 debt-ceiling deadlock in the United States caused multiple ratings agencies to downgrade significant amounts of sovereign bonds. The *Financial Times* estimated that the global supply of AAA-rated debt fell by 60 percent in the first five years of the financial crisis, to less than $4 trillion.[107] At the same time, as banks started complying with Basel III, BCBS and IMF officials estimated a new demand to acquire between $2 to $4 trillion in safe assets.[108]

While some of the downgraded debt would qualify as Level 1, the simultaneous decline in supply and spike in demand had the potential to distort capital markets.[109] Not surprisingly, the IMF warned in its 2012 *Global Financial Stability Report* that "the tightening market for safe assets can have considerable implications for global financial stability." The fund urged a more relaxed attitude towards the definition of safe assets to "ameliorate pressures" in this market.[110] So did British regulators, who had already instituted more stringent liquidity rules within the City of London. Mervyn King, the British central bank head, explained to the *New York Times* that "nobody set out to make [the liquidity rule] stronger or weaker, but to make it more realistic."[111] Given that the British were by far the most eager of the national regulators to ratchet up standards, their change of mind was significant. It was an indication that interest-group pressure was not the only causal logic at work. In this context, expanding the category of liquid assets to include private commercial paper is less surprising—and less indicative of regulatory capture.

Even with the relaxed LCR and slower implementation, the evidence suggests that systemically important global banks adjusted considerably to comply with Basel III. One BCBS survey showed that between December 2011 and June 2012 alone, systemically important global banks secured more than $200 billion—or 43 percent of the estimated shortfall in Tier 1 capital—necessary to comply with the capital adequacy standard due to be activated in 2015.[112] Parallel surveys by the European Banking Authority in the eurozone and the Clearing House in the United States showed significant increases in liquid assets on hand held by banks.[113] The worst-capitalized large European institutions, such as Deutsche Bank, continued to recapitalize in early 2013.[114] Further BCBS quantitative research suggests that banks have significantly augmented their capital reserves over the past few years—and, contrary to IIF warnings, did so while increasing lending.[115] Even if Basel III did not achieve everything that critics of big banks wanted, its implementation forced systemically important banks to make significant changes to their business model. The financial sector retains significant influence, to be sure. This influence may further increase as memories of the subprime mortgage collapse continue to fade.[116] At the same time, improved profits have undercut the banking lobby's arguments against further regulation.[117]

Overall, during the post-crisis response, the Basel Committee responded in a manner that belies the interest-group-capture argument. In expanding capital adequacy and establishing a macroprudential foundation at the outset of Basel III, BCBS regulators took significant steps to retard the probability of regulatory capture in the future. On this issue—where sectoral interests were at their most concentrated, and the tight links between regulators and bankers long-standing— regulatory capture of global economic governance did not take place.

Conclusion

This chapter has explored the question of whether material interests can explain how global economic governance functioned during hard times. The major strands of international political economy research would predict that a sufficient constellation of interests had a vested stake in ensuring an open global economy, thus empowering states to act in a cooperative manner. The global supply chain would ostensibly ensure that major importers would still not agitate for protectionism. Similarly, the privileged position of the financial sector in this era of globalization would ensure unfettered capital markets and a light regulatory touch.

An interest-based explanation goes part of the way in explaining why states did not defect from existing global economic governance structures. Among the G20 economies, there is a moderate correlation between exposure to globalization prior to the crisis and policy adherence to openness after the collapse of Lehman Brothers. Imbricated interests help to explain why countries refrained from trade protectionism. Nevertheless, a closer examination of Basel III reveals two significant flaws in a strictly interest-based explanation of post-crisis global governance: theory and practice.

Theoretically, the problem with the interest-based explanation is that it presumes a harmony of preferences when one did not exist. Recall the distinction between harmony and cooperation in international relations. In a harmony situation, the salient actors all share the same set of preferences. At best, only minor governance is necessary because there is minimal disagreement among the principal actors about what to do. This covers only a small fraction of possible cooperation problems in world politics, however. Even if a plethora of actors share a similar set of interests on the content of global governance, there are inevitably distributional issues that are zero-sum in nature.[118] Who pays for monitoring? Who pays for enforcement? Bargaining is an inevitable feature of global economic governance. In the case of Basel III, the cleavage of interests between coordinated market economies and liberal market economies demonstrated the distributional concerns among states affected by of global regulation.

The empirical problems are more formidable. There are simply too many instances of powerful interests either losing or compromising their positions. The pattern of capital market regulation after 2008 demonstrates the limits of an approach that explains global governance outputs as products of sectoral interests. Regardless of national origin, the financial sector was firmly opposed to the Basel III banking accord. It was a well-organized and well-funded interest group. Despite its opposition, both national regulators and Basel Committee officials crafted a set of regulations that ratcheted up capital adequacy and introduced macroprudential principles to determine liquidity minimums and leverage limits. The empirical evidence suggests that the banking sector exercised limited influence during the drafting of the rules. They did exercise greater influence over the implementation phase—but even here, the evidence points to both national and international regulators exercising autonomy in crafting new rules and regulations.

Basel III was not the only arena in which banks faced a regulatory setback. They also lost on the question of capital controls. For decades, the IMF had used its influence to pressure countries into liberalizing their capital accounts.[119] Some economists went so far as to accuse IMF officials of acting at the behest of the banks in pushing this agenda.[120] In the wake of the 2008 financial crisis, however, IMF economists began to change their minds about the wisdom of capital controls. In February 2010, an IMF staff paper concluded that under some circumstances, capital controls could be a legitimate and useful policy tool.[121] Dani Rodrik characterized the change in the IMF's tune as a "stunning reversal" of its previous orthodoxy.[122] By November 2012, the staff note had become the IMF's official position. Now, the fund allows that capital controls can be "useful" in some circumstances, and that "there is…no presumption that full [capital account] liberalization is an appropriate goal for all countries at all times."[123] Brazil even used the logic of macroprudential regulation developed in Basel III to justify the capital controls it imposed.[124]

The shift in the IMF's position on capital controls did not lead to a wholesale rejection of capital account liberalization. *The Economist* described these newer controls as "lighter-touch" and "market-based."[125] Still, this represented a shift in the global policy climate against the financial sector. To explain this development, Rodrik proposed an intriguing hypothesis: "What made finance so lethal in the past was the combination of economists' ideas with the political power of banks. The bad news is that big banks retain significant political power. The good news is that the intellectual climate has shifted decisively against them."[126] Rodrik's emphasis on the role of power and ideas in determining the outcome of global economic governance is intriguing. This chapter suggests the limits of material interests in explaining the functioning of global governance; the next two chapters turn to the role of state power and economic ideas.

5

The Role of Power

IN THE POST-2008 WORLD, the best place to look to get an analytical grip on relative economic power might be Iran. Focusing on a midsized economy that has been diplomatically isolated for a generation might seem odd to those interested in global economic governance. When we think about economic power, however, Iran is a revealing example. The recent economic sanctions imposed on Iran are a good test of the use of economic power as a means of constructing and enforcing the rules of the game.

In 2010, the United Nations Security Council voted to impose a fourth round of economic sanctions on Iran following its refusal to cooperate with the International Atomic Energy Agency. The United States and the European Union announced their intent to impose additional financial sanctions. Most observers doubted they would be effective.[1] After all, China, South Korea, and other Pacific Rim power-houses would simply buy up the oil that did not go to Europe. Indeed, Iran's lead negotiator on the nuclear question bragged to *Der Spiegel*, "Do you really believe there are sanctions that can hit us that hard? We've lived with sanctions for thirty years, and they can't bring a great nation like Iran to its knees. They do not frighten us. Quite the opposite—we welcome new sanctions."[2]

The United States and the European Union obliged. The financial restrictions were so comprehensive that the Society for Worldwide Interbank Financial Telecommunication (SWIFT) ended all transactions with the Iranian banks named in the sanctions. Iran was effectively cut off from twenty-first-century finance. In 2012, the European Union also implemented an embargo on Iranian oil. By 2013, it was clear that the sanctions had been more crippling than experts had thought they would be. Iran's oil export revenue was cut in half between 2010 and 2012, and overall oil production was at its lowest levels in twenty-five years. China has purchased Iranian oil in recent years, but Beijing has also exploited the sanctions regime to impose below-market purchase prices and payment in shoddy consumer goods rather than hard currency.[3] These moves have served China's interests—but China's behavior has also served the transatlantic goal of imposing economic costs on Iran.

Iran's economy, compared to its peer group of oil exporters, has deteriorated badly since 2010.[4] Iran's economy shrank in 2012 and 2013. Inflation increased to over 50 percent as the rial plummeted in value relative to other currencies. The combination of financial sanctions and reduced oil exports left Iran with useful currency reserves of less than $20 billion. By fall 2013, Iran's president Hassan Rouhani had publicly acknowledged that the effect of sanctions had been severe and said that quick negotiations were required to settle the nuclear question.[5] Despite widespread perceptions of receding Western influence, it appears that the US and EU actors wielded sufficient economic power to bring Iran to the negotiating table.

Global economic governance did what was necessary during the Great Recession. The previous chapter found that material interests can only partly explain why the system worked. This chapter assesses the crucial role that power plays in sustaining global economic governance, particularly when the global economy is experiencing downturns. In *Politics in Hard Times*, political scientist Peter Gourevitch observes:[6]

> In prosperous times it is easy to forget the importance of power in the making of policy. Social systems appear stable, and the economy works with sufficient regularity that its rules can be modeled as if they functioned without social referent. In difficult economic times this comfortable illusion disintegrates. Patterns unravel, economic models come into conflict, and policy prescriptions diverge. Prosperity blurs a truth that hard times make clearer: the choice made among conflicting policy proposals emerges out of politics. The victorious

interpretation will be the one whose adherents have the power to transfer their opinion into the force of law.

Gourevitch believes that hard times reveal the power politics that determine national policies. This applies to world politics as well.

Nevertheless, assessing economic power during the post-2008 era is not for the faint of heart. For the past few years, I have challenged the students in my global political economy classes to identify the actors belonging to the current roster of great powers. The answers I have received have been heterogeneous, to say the least. They range from safe choices like the United States to more unorthodox suggestions, such as Goldman Sachs, WikiLeaks, and the China Development Bank. A healthy fraction of my students has argued that there are no current great powers. This assessment reflects views expressed in the burgeoning literature about the diffusion of power in the world that was discussed in Chapter 1. The problem of accurately assessing economic power is not limited to students, however. Economists and political scientists are uncomfortable with such discussions. Most economists do not like to think about power. Many international relations scholars do not like to talk about economics.

How has the 2008 financial crisis affected the global distribution of power? The conventional wisdom is that power has shifted from the OECD economies to the BRIC economies. On one level the conventional wisdom is true; the BRIC economies are rising relative to the OECD countries. That statement, however, masks the divisions within each cluster of actors. China has risen to be a great power of the first rank; the rest of the BRIC countries have not. And, though China may be rising, it has not risen nearly as high as perceptions suggest. Similarly, although American economic power has declined, it has not declined by all that much—and it has declined from a position of unparalleled hegemony. The United States remains the most powerful economic actor in the global economy, permitting it to exercise leadership in global governance through a variety of means. When the United States, the European Union, and China act in concert, global governance rests on a strong foundation. Although the distribution of global power has become less concentrated, the perception that it is diffusing rapidly does not square with the reality.

In this chapter I briefly review the literature on the relationship between the distribution of power and the functioning of global economic governance. While a hegemon is commonly thought to be a necessary and sufficient condition of governance, the state of thinking is more complex than that simple statement suggests. Hegemonic actors need to attract supporters and discourage spoilers. I discuss elite and public perceptions about economic power, and why those perceptions might not be entirely accurate, and then section audit the capabilities of the great powers. As will be seen, popular perceptions about the global distribution of power are inaccurate; the BRIC economies are not as powerful as they are perceived to be, and the established powers are not as weak. The current global political economy rests on a troika of great powers—the United States, the European Union, and China—and the United States remains the first among equals. The chapter explains why this troika was able to make global governance function. The United States still exercised leadership on key policy dimensions. More intriguingly, China largely acted as a supporter rather than a spoiler of global economic governance.

Great Powers and Global Governance

Beginning with Charles Kindleberger, global political economy scholars have argued that the existence of a hegemonic power is necessary to sustain global economic order.[7] The empirical validity of "hegemonic stability theory," however, has been a running debate in global political economy for the past four decades. On the one hand, scholars now reject the notion that hegemony is either a necessary or sufficient condition for an open global economy. There are a welter of substitutes for hegemonic power in the international system. Formal or informal global governance structures can facilitate cooperation among a concert of powerful actors to provide global public goods in the absence of an undisputed hegemon.[8]

Furthermore, the mere existence of a liberal economic hegemon is not necessarily a sufficient condition for effective global governance. "Supporters" also play a crucial role in the spread of economic openness by buttressing and adhering to the rules of the global economic order.[9] Supporter states possess significant reservoirs of power in world politics, albeit fewer capabilities than the most powerful actor. Supporters can matter because of their strategic position within global economic networks.[10] For example, in the nineteenth century, the United Kingdom sponsored both the gold standard and the principle of free trade. Neither concept went global, however, until supporter states, such as France and Germany, also embraced these regimes.[11] The collapse of the interwar trading system happened when supporter states like Germany and the United States transitioned into spoiler states. Spoilers are revisionist actors relative to the status quo, with sufficient capabilities to disrupt preexisting regimes. As the United States' relative power waned during the Bretton Woods era, supporter states like Germany, Great Britain, and Japan played crucial roles in sustaining the system.[12]

Although the precise causal mechanisms remain disputed, it is nevertheless true that hegemonic eras are strongly correlated with greater levels of globalization.[13] If one updates Stephen Krasner's oft-cited analysis about the distribution of state power and the structure of foreign trade, the correlation between hegemonic power and economic openness seems clear. In five of seven eras since 1820, the presence of a strong or rising hegemon is correlated with greater openness, while a declining hegemonic power was correlated with greater levels of closure.[14] Furthermore, institutionalists acknowledge that power is still the crucial criterion for membership in any "k-group" or "hegemonic coalition"—the concert of great powers that must cooperate in order to articulate and enforce global economic governance.[15] Should the hegemonic coalition agree to coordinate policy, those nations can jointly supply the necessary global public goods for proper implementation.[16] If the distribution of power diffuses, the requisite membership in the hegemonic coalition increases.

Although an economic hegemon would appear to be strongly correlated with effective global governance, it is really the existence of a hegemonic coalition that is the necessary and sufficient condition.[17] If a great-power concert exists, global governance structures are seen as critical actors in the coordination process. Whether the governance outcome is achieved through consensus or coercion, it will be viewed as effective. However, if no bargain can be struck among the potential coalition members exists, then these same global economic governance structures will experience intractable deadlocks, inconsistent articulations of policy, forum shopping, and weak enforcement. If one rationale for global governance structures is that they can bring about effective multilateral cooperation, then this ability is irrelevant if either the distribution of power or the distribution of interest is too diverse.[18]

As noted in chapter 1, the conventional wisdom about post-crisis world politics is that the distribution of power has become widely diffused. Compared to the pre-crisis era, any expected hegemonic coalition needs to be larger. An increase in the number of great powers automatically decreases the likelihood of effective governance outcomes. Most formal models of cooperation demonstrate that as the number of relevant actors increases, the transaction costs of creating a functioning concert increase as well.[19] Introducing more actors into a small group also decreases the likelihood of finding a bargaining core existing among the participants. The number of issue areas in which governance should function is automatically reduced.

Perceiving, Measuring, and Defining Economic Power

After the Lehman Brothers collapse, which actors qualified for membership in the hegemonic coalition? Who are the great powers in the Great Recession? Before the 2008 crisis, it was a straightforward matter to identify the great powers in the global political economy as the United States and the European Union.[20] Even then, however, there was considerable talk about the rise of the BRIC economies and their effect on the global political economy.[21] The outward signs seemed manifestly clear. Even before the collapse of the subprime mortgage bubble, for example, India and Brazil were invited into the "green room" of key negotiators during the Doha Round, effectively wielding veto power when necessary. In 2008, it was China, not the United States, that applied the coup de grace to Doha. Russia attempted to jump-start a natural gas cartel that could match OPEC in global influence. All the BRIC economies took steps to invoice trade in their national currencies rather than dollars, with no retaliation from either the G7 economies or the IMF.[22] Post-crisis, new terms such as the "Second World," "BRICSAM" (the BRIC countries plus South Africa and Mexico), and

"Global Growth Generators" were bandied about to describe other emerging powers.[23]

The power of these actors, particularly China, flourished at the same time the power of United States and the European Union seemed to wane. In 2010, China officially surpassed Japan as the world's second-largest economy, and in 2012, China displaced the United States as the largest trading state in the global economy. The IMF projected that China would overtake the US economy in terms of purchasing power parity by 2016. The US National Intelligence Council predicted that by 2025, China's power would approximate that of the United States.[24] According to at least one estimate, by 2011, China already had a larger GDP than the United States, beginning in 2011.[25] Part of China's power comes from this perception of its inexorable rise. Multiple projections have identified China as the economic hegemon by the year 2050.[26]

With the onset of the Great Recession, China began to use its economic power to influence its near abroad.[27] Holding substantial dollar-denominated debt, Beijing pressured the United States to alter its economic policies.[28] In assessing the post-crisis distribution of power, two analysts from the US National Intelligence Council concluded, "The state wealth Beijing has already amassed, over $1 trillion of which resides in U.S. government-backed securities, gives China ample leverage in shaping the future economic landscape. . . . The manner in which China deploys its reserves is among the most decisive factors determining global outcomes to the current crisis."[29]

This perceived shift in the distribution of power is revealed in both public opinion and elite discourse. Since 2008, the Pew Global Attitudes survey has included a question asking respondents to identify the world's leading economic power. The answers have been telling, as figures 5.1–5.4 demonstrate. In 2008, pluralities or majorities in twenty of the twenty-two countries that were surveyed (and ten of the twelve G20 members surveyed) said that the United States was the world's leading economic power—including Chinese and American respondents. Clear majorities in ten of the twenty-two countries surveyed said the United States. In no country did a majority of respondents say China. By 2012, however, there had been a wholesale shift in public attitudes. Pluralities or majorities in eleven of the twenty-two countries now said China was the world's leading economic power. Clear

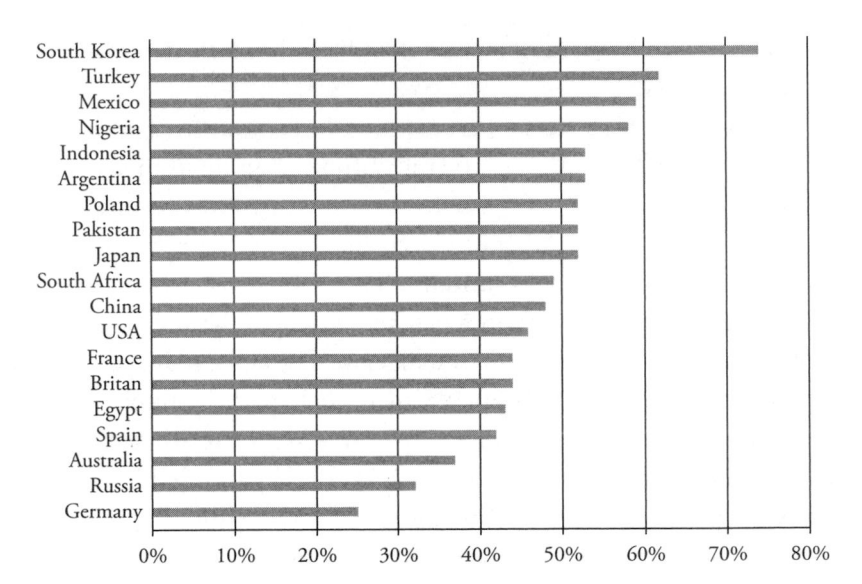

FIGURE 5.1 Respondents in 2008 Who Said the United States Was the World's Leading Economic Power

Source: Pew Research Global Attitudes Project, Global Indicators Database, http://www.pewglobal.org/database/indicator/17/survey/all/

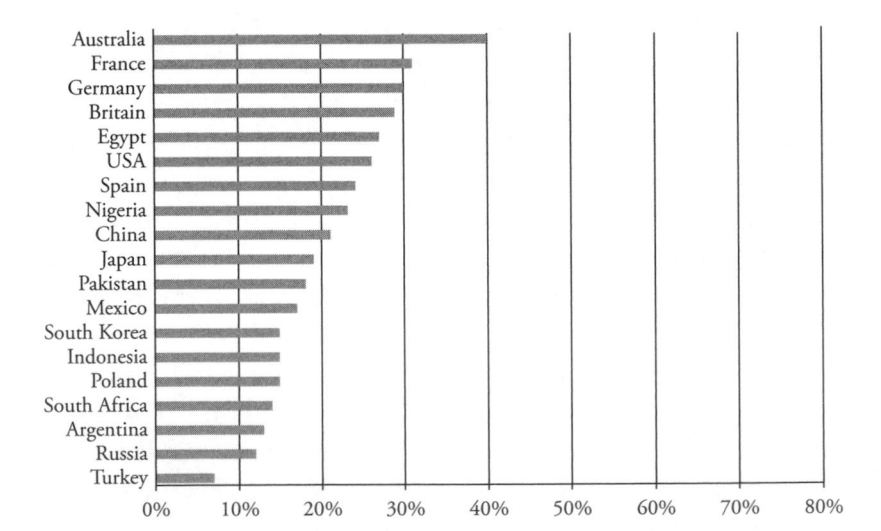

FIGURE 5.2 Respondents in 2008 Who Said China Was the World's Leading Economic Power

Source: Pew Research Global Attitudes Project, Global Indicators Database, http://www.pewglobal.org/database/indicator/17/survey/all/response/China/

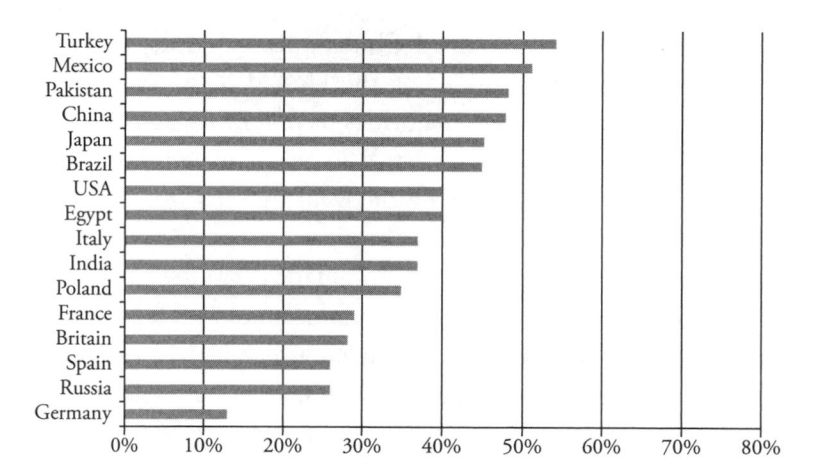

FIGURE 5.3 Respondents in 2012 Who Said the United States Was the World's Leading Economic Power

Source: Pew Research Global Attitudes Project, Global Indicators Database, http://www.pewglobal.org/database/indicator/17/survey/all/

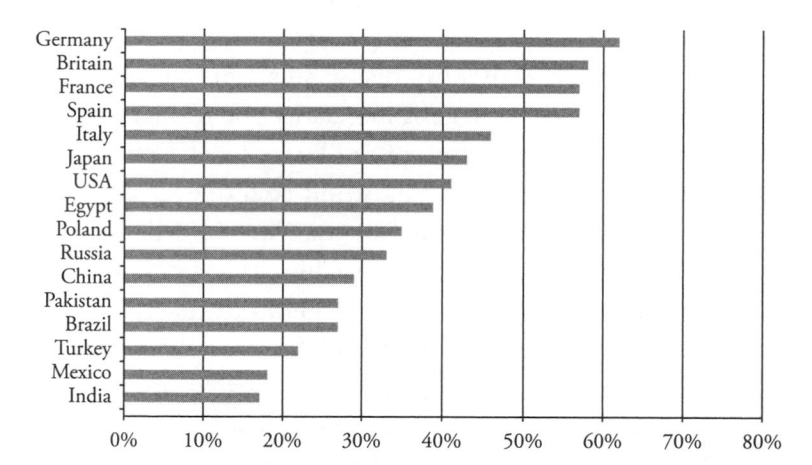

FIGURE 5.4 Respondents in 2012 Who Said China Was the World's Leading Economic Power

Source: Pew Research Global Attitudes Project, Global Indicators Database, http://www.pewglobal.org/database/indicator/17/survey/all/response/China/

majorities in five countries named China; only in Turkey and Mexico did majorities of respondents name the United States. In five of the original G7 economies strong majorities or pluralities named China as the world's leading economic power. When the survey results are combined, there is an aggregate swing of twenty points from the United States to China between 2008 and 2013.

Both public rhetoric and private diplomatic discourse suggested that US policymakers shared this view of China's new superpower status. On the US side, for example, the official assessment of Chinese economic power was reflected in Secretary of State Hillary Clinton's 2009 conversation with Australian prime minister Kevin Rudd. In response to Rudd's suggestion that the US should pressure China, she asked rhetorically, "How do you deal toughly with your banker?"[30] Similarly, in 2012, prominent Chinese international relations scholar Wang Jisi summarized the worldview of the top Chinese leadership, "The rise of China, with its sheer size and very different political system, value system, culture, and race, must be regarded in the United States as the major challenge to its superpower status."[31]

If there is a strong consensus that China's power has increased vis-à-vis the United States, there is less clarity about the extent of the redistribution. The 2013 iteration of the Pew Global Attitudes survey covered a wider array of developing-world countries, and the results were more favorable to the United States. Pluralities in both North America and Europe still believed that China was the most powerful economy in the world. In every other region in the globe, however—Asia, Latin America, Africa, and the Middle East—a plurality or majority of respondents said the United States. It is particularly striking that the Chinese did not agree with the assessment that China is the world's most powerful economy. In the 2013 Pew survey, 46 percent of Chinese respondents believed the United States' economy was the most powerful, whereas only 30 percent said China.[32] The Chinese public may well be correct. China's per capita income remains about one-sixth that of the United States. If one relies on the UN human development indicators or the Legatum Prosperity Index, China and the rest of the BRICs lag far behind the United States.[33] Furthermore, there are excellent reasons to doubt the straight-line extrapolation of China's continued economic ascent.[34]

The lack of clarity in the conversation reflects, in part, the evolution of the discussion in policical science of power as a concept. The attempts to define power stretch back to the very origins of the field, and the debate continues to animate international relations scholars.[35] It started with a narrow, coercive definition—Robert Dahl's famous contention that power is the ability of actor A to get actor B to do what B would otherwise not want to do. Later generations of political scientists expanded the concept beyond coercion to focus on the ways in which power can affect the preferences and perceptions of other actors. Robert Gilpin discussed the significance of having a "reputation for power."[36] Susan Strange has emphasized the ways in which structural power can empower its architects more than other actors.[37] Joseph Nye's concept of "soft power" focuses on how actor A can get actor B to want what actor A wants.[38] Some scholars have talked about the power of discourse to socially construct common worldviews among actors.[39] Others have emphasized the role that networks play in concentrating or exercising power.[40]

This evolution in the discussion of power reveals the ways in which state actors must contend with powerful structural forces in the global political economy. The global political economy comprises material and social structures that constrain all actors in the system. Capital markets, global civil society, and voting selectorates shape and limit the ways in which governments exercise power in the world. States' ability to affect, alter, or resist these structures in ways that advance their own interests is also a clear sign of their power. Indeed, as noted in chapter 1, one of the primary reasons for the skepticism about the future of global governance is the belief that global power is diffusing, shifting away from all the historically significant actors and stripping them of the ability to set agendas, negotiate rules, or implement regulations.[41]

In my previous work, I have stressed effect of market size on global regulations.[42] When it comes to setting standards, having power over the demand side matters far more than having power over the supply side. For global economic governance more generally, however, other metrics also come into play. Producer power—control or ownership of key production capabilities—might matter in some instances. In trying to coordinate or enforce global rules or regulations, state capacity can be significant as well. Governments that command greater expertise, experience, or network centrality with respect to the issue at hand often carry that advantage into international negotiations.[43]

There is another set of useful metrics to consider—the response of private-sector actors to public policies. Is the dollar still being used to invoice most of global trade? Have sovereign borrowing rates changed over time? Unlike public opinion surveys, in which respondents frequently have a low level of information, market participants have a vested interest in making sure that their judgments are grounded in a high level of information. Therefore, market evaluations of national economies—through such measures as sovereign borrowing rates, FDI inflows, and the ratings of outside market observers—represent a complementary means to measure economic power.

A Power Audit

Figures 5.5 and 5.6 show shares of global economic output measured using purchasing power parity and market exchange rates for the United States, the European Union, Japan, and the BRIC economies. Even a glance at these figures makes three facts abundantly clear. First, commentators are correct in observing that China's power is rising. In just a dozen years, China has moved from being a middle-rank economy to being one of the biggest in the world. When measured by purchasing power parity, China has moved much closer than the other emerging markets to the United States and the European Union. Second, despite lagging growth since the start of the Great Recession, the United States and the European Union are still the two largest markets, regardless of whether one is measuring GDP by market exchange rates or purchasing power parity. If one relies on market exchange rates, then the United States and the European Union still exercise outsized influence compared to the other candidate countries. This matters because both economists and political scientists argue that using market exchange rates is more appropriate when thinking about relative power in the global economy. [44] The third observation is that only the United States, the European Union, and China stand out. The other BRIC economies and Japan look like middle-range powers in comparison. At no point in the post-crisis era has any of these economies possessed even

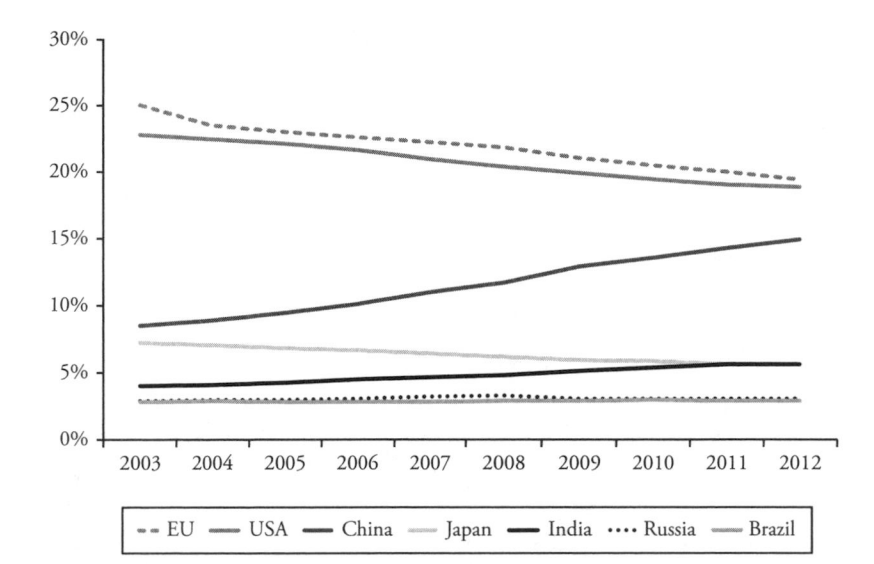

FIGURE 5.5 Share of Global Economic Output as Measured by
Purchasing Power Parity

Source: International MonetaryFund's World Economic Outlook database, October
2013, http://www.imf.org/external/pubs/ft/weo/2013/02/weodata/index.aspx

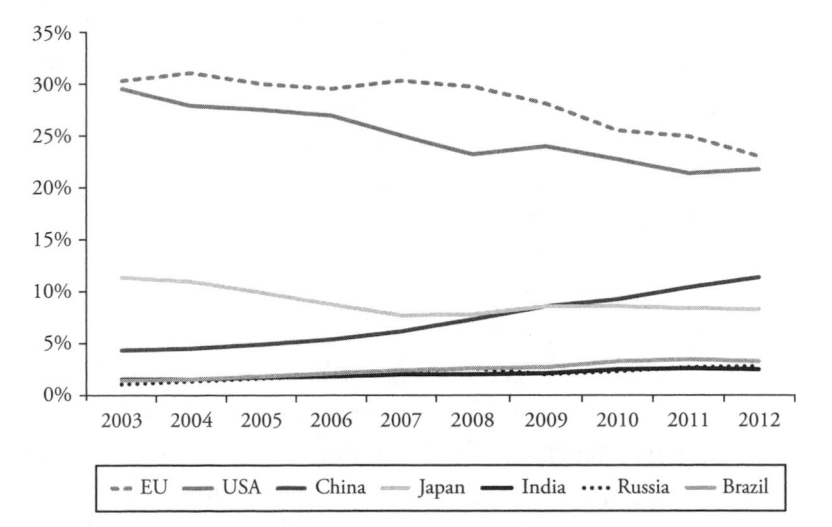

FIGURE 5.6 Share of Global Economic Output as Measured by Market
Exchange Rates

Source: International MonetaryFund's World Economic Outlook database, October
2013, http://www.imf.org/external/pubs/ft/weo/2013/02/weodata/index.aspx

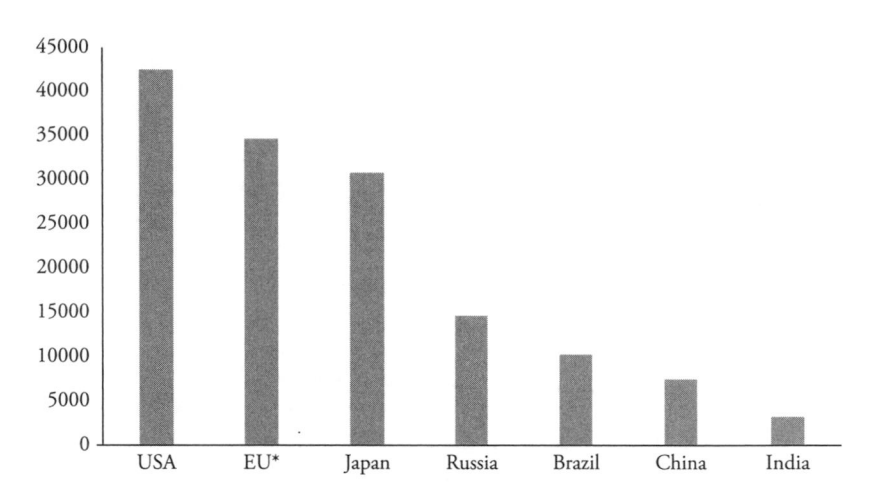

FIGURE 5.7 GDP per Capita, 2011
Source: World Bank's World Development Indicators, October 2013, http://data.
worldbank.org/data-catalog/world-development-indicators?cid=GPD_WDI
*Germany was used as a proxy for the European Union. This overstates per capita
income in the EU.

half the size of either the United States or the European Union when
measured using purchasing power parity. Using market exchange rates,
the gap is even greater.

Some scholars have argued that when one is assessing wealth,
aggregate economic size is less important than per capita income.[45]
According to this logic, countries with higher per capita incomes have
more resources left after fulfilling subsistence needs and can thus devote
more resources to projecting power. Figure 5.7 shows a snapshot of per
capita GDP figures for 2011.[46] The chart reveals the continued and pronounced gap between the developed world and the BRIC economies.
Despite a decade of rapid economic growth, none of the BRIC economies had a per capita income level that was more than half the levels of
the United States, Japan, or the European Union. Using this metric,
the distribution of power has not shifted much at all.

In terms of trading influence, figure 5.8 shows each jurisdiction's
share of global merchandise imports in 2011.[47] Imports represent the
extent to which an actor commands an attractive market.[48] The findings are similar to the data on national income. The European Union,
the United States, and China are the three most significant importers.

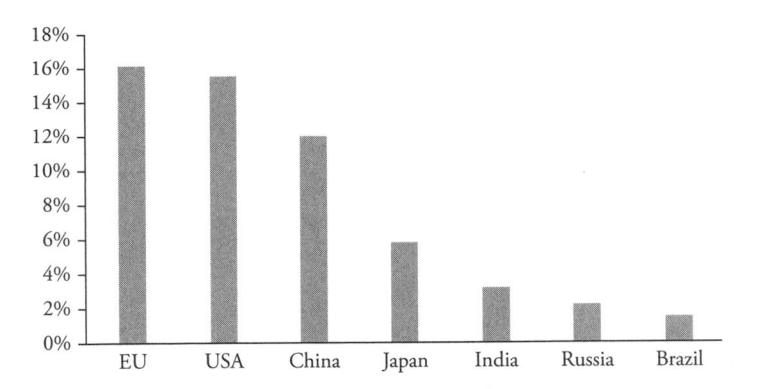

FIGURE 5.8 Share of Global Imports, 2011
Source: World Trade Organization's International Trade Statistics 2012, July 2013,
http://www.wto.org/english/res_e/statis_e/its2012_e/its12_toc_e.htm

The next-largest trading state, Japan, imports less than half of what China imports. The rest of the BRIC economies are far less influential; indeed, South Korea is a more significant trading state than any of them. Network analyses of trading patterns tell a similar story—the pre-eminence of the OECD economies relative to the BRIC economies.[49]

The data for FDI inflows is somewhat more difficult to analyze, because it does not exclude intra–European Union cross-border investment. This significantly inflates the European Union figure. Nevertheless, the UNCTAD data on inward FDI paints a picture similar to that of the trade and output data, as can be seen in figure 5.9. The United States, the European Union, and China again outclass all other great-power candidates; the next-largest economy is not half as influential as the smallest of the Big Three. There are two other noteworthy trends. The rise of China is again quite clear. Its share of FDI inflows more than doubled between 2007 and 2012. The decline of the European Union is equally dramatic—its share of global FDI inflows fell by more than 50 percent. It is likely that this number overstates the extent of Europe's fall as an FDI magnet because much of that decline likely resulted from the drying up of intra-European investment. Still, the latest figure is also the best measure of Europe's waning market power in investment.

The last major dimension of market size is in global capital markets. The IMF's Global Financial Stability Report provides the most

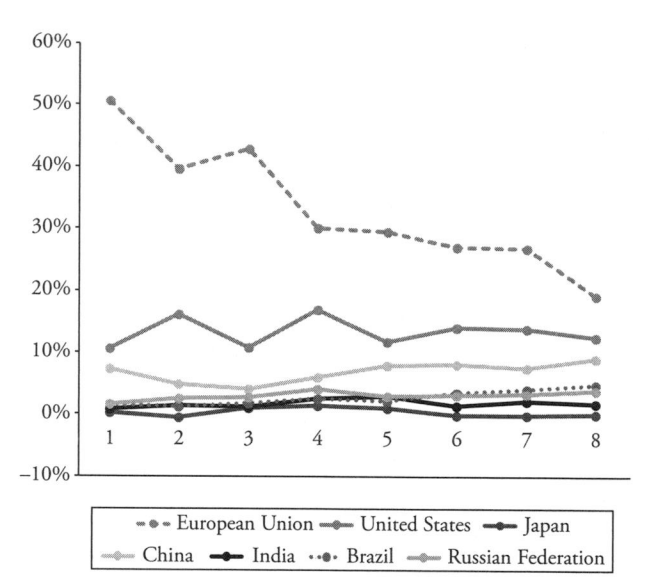

FIGURE 5.9 Share of Worldwide Inward Foreign Direct Investment
Source: UN Conference on Trade and Development, *World Investment Report 2013*,
http://unctad.org/en/PublicationsLibrary/wir2013_en.pdf
Note: Does not exclude intra-EU investment.

readily available data on the size of capital markets. The results, shown
in figure 5.10, point to a different distribution of market power. The
United States and the eurozone maintain market dominance.[50] Again,
both jurisdictions dwarf Japan, possessing capital markets roughly
twice as large as that country's. On this dimension, the United States
and the European Union also dwarf all the BRIC markets. Indeed,
the financial markets of all the emerging markets combined are still
smaller than either the US or eurozone capital markets. Based on
the regional breakdown, no individual member of the BRIC club—
including China—is even remotely close to either the United States or
the European Union.

Using a network model to chart global financial flows reveals even
more clearly the power of the United States. The United States is the
most central actor in the network of global finance, with the United
Kingdom a distant second. Indeed, the network centrality of the United
States *increased* after 2008. As one recent analysis concluded: "the
U.S. is more firmly ensconced at the center of the global financial

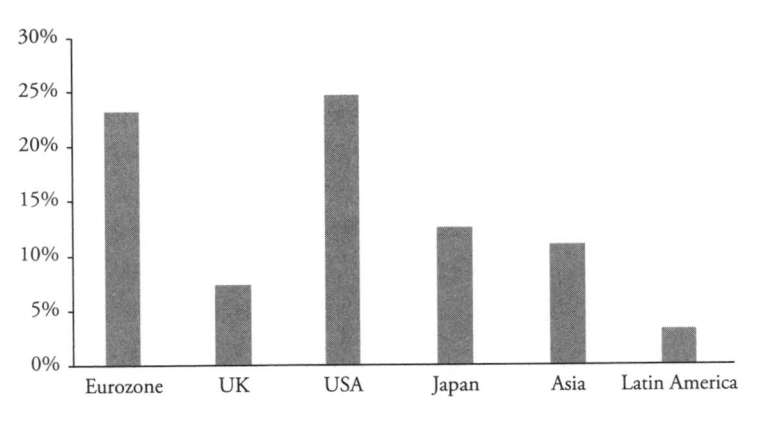

FIGURE 5.10 Share of Global Capital Markets, 2011
Source: International MonetaryFund's World Economic Outlook database, October 2013, http://www.imf.org/external/pubs/ft/weo/2013/02/weodata/index.aspx

system than commonly appreciated.... The EU's struggles and China's lack of financial development and extant positive feedback effects interact to keep the United States at the center of the global financial system for the foreseeable future."[51] Economist Hélène Rey argues that in a world of capital mobility, the US Federal Reserve essentially controls the global business cycle.[52] This explains why the financial sanctions imposed by the United States and the European Union worked so well against Iran. The significance of these economies to global finance was so great that the costs to any bank in defying them was prohibitive.

Some scholars argue that commanding the power of production is equally important. On this dimension, China's exporting prowess becomes quite clear, as the WTO data in figure 5.11 demonstrate. China is the world's largest exporter if one disaggregates the European Union, and has eclipsed the United States as an export powerhouse. This overstates Chinese trading power in two crucial ways, however. First, China's gross export statistics exaggerate its real productive capacity. As discussed in the chapter 4, China's export prowess rests on its being the location for the final assembly stage of production. But in the global value chains of the twenty-first century, much of the value added in manufactured goods comes from earlier stages of production. These intermediate goods are then imported by China for final assembly. In 2013, the WTO and OECD estimated export shares

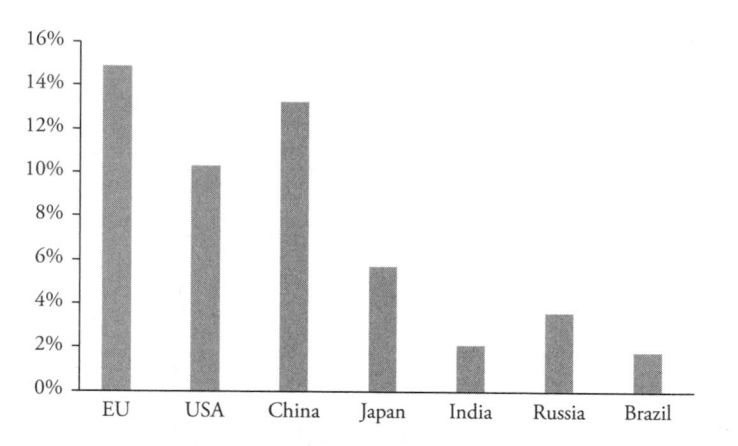

FIGURE 5.11 Share of Global Exports, 2011
Source: World Trade Organization's International Trade Statistics 2012, July 2013,
http://www.wto.org/english/res_e/statis_e/its2012_e/its12_toc_e.htm

using a value-added calculation. Figure 5.12 shows that in 2009, the
European Union remained the world's largest exporter, with 21.8 percent of global exports. The United States was second, responsible for
14.4 percent. Using value-added calculations, China falls to third, with
10.1 percent of global exports.[53] As with GDP, the trade data suggest
that the post-crisis world has three—and only three—great economic
powers.

The second way gross exports potentially misrepresent productive
capacity is by overlooking the issue of ownership. A large fraction of
productive capacity in the European Union, the United States, and
China is based on FDI. On the one hand, large FDI inflows represent a
source of economic strength. On the other hand, where the profits go is
also a source of economic power. Figure 5.13 shows global shares of FDI
outflow. Again, this figure overstates the influence of the European
Union because it includes intra–European Union FDI. The results are
nevertheless indicative, and suggest a concentrated distribution of productive power. The United States and the European Union both command more than 20 percent of FDI outflows, and no other country
commands even half that share.

The distribution of productive power is likely even more concentrated than figure 5.13 suggests. Sean Starrs analyzed data on corporate
ownership from the Forbes Global 2000 lists of the top twenty-five

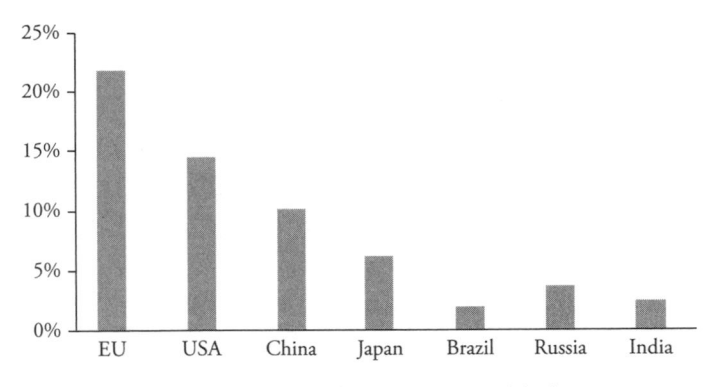

FIGURE 5.12 Share of Global Exports in Value Added, 2009
Source: OECD/World Trade Organization

global companies from 2006 and 2012 and concluded, "Corporations domiciled in the United States continue to dominate by far the largest range of sectors, in particular, those involving advanced technology and knowledge. In fact, since 2008, American dominance has increased in key sectors such as financial services and software, with no serious contenders on the horizon, including China." More than 45 percent of the top 500 multinational corporations are headquartered in the United States. This figure may be deceptive, because the cross-national ownership of firms can render corporate nationality less meaningful. Nevertheless, when Starrs analyzed that data, he found that in 2012 Americans possessed 41 percent of all household wealth in the world. He observed that "American citizens continue to own the predominant share of the world's wealth—much more so than America's declining share of GDP would suggest."[54] Starrs's findings buttress other research on the distribution of global wealth and corporate control that finds US firms and households at the apex.[55]

There are two other relevant dimensions of productive power in which the United States has maintained uncontested hegemony since the 2008 financial crisis. The first is that the dollar remains the world's reserve currency. Despite claims and concerns to the contrary,[56] the Great Recession's effect on the dollar's status has been minimal. Between 2007 and 2010, for example, the dollar's share of the international banking market increased from 41.9 percent to 43.7 percent. Between 2007 and 2013 the dollar's share of official currency reserves

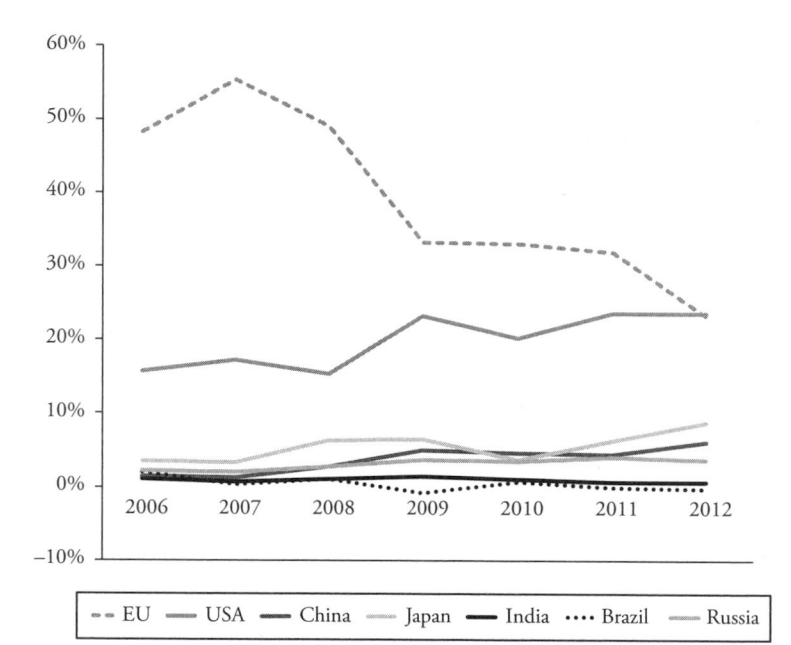

FIGURE 5.13 Share of Worldwide Outward Foreign Direct Investment
Source: UN Conference on Trade and Development, *World Investment Report 2013*,
http://unctad.org/en/PublicationsLibrary/wir2013_en.pdf
Note: Does not exclude intra–EU investment.

declined from 64.1 percent to 61.4 percent. This is still above the dollar's 56.8 percent share in the mid-1990s. As a medium of exchange, the dollar has shifted from being responsible for 85.4 percent of the global foreign exchange market in 2007 to being responsible for 87.0 percent in 2013.[57] Multiple analyses confirm that even after the 2008 crisis, more countries peg their currency to the dollar than to any other currency.[58] The dollar is still a global currency; the euro functions as a regional currency; and no other national currency has attained significance—including the renminbi, which remains inconvertible.[59] Doug Stokes concludes that by all conventional measures of market concentration, "the dollar continues to remain the key *global* currency by a considerable margin, with no other currency even close to competing."[60] Possessing the global reserve currency carries certain structural advantages. This status helps insulate the US economy from foreign shocks while making other economies more sensitive to fluctuations in the dollar's value.[61]

The utility of using military power to affect the global political economy is a matter of some debate.[62] Nevertheless, even skeptics of the fungibility of military power acknowledge that in some economic issue areas, the capacity to use force matters. Military power provides the ultimate means of enforcing the rules of the game.[63] As with currency use, the United States retains hegemonic levels of power in its military capabilities. The Stockholm International Peace Research Institute (SIPRI) data on worldwide military expenditures show that, in 2012, the United States was responsible for approximately 40 percent of worldwide military expenditures and more than 60 percent of great-power military expenditures.[64] These figures have been roughly constant for the past two decades. The distribution favors the United States more than any prior distribution of military expenditures has favored a great power since the 1648 Peace of Westphalia.[65] These data do not treat the European Union as a single actor—but even if they did, the amalgamated military expenditures of the European Union would still be less than half of US defense spending.[66] China's military, while undeniably growing, remains much poorer than the American armed forces. Despite ramping up its defense budget, in 2012 Beijing spent less than a quarter of what Washington spent on defense. Even skeptics of US capabilities, such as Christopher Layne, concede that "the United States still wields preponderant military power."[67]

China has become the hegemonic actor in one arena: official currency reserves. China has accumulated the world's hard currency reserves, swelling from close to $2 trillion in 2008 to more than $3.4 trillion five years later,[68] a figure that dwarfs the reserve assets of any other actor, including both the United States and the European Central Bank. As of June 2013, the United States possessed roughly $145 billion in official reserves, while the European Central Bank possessed less than $75 billion.[69] Indeed, Japan, Russia, India, and Brazil each possess reserves that are several multiples of those of the United States and the eurozone.

China has undeniably leveraged these reserves to increase its power vis-à-vis smaller countries[70] and to exercise economic statecraft in some new and influential ways. China ratcheted up its foreign aid through its own state-run banks. The *Financial Times* reported that between mid-2008 and mid-2010, Chinese loans to developing countries and companies exceeded those of the World Bank.[71] Bloomberg reported that in 2010, Chinese lending to Latin America exceeded that of the World Bank, Inter-American Development Bank, and US Export-Import Bank combined.[72]

That said, China's ability to translate its economic clout to political influence has been limited to its interactions with smaller states. China's fitful efforts to use its reserves to economically pressure the United States have yielded few, if any, concessions.[73] Indeed, despite considerable hype among pundits, in 2012 the Defense Department concluded that "attempting to use US Treasury securities as a coercive tool would have limited effect and likely would do more harm to China than to the United States.... The threat is not credible and the effect would be limited even if carried out."[74] Similarly, China has not demanded any quid pro quo for assisting the eurozone economies.

The data for each of the foregoing measures are flawed. As with intra-European trade and investment, the existence of Hong Kong distorts some of the figures for China's influence. The rise of offshore financial centers can skew the data on capital and investment flows as well.[75] Brazil's, India's, and Russia's output data might undercount gray market activities. Chinese data have long been suspect because of the political incentive for provincial leaders to inflate output figures at key moments.[76] Still, the picture these aggregate figures paint is clear enough. The United States and the European Union still command significant amounts of market power. On most dimensions, China is almost as significant an actor. Based on the trend lines, it is not surprising that observers expect it to be more powerful in the future. Japan is no longer in the first tier of great powers, and Russia, Brazil, and India are not close to ascending to that first tier as well. Only on the dimension of currency reserves does the distribution of power resemble the perceptions discussed in the previous section. Therefore, the primary focus of the rest of this chapter is on the capabilities of the United States, the European Union, and China.

How have markets rewarded the policies of the United States, the European Union, and China? At first glance, the financial crisis would seem to have clarified the hard limits of US power. The ability of the US government to sway market actors appeared to be on the wane. Ratings agencies, for example, put the United States on notice that there were limits to its attractiveness. Standard & Poor's downgraded the US credit rating after the debt-ceiling negotiations in the summer of 2011; Egan-Jones downgraded US government debt on numerous occasions after 2008.[77] The World Economic Forum downgraded the competitiveness ranking of the United States because of its mounting fiscal problems, as did the Legatum Prosperity Index. US businessmen became extremely gloomy. In a 2011 survey, only 9 percent of Harvard Business School alumni thought the United States would outperform the other advanced industrialized states; 21 percent thought the US would be an economic laggard. Two-thirds of respondents expected America to lose ground to Brazil, India, and China.[78] Economics commentators debated the Federal Reserve's waning ability to move markets in the desired direction. Both the second and third rounds of quantitative easing had underwhelming effects on aggregate economic growth.

It is worth distinguishing between the actions of ratings agencies, however, and the actions of markets. On the latter front, the influence of the US government and the attractiveness of the United States economy remained unbowed. Despite the actions taken by S&P's and others, for example, market actors did not punish the US economy. As Bloomberg reported a year after the S&P downgrade: "mortgage rates have dropped to record lows, the government's borrowing costs have eased, the dollar and the benchmark S&P's stock index are up, and global investors' enthusiasm for Treasury debt has strengthened."[79] As figure 5.14 shows, benchmark borrowing rates continued to decline for the United States until June 2013, after the Federal Reserve indicated an eventual tapering of quantitative easing in its forward guidance. These responses contradict the claim that markets did not respond favorably to US policy measures.[80]

In terms of economic fundamentals, the United States has weathered the Great Recession better than other developed economies. US job creation and GDP growth outpaced most of the other advanced industrialized economies. At the same time, the United States has gone further than other OECD economies in deleveraging its consumer and business sectors.[81] This success in deleveraging carried over into the public sector as well. The federal budget deficit as a percentage of GDP declined from over 10 percent in 2009 to 4 percent in 2013. It was the

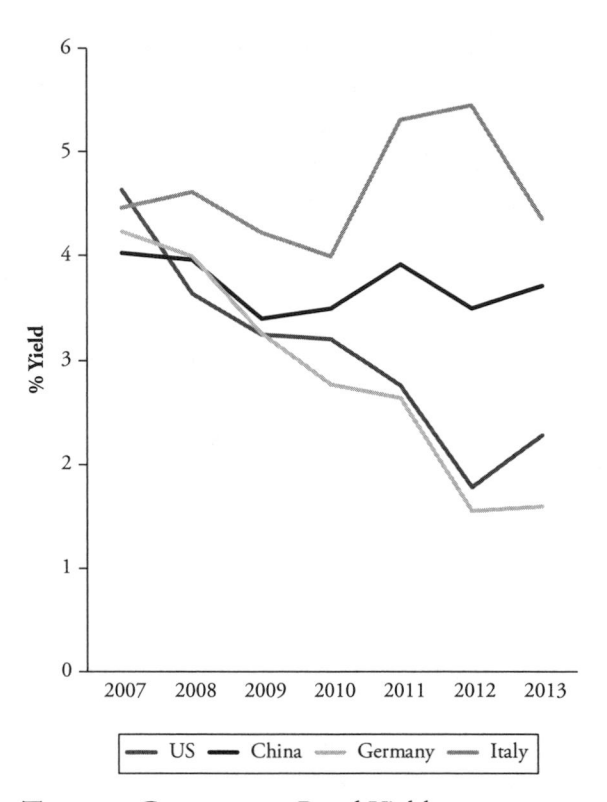

FIGURE 5.14 Ten-year Government Bond Yields, 2007–2013
Source: Trading Economics, http://www.tradingeconomics.com

fastest-paced decline in US postwar economic history—including the military drawdowns following the Vietnam War and the end of the Cold War.[82] Eventually, the observers caught up: Standard & Poor's upgraded its outlook on US debt in June 2013.[83] The same month, A. T. Kearney ranked the United States as the most attractive place for FDI—the first time the United States had been ranked first in that index since 2001.[84] In all, the market's responses to the United States suggest that America remains attractive to both financial and human capital.

But when we examine the market dimension, the European Union runs into difficulties as a great power. Prior to the crisis, many scholars posited that the European Union was an emergent hegemonic power, even raising the possibility that the euro would join the dollar as an international reserve currency.[85] The sovereign debt crisis scuttled such talk, however.[86] Since the start of the Great Recession, the use of the euro as a means to store value and as a medium of exchange has either stalled or declined. Use of the euro remains well below that of the dollar.[87] Since the start of the sovereign debt crisis, the ratings agencies have repeatedly downgraded the bond ratings for most of the European economies. And national governments, as well as myriad European Union bureaucracies, face far stronger constraints from both markets and voters. The sovereign debt crisis in Greece caused financial markets to apply pressure on other eurozone economies that looked vulnerable. The spreads between the sovereign borrowing rates of the Southern Mediterranean countries, such as Italy, widened in comparison to Northern European countries, such as Germany.[88] The result has been years of lackluster growth and in which no steps have been taken toward public-sector or private-sector deleveraging. The austerity measures proved to be deeply unpopular with wide swaths of the voting public. Indeed, as time passed, most of the European Union economies found themselves stuck between two diametrically opposed structural forces. On the one hand, capital markets demanded more credible fiscal policies and promises of backstopping from the European Central Bank. On the other hand, irate publics opposed cuts to social services—sometimes violently. For the first time in decades, European officials found themselves on the receiving end of IMF criticism.

Markets have not constrained all elements of the European Union equally. As figure 5.14 shows, German borrowing rates remained low during most of the sovereign debt crisis. Furthermore, after European Central Bank president Mario Draghi announced in September 2012 that the bank would fully backstop sovereign debt in the eurozone economies, the market panic began to ease and borrowing rates started to drop in the distressed parts of the eurozone (such as Italy). Still, financial pressures have forced significant changes in the continental version of the coordinated market economy, including imposing austerity on the macroeconomic side and forcing the liberalization of labor and product markets on the microeconomic side. Even countries that are not in the eurozone—such as Great Britain—felt compelled to take similar actions. Markets imposed tight constraints on the European economy.

If market actors imposed hard constraints on the eurozone, the opposite seemed to be the case for China. Yet, there were still some warning signs. The World Economic Forum ranked China's competitiveness between twenty-sixth and twenty-ninth in the world for a five-year period after the 2008 financial crisis. While this was well above the rankings of the other BRIC economies, China still was well below the United States and ten of the eurozone economies.[89] High-profile investors made very public bets against continued Chinese growth.[90] In 2013, Fitch downgraded China's sovereign debt rating because of concerns about its shadow banking system, excessive credit expansion, and the mounting unsecured debts of local governments.[91] China's low ranking in the 2013 World Bank's Ease of Doing Business Index—ninety-first—highlighted gaps in the rule of law between Beijing and the OECD economies.[92]

As with the United States, however, China's market performance belied the assessments of ratings agencies and ranking exercises. China's primary problem both before and after the Great Recession was trying to contain massive inflows of foreign capital because of its dynamic and growing market. A. T. Kearney had ranked China as the most attractive locale for FDI for the five years prior to 2013.[93] Multiple private-sector assessments predicted increasing flows from the developed world to emerging markets in general and to China in particular.[94] China's fiscal and trade surpluses meant that its international borrowing needs were close to nil, and that it could access capital with a minimum of fuss. Many of the OECD economies' sovereign debt ratings fell further and faster than China's.

Measuring state capacity is a murkier project; few objective metrics are available. Yet, one can still argue that in this arena, the United States possesses significant network and structural advantages over both the European Union and China. The advantage the United States has over the European Union on this dimension is its degree of centralization. No one doubts the existence of the United States as a coherent actor in the global political economy. Matters are less clear with the European Union. The division of authority between the European Commission, European Council, European Central Bank, and national governments in dealing with the outside world varies widely across issue areas. When the European Union can act as one, its capacity is formidable. When it

is politically or legally divided, that collective strength begins to dissi-
pate—and, as we shall see in chapter 6, the European Union was deeply
divided on important policy dimensions. In contrast, the United States
federal government can be discussed as a more coherent actor. It also
possesses more network centrality across a range of governance structures.[95] At a minimum, the European Union's internal divisions have
stripped away the agenda-setting power it had begun to demonstrate in
the pre-crisis years.

The United States also possesses much greater state capacity than
China in dealing with matters of global governance. As Amitav Acharya
puts it, "While China has increased its *participation* in multilateralism and global governance, it has not offered *leadership*."[96] Indeed,
on numerous metrics, China's engagement with global governance
structures is even less than that of the other BRIC economies.[97] One
scholarly assessment observed that "China's political elites and bureaucracies [were] ill-prepared for the country's sudden high-profile in
global affairs."[98] Part of this is due to legacy effects; China only joined
most global governance structures beginning in the early seventies,
whereas the United States founded or co-founded most of the salient
international organizations.[99] Furthermore, the Chinese policymaking
apparatus suffers from other flaws. One recent assessment compared
China to other East Asian development states and concluded, "Intense
rivalries among Chinese state agencies and local governments put
considerable implementation constraints on indicative planning and
market-conforming state interventions."[100] Corruption also remains
an intractable issue within the Chinese state.[101] These disadvantages
may ebb over time as China modernizes. Still, during the period under
question, China's state capacities were more constrained than those of
the United States.

Tables 5.1 and 5.2 summarize the results of the power audit. Clearly,
for global economic governance, the great powers are the United
States, the European Union, and China—the other BRIC economies,
as well as Japan, can be considered first tier on only a few dimensions.
While the hegemonic coalition of great powers has expanded, it has not
expanded by as much as BRIC enthusiasts predicted. Just as clearly,
table 5.2 reveals that the United States retains primacy in the global
economy. The United States possesses great-power status across the

most dimensions. Even if its relative share of state power is not the same as it was at the turn of the century, the United States has demonstrated full-spectrum resiliency in the wake of the 2008 financial crisis. If the European Union functioned as seamlessly as a single actor, then on many dimensions its power would exceed that of the United States. As it stands, however, the weakened capacity and integrity of the eurozone have sapped its convening power. Only in a few areas, such as trade and regulatory matters, does the European Union function as a great power equal to the United States. Finally, China is indeed rising. It possesses capabilities that it did not possess even a decade ago across several dimensions. That said—and contrary to public perceptions—it is still the weakest of the great powers.

Stepping back to take a broader view, we find that both public and elite perceptions about the distribution of power are at variance with the reality. To be fair, these perceptions contain an important kernel

TABLE 5.1 Great-Powers Assessment

POWER DIMENSION	USA	EU	China	Japan	India	Russia	Brazil
Gross domestic product	X	X	X	--	--	--	--
GDP per capita	X	X	--	X	--	--	--
Global import share	X	X	X	--	--	--	--
Global export share	X	X	X	--	--	--	--
Exports in value-added	X	X	X	X	--	--	--
FDI inflows	X	X	X	--	--	--	--
FDI outflows	X	X	--	--	--	--	--
Capital market size	X	X	--	--	--	--	--
Asset ownership	X	X	--	--	--	--	--
Currency use	X	X	--	--	--	--	--
Currency reserves	--	--	X	X	X	X	X
Military power	X	--	X	--	--	X	--
State capacity	X	--	--	X	--	--	--
QUALIFYING CATEGORIES	12	10	7	4	1	2	1

TABLE 5.2 Great-Power Rankings

POWER DIMENSION	United States	European Union	China
Gross domestic product	2	1	3
Per capita income	1	2	3
Global import share	2	1	3
Global export share	3	1	2
Exports in value-added	2	1	3
FDI inflows	2	1	3
FDI outflows	2	1	3
Capital market size	1	2	3
Asset ownership	1	2	3
Currency use	1	2	3
Currency reserves	2	3	1
Military power	1	3	2
State capacity	1	3	2
AVERAGE RANK	1.61	1.76	2.62

of truth. China's power *is* rising, as are the BRIC economies generally. Across numerous dimensions, the power of the advanced industrialized democracies *has* declined. Nevertheless, most commentators miss three salient facts. First, China is vastly more powerful than the other BRIC economies. Brazil, India, and Russia are important middle-rank economies that belong in groupings like the G20—but they are not catching up with the United States or the European Union on most dimensions. Second, while China has become a great power, it is still demonstrably weaker than the United States and the European Union on multiple dimensions. Ironically, the Chinese seem perfectly aware of this—it is Western analysts who make this error. Finally, on some significant structural dimensions—currency use, asset ownership, military power, and network centrality—the United States remains the uncontested hegemon.

How Have the Great Powers Made Global Governance Work?

Based on the audit just conducted, one can find reasons commentators would be dubious about the ability of powerful actors to manage the global economic order. First, the Great Recession weakened the post–Cold War hegemonic coalition, and weakened it badly. The United States suffered a modest relative decline; traditional allies, such as the European Union and Japan, were hit hard by the crisis. Japan fell from the ranks of first-tier great powers. In some arenas, such as trade or anti-piracy operations, the pre-crisis hegemonic coalition was insufficient to guarantee robust global governance. In other arenas, such as reforming the international financial institutions, the European Union countries resisted reforms because the proposed changes weakened their influence. China, a country that looks very different from the United States or Europe, is now a first-tier great power. With this new managing coalition, making the system work is simply more difficult.[102]

Another reason for pessimism is the mismatch between perception and reality. The previous section showed the gap between the United States, the European Union, China, and everyone else. Other commentators include the other BRIC countries, as well as the other actors in the great-power club.[103] So do many global governance structures, as noted in chapter 2. The debate about which actors belong in the hegemonic coalition raises an important point: the uncertainty about which countries belong must be factored into any analysis of the future of global economic governance. A lack of consensus in this regard allows misperceptions to fester. If enough actors believe that the distribution of power has shifted in a particular direction, then those perceptions can socially construct that reality for a limited period of time. If India is granted the perquisites of economic great-power status, for example, it will also be expected to assume the responsibilities that go along with that status. Collective perceptions can force countries to either shirk or take on ill-suited obligations—particularly if the perceptions deviate significantly from the material facts of life. This explains some commentators' frustration with the failure of the BRIC economies to shoulder the burden of leadership in global governance structures.[104]

Still, the system worked as well as it did for a few very simple reasons. The United States continued to exercise leadership across a wide variety of issue areas, while the European Union acted as a traditional supporter on questions of maintaining economic openness. China acted more like a supporter and less like a spoiler of the system. When they were in agreement, the collective capability of these three economies was sufficient to ensure that their preferred governance solutions won out.[105] When they disagreed, the status quo bias was in favor of policies that promoted openness.

Claiming that the United States was the global economic leader during the Great Recession might sound odd. After all, US influence over global governance structures certainly declined. As is discussed further in chapter 6, the G20 governments rejected the Obama administration's push for continued fiscal stimulus at the June 2010 G20 leaders' summit in Toronto. Later in 2010, G20 leaders categorically rejected Secretary Geithner's suggestion to apply quantitative limits on macroeconomic imbalances. Looking at governance structures, the expansion of the Basel Committee on Banking Supervision and the Financial Stability Forum to encompass all G20 countries showed the apparent dilution of US hegemonic power.[106] At the same time, countries as variegated as Cyprus, Thailand, and Colombia made contributions to double the IMF's lending capacity in 2012, while the United States was domestically constrained from proffering a dime.[107] As of the end of 2013, the United States had not passed the necessary legislation to allow IMF quota and governance to proceed. The limited ability of the United States to manage the Doha Round was likely due to its declining share of global imports and Congress's failure to give the president trade promotion authority.

American leadership during the recent crisis nevertheless turned out to be more robust than many experts perceived.[108] In some areas, such as combating antipiracy, the leadership of the United States was not surprising given its capabilities. The United States organized the Contact Group on Piracy off the Coast of Somalia in early 2009, which coordinates antipiracy activities in the region. Indeed, the creation of Combined Task Force 151 was announced at the headquarters of the US Navy's Fifth Fleet in January 2009, and a US Navy admiral was named its first commander. While numerous other countries have cooperated, the United States took the lead in coordinating antipiracy operations.[109] The Brookings Institution's Bruce Jones concluded, "That force was a visible manifestation of America's alliance reach."[110]

Though perhaps hidden from public view, US leadership also mattered in other areas. This was particularly true in the financial realm. As early as 2007, the Federal Reserve's decision to announce currency swaps provided a way for European financial institutions to improve their positions. Indeed, in 2008, foreign banks made up a majority of the top twenty borrowers from the Fed's emergency lending programs.[111] In agreeing to currency swaps in fall 2008, the Fed prevented a global liquidity crisis. As one European central banker put it, "In a way, we became the thirteenth Federal Reserve district."[112] The 2008 TARP, the AIG bailout, and the Federal Reserve's myriad emergency credit facilities did not just stabilize the US financial sector—these funds also found their way onto the balance sheets of European financial institutions, helping to prevent a meltdown on that continent as well. In opening up those swaps again to the European Central Bank in May 2010, the Fed helped avert a crisis in the European financial markets.[113] After the crisis abated, and US capital rushed out to the rest of the world, the United States functioned "as a global insurer," in the words of one economist.[114] Other great powers rapidly discovered that US dollar hegemony anchored their economies to the United States on financial issues. It is therefore unsurprising that United States–led and European Union–supported financial sanctions exacted a significant toll on the Iranian economy.

Domestic politics may have prevented a more robust US policy response. Partisan gridlock, however, did not prevent the United States from pursuing a plethora of emergency rescue packages (via TARP), expansionary fiscal policy (via the 2009 American Recovery and Reinvestment Act), stress tests of large financial institutions, expansionary monetary policy (via interest rate cuts, three rounds of quantitative easing, and Operation Twist), and financial regulatory reform (via Dodd-Frank). These actions helped to secure multilateral cooperation on macroeconomic policy coordination for two years, as well as Basel III. Moreover, even though the United States has been slow to pass quota reform legislation through Congress, by most accounts America played a leadership role in negotiating the IMF reform.[115] On financial regulation, the United States exercised leadership using myriad dimensions of its power.

The United States also demonstrated leadership in other issue areas in which China was initially reluctant to cooperate. On the question of macroeconomic imbalances, the United States took the lead in pressuring Beijing to allow the renminbi to appreciate and to allow G20 monitoring. China initially stonewalled the G20 information-sharing process because of a reluctance to discuss its exchange-rate policies and a desire to avoid external pressure to revalue. Beijing missed a November 2009 deadline to provide information about China's economic plans going forward. When Chinese officials did submit information, it was historical and vaguely worded rather than forward looking.[116] In response, the United States coordinated a March 2010 letter from the leaders of five countries—the United States, Canada, Great Britain, France, and South Korea—to the other G20 members. The letter raised the issue of exchange rates in relation to reducing trade imbalances, and urged all members to accelerate their compliance with G20 processes.[117] In June 2010, President Obama sent another letter to his G20 colleagues stressing the importance of "market-determined exchange rates." Three days later, the People's Bank of China announced that it would "enhance the RMB exchange rate flexibility."[118] The slow appreciation of the renminbi, then, began after US-coordinated application of pressure. Even after the announcement, the United States continued to coordinate action within the G20 to maintain pressure on China.[119]

Another example of US leadership was the creation of a transparency regime for sovereign wealth funds. The United States led the way in calling for action in this area. In spring 2007, the Treasury Department stated publicly that the funds raised "broad, strategic issues for the international financial system" and called for the IMF to draft best practices to address these issues.[120] The United States then used the size of its capital markets to secure cooperation from capital exporters. For example, a key step in securing the 2008 Santiago Principles came when the United States persuaded two of the largest sovereign wealth funds—the United Arab Emirates' Abu Dhabi Investment Authority (ADIA) and the Government of Singapore Investment Corporation (GIC)—to jointly issue a set of policy principles regarding the funds and recipient countries. They included commitments to governance and to transparency standards, as well as a pledge to use commercial, not political, criteria to evaluate investments.[121] Because ADIA's and GIC's transparency scores ranked among the lowest of all sovereign wealth funds, their commitment to these US-articulated principles signaled a clear policy reversal.[122] Both funds subsequently agreed to accept the voluntary Santiago Principles as a way of securing access to the US market. GIC's deputy chairman explained, "The greatest danger is if this is not addressed directly, then some form of financial protectionism will arise and barriers will be raised to hinder the flow of funds."[123] A few days before the policy principles were articulated, Abu Dhabi's director of international affairs wrote an open letter to the *Wall Street Journal* stressing the importance of maintaining an open investment climate.[124] An Arab League report urged acceptance of a code of conduct, arguing that it would alleviate Western pressure to restrict sovereign wealth funds' access to their capital markets.[125] Survey evidence also indicates that fund managers believed there was a linkage between agreeing to a code of conduct and warding off investment protectionism.[126]

China initially resisted these pressures to form a new regime. At one point during the negotiations of the Santiago Principles, Gao Xiqing, the president of the Chinese Investment Corporation, told *60 Minutes* that an IMF code would "only hurt feelings" and characterized the idea as "politically stupid." Later, he was more blunt, characterizing the process as "political bullshit."[127] In the end, however, US power and European Union support mattered. At the key meeting in Santiago in 2008, the more-established sovereign wealth funds, together with the recipient countries, were able to apply sufficient pressure on new capital exporters to ensure agreement.[128]

The eventual Chinese accommodations on these issues highlight the second major contributor to functional global governance—China's surprising role as a key supporter of the status quo. This assertion is counterintuitive, given the raft of arguments that Beijing has acted as a revisionist actor in the global political economy.[129] It is true that in some arenas—such as export subsidies, cyberattacks, and territorial disputes—China has been reluctant to engage constructively with other actors. Nevertheless, on a number of key policy dimensions, China bolstered the power of existing policy coordination rather than undermine it. Furthermore, the arenas in which China dissented from the global consensus were those in which its voice mattered the least.

China acted like a supporter rather than a spoiler in multiple issue areas. On antipiracy, China dispatched a naval task force to the Horn of Africa soon after the salient UN Security Council resolutions were passed in December 2008. This represented the first sustained Chinese naval presence in the region in 500 years. Although Beijing has its own commercial incentives to protect shipping, the Chinese government stressed that it was honoring its obligations as a responsible global actor.[130] US officials repeatedly praised China's ongoing participation in the task force, and the two countries began conducting joint military exercises on antipiracy techniques in 2012.[131]

Evidence of Chinese supportership can also be seen in macroeconomic policy coordination. In 2008 China enacted one of the largest packages of fiscal spending as a percentage of GDP among the G20 economies. China acted out of self-interest in doing this, but the salutary effect on the global economy was still significant.[132] Beijing also extended swap lines and dollars to distressed trading partners during the depths of the 2008 financial crisis.[133] Beginning in 2010, China also took steps to reduce its role in rising macroeconomic imbalances. It allowed the yuan to appreciate slowly over the next few years. Combined with higher domestic inflation, China's real exchange rate showed significant appreciation, with a concomitant effect on macroeconomic imbalances. According to a Peterson Institute for International Economics study, by fall 2012, the renminbi was only "modestly" undervalued. The McKinsey Global Institute estimated that, due in no small part to the appreciation of the renminbi, the overall size of macroeconomic imbalances shrank by 30 percent in the first four years after the 2008 financial crisis.[134]

On trade matters, China's role as a supporting state becomes manifestly clear. On the one hand, China exploited loopholes in global economic governance to keep its currency undervalued. In doing so, China violated the spirit of the rules of the game.[135] At the same time, China also adhered to the letter of the law in implementing its trade policy—and for China, the letter of the law imposes significant constraints.[136] When China entered the WTO in 2001, the accession negotiations imposed significant strictures limiting Beijing ability to raise China's protectionist barriers. In contrast to other developing economies, for example, China's "bound" tariffs—the highest rate at which tariffs can be set—were at a comparatively low level when they joined the WTO. Similarly, stricter limits were placed on its ability to use nontariff barriers as well.

Despite China's rising power, the hard law of the WTO, along with its myriad bilateral and regional free-trade agreements, functioned as a binding constraint on China's trade measures. A World Bank research paper on movement in Chinese tariff rates since 2008 concluded that China's commitments to the WTO and other preferential trade agreements explained more than 95 percent of the variation.[137] An analysis of China's use of temporary trade barriers reveals a similar finding. Compared to the other developing country members of the G20, China's use of those measures covers the smallest trade-weighted share of imports—smaller, in fact, than the share covered by US temporary trade barriers.[138] China's compliance with adverse WTO rulings has been better than that of either the United States or the European Union.[139] Christopher McNally concludes, "China has adopted largely non-disruptive policies supportive of the rules-based multilateral order. China's economy has been integrated globally by relying on multilateral institutional frameworks, especially the WTO. And so far China has mostly complied with its WTO commitments and avoided any aggressive role in trying to change the nature or rules of the organization."[140]

Stepping back to view the bigger picture, we see that China largely refrained from challenging the status quo in global economic governance.[141] It requested and received larger quotas in the IMF and the World Bank, as well as a larger voice in other global governance clubs. Still, none of these moves involved a shift in the underlying rules of the game. Most of China's demands were designed to give Beijing a greater voice in existing global governance structures—not to revise the purpose of their missions. When opportunities arose for China to subvert these regimes—such as when Pakistan sought Chinese aid as a substitute for IMF loans in fall 2008—Beijing did not take action.[142] The biggest exception to Chinese quiescence proved the rule.

In 2009, the head of the People's Bank of China suggested ending the dollar's status as the world's reserve currency. This was clearly a revisionist aim, but China's government had neither the resources nor the inclination to do so. Other central bankers were aware of the People's Bank's constrained influence within the Chinese state.[143] Even China's fellow BRIC partners resisted the proposal.[144] In the end, the suggestion was mostly symbolic. For the issue areas where China did have the power to alter global governance rules—as in trade—Beijing adhered to the status quo.

China was the only actor powerful enough and distinct enough from the established great powers to act as a truly revisionist actor in the world of global economic governance. However, China did not act in this manner at all (see chapter 6). On the contrary, in the first five years following the 2008 crisis, China acted primarily as a responsible stakeholder. It did not advocate abandoning either the open trading system or the open investment regime. This behavior is consistent with the assessment by China scholars that the country will continue to demonstrate willingness to comply with other global governance mechanisms over time, and remain reluctant to articulate a truly revisionist set of policy demands.[145] Iain Johnston provides a concise snapshot of China's post-crisis behavior.[146]

> The pundit and media world thus tended to miss a great deal of ongoing cooperative interaction between the United States and China throughout 2010. Examples include the continued growth of US exports to China during the year ... [and] a Chinese decision to continue the appreciation of the renminbi prior to the Group of Twenty meeting in Toronto in June 2010. . . . .
>
> In addition to these U.S.-specific cooperative actions, throughout 2010 China continued to participate in all of the major multilateral global and regional institutions in which it had been involved for the past couple of decades, including the World Trade Organization, the International Monetary Fund, the United Nations Security Council, the Association of Southeast Asian Nations (ASEAN) Plus 3, the China-ASEAN Free Trade Agreement, UN peacekeeping operations, and antipiracy activities in the Gulf of Aden. There is no evidence that ... it began to withdraw from global institutional life or to dramatically challenge the purposes, ideology, or main organizational features of these institutions to a degree that it had not in the past.

Since the start of the Great Recession, China's behavior has reinforced rather than subverted the existing set of global governance rules. China was a supporter and not a spoiler.

There is one final aspect of the post-2008 distribution of power that aided in the functioning of global economic governance. It is certainly true that the post-2008 hegemonic coalition was larger and more heterogeneous than the pre-2008 coalition. The cumulative effect of such a power shift, however, is to reinforce preexisting policies in the absence of any overwhelming consensus for change. Because changing the status quo becomes hard for all actors, such change is more likely to persist. In the case of global economic governance, this path-dependent effect was fortuitous. Pre-crisis global economic governance was already locked in with a bias toward greater openness. The response to the crisis was crafted with the assumption that this openness was locked in. The erosion of coercive power made it difficult for any actors eager to dislodge Washington Consensus norms to actually do so.

Conclusion

This chapter has examined the distribution of power in the wake of the 2008 global financial crisis to understand why the system worked reasonably well. Despite some decline, the United States possessed sufficient reservoirs of power to take an active leadership role. Even though America's traditional supporters had also declined in influence, the European Union was still powerful enough to matter as a key supporter of US leadership. Equally important, China acted like a responsible stakeholder after the 2008 financial crisis. In the arenas in which China could have blocked neoliberal norms, it refrained from doing so. On key aspects of global governance, the troika of the United States, the European Union, and China formed a sufficiently large hegemonic coalition to maintain the relevance of the principal rules of the global economic game. Although the distribution of power diffused somewhat, there remained a sufficient concentration for a great-power concert to preserve the system.

Comparing the current situation with the analogous moment during the Great Depression, we can discern why events unfolded differently this time around. Looking at the distribution of power, for example, the interwar period was truly a moment of great-power transition. At the start of the Great Depression, the United Kingdom's lack of financial muscle badly hampered its leadership efforts. Even as it was trying to maintain the gold standard, Great Britain held only 4 percent of the world's gold reserves.[147] The United States had amassed much of the world's gold reserves, but the US government was unwilling to aid the beleaguered European economies. The situation was very different in fall 2008. The United States still possessed significant material capabilities, as did the European Union. China, the most likely challenger to the liberal international order, acted to support rather than spoil the system. Combined, the great powers were able to avert the worst-case scenarios.

The distribution of power played a contributing role in the continued functioning of global economic governance—but power alone is an insufficient explanation. Why did the American and Chinese governments continue to comply with WTO norms? What explains the preferences of the great powers? To answer these questions, we need to turn to the role of economic ideas.

6

The Role of Ideas

AS WE HAVE SEEN, global economic governance has functioned surprisingly well since the 2008 financial crisis. This is due in part to shared material interests and in part to resilient American leadership and robust Chinese supportership. The question of why the system worked remains somewhat unresolved, however. Arguments grounded only in material power and interest cannot explain everything. There are simply too many instances in which powerful national or sectoral interests compromised. As we shall see, Germany was not enthusiastic about the notion of Keynesian stimulus at the outset of the economic crisis. In the end, however, the German government was responsible for some of the largest stimulus spending among the G20 economies.[1] Chinese princelings resisted any move by the Chinese government to allow the remninbi to appreciate—and yet, beginning in 2010, the government allowed the currency to rise relative to the dollar. European governments resisted the dilution of their influence in the World Bank and the IMF, but eventually acquiesced. And the negotiations over Basel III suggested the limits of an approach based solely on material interests. More generally, neither interest nor power alone explains why the United States chose to perpetuate the system of global economic openness, and why China supported that decision.

This chapter considers the role that economic ideas played in fostering the necessary comity for global governance to function. Ideas can provide a powerful guide for action during times of crisis—provided they are shared. There were excellent reasons to believe that the 2008 financial crisis would delegitimate the economic principles that undergirded the open global economic order. Despite this expectation, delegitimation occurred only on the margins. Because rising actors failed to articulate a coherent alternative, the neoliberal ideas of the Washington Consensus continued to act as a guide for key actors in the post-crisis world.

In this chapter I look at why there were excellent reasons to believe that the 2008 crisis could have been a game-changer in how elites and publics viewed the global economy in general and neoliberalism in particular, and then review the data confirming that there has been no sea change in public attitudes and only minimal changes in policy content. Then I discuss the conditions for ideational change in times of economic crisis, and follow with discussions of two ideational debates that played out in the five years after the financial crisis: the competition between the Washington Consensus and the Beijing Consensus, and the battles over austerity in fiscal and monetary policy.

Why the Great Recession Could Have Been an Existential Crisis

The dominant theme of global economic policy for the three decades prior to 2008 was the retreat of the state from the commanding heights of the economy.[2] The embodiment of this trend was the articulation of a set of ideas that was sometimes labeled "neoliberalism" and sometimes labeled the Washington Consensus. Economists have developed the core of neoliberalism over the previous half-century.[3] Its central argument is that the world is most likely to prosper if the state adopts a hands-off attitude to markets. At the international level, the embrace of market forces led to a series of policies that pushed toward reducing restrictions on cross-border exchange: freer trade, capital account liberalization, and fewer restrictions on foreign investment. In finance, the efficient-market hypothesis held that state regulation is essentially unnecessary, since all information about any financial asset is encapsulated in its price.[4] Via privatization, liberalization, and deregulation, governments across the globe increasingly accepted the idea that markets represent the most efficient method of resource allocation. At the most abstract level, the spread of neoliberalism was a strong affirmation of Francis Fukuyama's "end of history" thesis—the idea that no universally viable challenger to liberal capitalist democracy would emerge as an alternative mode of domestic governance.[5]

Even in the run-up to the subprime mortgage crisis, however, there were signs that both American politicians and the American body politic were souring on globalization. According to a recent Gallup poll, at the peak of the late-1990s economic boom, 56 percent of Americans believed that the economic opportunities created by foreign trade outweighed the costs; only 36 percent thought the costs outweighed the benefits. By 2008, however, that support for freer trade had collapsed. As the financial crisis was growing more acute, 52 percent of Americans thought the costs had become prohibitive; only 41 percent thought otherwise.[6]

The attitudes of US political and business elites matched the public's turn against the global economy. Most business interests didn't exactly clamor for a return to protectionism, but neither were they terribly enthusiastic about lobbying for the completion of the Doha Round. Political elites paid lip service to supporting free trade—unless Dubai Ports World tried to acquire holdings in US ports or foreign sovereign wealth funds tried to invest in the United States. Still, the number of congressional bills targeting China as an unfair trader exploded.[7] And during the 2008 presidential campaign, one of Barack Obama's sharpest conflicts with then-rival Hillary Clinton was over which candidate would renegotiate the North American Free Trade Agreeement (NAFTA) more favorably in America's direction.

Chinese preferences for trade liberalization were relatively robust before the crisis—but resentment against the US-created international economic order was simmering. The US response to the Asian financial crisis in 1997–98 had already created layers of hostility to the Washington Consensus across the Pacific Rim.[8] The Chinese public also resented the US-imposed terms for China's WTO membership in 2001, viewing them as onerous.[9] US pressure on China to liberalize its financial sector and allow the remninbi to appreciate also generated hurt feelings. A December 2007 survey of Chinese citizens and opinion leaders revealed that a plurality of both sets of respondents believed that the United States was trying to prevent China from becoming a great power.[10] Chinese officials ratcheted up their criticism of the

US-led economic order. China's Communist Party authorized party critiques of the Washington Consensus.[11] A senior Chinese banking official publicly blasted the United States for having a "warped conception" of financial regulation. Chinese trade officials accused the United States of engaging in its own form of protectionism because of dollar depreciation.[12]

Once the acute phase of the crisis hit there were excellent reasons to believe that the animating ideas of the Washington Consensus would lose their legitimacy. In 2008, global markets in financial assets, food, and energy were buffeted by a series of shocks, and none of them appeared to respond terribly well. The great powers responded by increasing state intervention in all three sectors. In the United States and United Kingdom, the Great Recession rattled even the most devout free-market enthusiasts. Former Federal Reserve chairman Alan Greenspan made headlines when he testified before Congress that his faith in the "intellectual edifice" of self-correcting markets had "collapsed."[13] At the 2009 G20 London summit, British prime minister Gordon Brown flatly declared that "the old Washington Consensus is over."[14] Press reports suggested that the consensus among economists about the virtues of an open global economy was cracking.[15] Over the next few years, book after book blasted the intellectual edifice of neoliberalism and the Washington Consensus.[16]

If the financial crisis caused a crisis of capitalist faith in the United States, it appeared to encourage more revisionist thinking in China and elsewhere. The contrast between the successful 2008 Beijing Olympics and persistent US malaise convinced many observers that China's moment to supplant the United States had arrived.[17] China's economic success in the wake of the 2008 financial crisis stood in stark contrast to the stagnation in the advanced industrialized economies. In early 2010, the *New York Times* noted the shift: "As developing countries everywhere look for a recipe for faster growth and greater stability than that offered by the now-tattered 'Washington consensus' of open markets, floating currencies and free elections, there is growing talk about a 'Beijing consensus.'"[18] As we shall see, there were multiple definitions of the Beijing Consensus, but a common denominator was the prominent role of state institutions and state-owned enterprises. In 2006, the Chinese government had declared seven strategic sectors in which the state would retain absolute control, signaling a move away from fostering private enterprise in leading sectors.[19] China's massive 2008 fiscal stimulus focused on infrastructure investments, disproportionately empowering those sectors even more.[20] Beyond those sectors, China facilitated the development of sovereign wealth funds, national oil companies, and state-run development banks.[21] The goal of all of these structures was to ensure that the state could direct resources toward favored and strategic sectors that were considered crucial to economic development.

Multiple Western analysts argued that the relative success of state-directed growth among energy and manufacturing exporters augured a rise in "authoritarian capitalism" or "state capitalism."[22] China was clearly the most powerful and most potent of these countries. Stefan Halper was even more explicit, arguing that "the terms, the conditions and arrangements, of state-directed capitalism give Beijing a distinct edge over Western competitors."[23] Martin Jacques noted, "China's success suggests that the Chinese model of the state is destined to exercise a powerful global influence, especially in the developing world, and thereby transform the terms of future economic debate."[24] Even former enthusiasts of neoliberalism, such as Francis Fukuyama and Thomas Friedman, began to wonder if the China model was superior.[25] At a minimum, the demonstration effect of China's phenomenal growth suggested that there were pathways to economic development that deviated from the Washington Consensus—and maybe other developing countries would try to adopt its features.[26]

The interest in a Beijing Consensus mirrored shifts in elite and public attitudes inside China that were more hostile toward the United States. As China scholars Andrew Nathan and Andrew Scobell observed, many Chinese elites viewed economic competition with the United States through a relative gains lens in which "China expects Western powers to resist Chinese competition for resources and higher-value-added markets."[27] Chinese officials publicly scorned the flaws of the Washington Consensus and began to talk privately about the virtues of their own development path. Wang Jisi noted in 2012, "It is a popular notion among Chinese political elites, including some national leaders, that China's development model provides an alternative to Western democracy and experiences for other developing and political systems are experiencing disorder and chaos. The China model, or Beijing Consensus, features an all-powerful political leadership that effectively manages social and economic affairs."[28] Post-crisis public opinion polls also revealed that an increasing number of Chinese citizens believed that US-led global governance structures were designed to contain Chinese power.[29] According to the Pew Global Attitudes survey, there was a demonstrable shift in Chinese public attitudes between 2010 and 2013. The attitudes of Chinese citizens toward the United States went from a net 21 percent positive to net 13 percent negative—a considerable swing.[30] Chinese questioning of the American model dovetailed with nationalist preferences to challenge US hegemony. Many Chinese hawks urged Beijing to use its holdings of dollar-denominated assets to subvert American foreign policy and delegitimize the US-created international order.[31]

During the depths of the Great Recession, there were excellent reasons to believe that the open, liberal international order faced an existential threat. The proponents of the Washington Consensus were no longer so confident in their ideas, and there seemed to be an intellectual movement coalescing toward an alternative paradigm based on China's growth model. What actually happened over the next five years, however, was something altogether different.

The Resilience of the Open Global Economy

As discussed in chapter 2, matters played out quite differently from expectations. Global governance structures mostly doubled down in committing to an open global economy. Trade protectionism did not increase as predicted, and trade flows recovered quickly. Despite concerns about state-led foreign investment, the actual steps taken to restrict such investments were minimal.[32] Only in the financial sector were there appreciable changes in the rules of the game—but even here the changes were designed to restore confidence in the markets rather than promote closure.

It is also noteworthy that, despite enthusiasm in some quarters for the China model, official rhetoric, public attitudes, and state actions have not shifted against either free trade or the free market. One of the key elements of the G20's "Framework for Strong, Sustainable, and

TABLE 6.1 Global Public Support for Free Markets

COUNTRY	2007	2009	2010	2011	2012
Argentina	43	56	—	40	—
Great Britain	72	66	67	64	61
China	75	79	—	84	74
Egypt	50	60	—	51	50
France	56	57	61	67	58
Germany	65	61	65	73	69
Indonesia	45	49	—	63	—
Italy	73	—	75	—	50
Japan	49	41	—	43	38
Jordan	47	54	—	48	43
Kenya	78	84	—	72	—
Lebanon	74	64	—	60	62
Mexico	55	52	—	44	34
Nigeria	79	66	—	82	—
Pakistan	60	65	—	57	48
Poland	68	65	70	68	53
Russia	53	51	52	60	47
South Korea	72	76	—	78	—
Spain	67	57	59	62	47
Turkey	60	60	—	64	55
United States	70	76	—	68	67

Source: Pew Research, Global Attitudes Project, http://web.archive.org/
web/20130310095600/http://www.pewglobal.org/database/?indicator=18&survey=12
&response=Agree&mode=table

Balanced Growth" articulated at the Pittsburgh summit in September 2009 was to maintain an open global economy. It included pledges to "stand together to fight against protectionism" and "minimize any negative impact on trade and investment of our domestic policy actions" and "not retreat into financial protectionism."[33] Pledges like these have littered G20 statements since Pittsburgh as well. One can argue that these endorsements were, to use the argot of policymakers, "boilerplate"—statements cut and pasted from previous communiqués and official documents. They were therefore simply unthinking reiterations of past pledges. This is the point, however: these statements were unthinking because they had been already accepted as given for quite

TABLE 6.2 Global Public Support for Free Trade

COUNTRY	2007	2008	2009	2010	2011
Argentina	68	62	65	72	—
Great Britain	78	77	82	84	87
Canada	82	—	85	—	—
China	91	87	93	93	89
Egypt	61	57	67	64	—
France	78	82	83	79	83
Germany	85	87	85	90	95
Indonesia	71	71	79	82	83
Israel	90	—	88	—	95
Japan	72	71	73	72	—
Jordan	72	65	60	71	77
Kenya	93	—	80	90	91
Lebanon	81	85	90	93	97
Mexico	77	69	79	71	79
Nigeria	85	91	90	84	—
Pakistan	82	78	79	86	81
Poland	77	85	81	84	78
Russia	82	82	80	86	83
South Korea	86	88	92	88	—
Spain	82	89	89	90	96
Turkey	73	67	64	83	82
United States	59	53	65	66	67

Source: Pew Research, Global Attitudes Project, http://web.archive.org/
web/20120310024942/http://www.pewglobal.org/database/?indicator=16&survey=13
&response=Good%20thing&mode=table

some time. These communiqués failed to include any language that suggested any kind of fundamental rethinking of the merits of an open global economy.

A similar story can be told about the BRICS summits.[34] Beginning in fall 2008, policymakers from Brazil, Russia, India, and China turned what had been a Goldman Sachs marketing term into a real international grouping with regular summit meetings and working groups. In December 2010, South Africa formally joined the grouping, making them the "BRICS." The BRICS have called repeatedly for "the reform of international financial institutions and global governance," as they did in their November 2008 communiqué.[35] When examining BRICS statements to determine their preferences, however, what emerge are demands that represent the international side of the Washington Consensus. This began with the November 2008 statement of the BRIC finance ministers, which called for taking actions to unfreeze private credit markets and prevent trade protectionism. The statement from their March 2013 summit in Durban noted strong support for "an open, transparent and rules-based multilateral trading system." These themes reverberate in every communiqué.[36] The BRIC Leaders 2010 statement did note: "Recent events have shattered the belief about the self-regulating nature of financial markets." But as chapter 4 shows, similar language also appeared in G7 and G20 communiqués.[37] After five years of summits, the only tangible step toward alternative institution-building was the March 2013 announcement that a BRICS Development Bank would be created.[38] Even this bank, however, was originally projected to have a total capitalization of approximately $50 billion—less than what the World Bank loans out in a single year.[39]

Public attitudes about the global economy also failed to shift all that much given the vicissitudes of global markets in 2007 and 2008. One would have expected eroding support for free markets and free trade. Given the prominence of the Washington Consensus, it would have been natural for publics across the globe to push back on the principles of laissez-faire capitalism. To be sure, one can find post-2008 global public opinion polls suggesting hostility to global capitalism, particularly with respect to finance.[40] Most of these surveys, however, lack a pre-crisis baseline. Evidence of a broad-based global turn in public opinion would only be convincing if there were an appreciable shift in public responses to questions that were asked both before and after the 2008 financial crisis.

Fortunately, the Pew Global Attitudes Project has surveyed a wide spectrum of countries since 2002, asking people about their opinions on both international trade and the free market more generally.[41] Surprisingly, the survey results (table 6.1) suggest that the Great Recession did *not* lead to a drop in support for either free markets or free trade. Pew surveyed people in more than twenty countries before and after the 2008 crisis on the question of whether people were better off in a free market economy.[42] There was no immediate drop in support following the crisis, and similar results were found in 2011. In 2007, the unweighted average of the twenty-three countries surveyed showed that, on average, 62.5 percent of respondents believed in the benefits of a free market. In early 2009, in response to the same question, those same countries produced an unweighted average of 62.7 percent in support. For those countries surveyed in 2007 and 2011, support for free markets increased from 61.9 percent to 62.4 percent. This is hardly a significant increase, but it demonstrates that there was no erosion of support for free markets either. Once the eurozone crisis deepened, support did plummet in European countries, such as Italy and Spain. But on the whole, and particularly in the developing world, support for free markets remained strong and robust.

The support for liberalizing trade with other countries was even more resilient, as table 6.2 demonstrates.[43] Twenty-four countries were surveyed in 2007 and in at least one year after 2008, including a majority of the G20 economies. Overall, eighteen of those twenty-four countries showed equal or greater support for trade in 2009 than in 2007. In the countries surveyed in 2007 and 2009, the unweighted average support of free trade increased from 78 percent to 79.5 percent. By 2011, twenty of twenty-four countries showed greater or equal support for trade compared to the 2007 surveys. Between 2007 and 2011, the unweighted average support for increased trade in the countries surveyed rose from 78.7 percent to 84.4 percent. Indeed, according to a Gallup poll, Americans were more positive about international trade in February 2013 than at any point in the previous twenty years.[44] Contrary to expectations, there was no public rejection of either the free market or the open global economy. Furthermore, any measurable dips in national support that did occur did not come from the developing world or BRICS, but from eurozone economies beset with multiple economic travails.

The absence of an ideational shift away from neoliberalism is consistent with the actual behavior of the BRICS economies. A glance at the scores on the Heritage Foundation's economic freedom index, for example, shows that trade freedom rose in all the BRICS countries between 2008 and 2013. This matches the BRICS' own rhetoric. As

Miles Kahler observes, "The Great Recession did not produce a redefinition of their interests away from international economic integration. Rather than delinking, as they had in the 1930s, or demanding a new international economic order, as they had in the 1970s, the developing world remained invested in the existing order and served as a key constituency in its defense."[45]

Despite the potential for transformation, the ideas animating the Washington Consensus emerged from the 2008 financial crisis relatively unscathed. Even though a few practices changed—such as the legitimation of capital controls—the basic premises of neoliberalism went unchallenged. Mercantilism and protectionism were rhetorically eschewed. Capital account liberalization remained a goal of global economic governance, albeit a less important one. Conservative macroeconomic policies were encouraged. The Washington Consensus continued to function as the "privileged" set of economic ideas in global economic governance. As Sarah Babb concludes, "Neither the policy changes recently adopted by national governments nor those adopted within the [international financial institutions] qualify as a paradigm shift. In this sense, the Washington Consensus lives on."[46]

This failure by elites and publics to overtly reject the Washington Consensus has nettled its critics. John Quiggin noted, "The zombie ideas that brought the global financial system to the brink of meltdown, and have already caused thousands of firms to fail and cost millions of workers their jobs, still walk among us." Colin Crouch observed, "Neoliberalism is emerging from the financial collapse more politically powerful than ever...and the issue today is not limited to a single country, as neoliberalism is an international, even global, phenomenon. What we have to understand today is, therefore, the strange non-death of neoliberalism."[47] Whatever new ideas have been introduced into the global public sphere, they have not reconstituted the core elements of the system.

The Necessary Conditions for Ideational Change

To understand why there was no fundamental challenge, it is worth considering how economic ideas matter in world politics. International relations scholarship on economic ideas comes from heterogeneous worldviews, but there are commonalities in the literature that are worth exploring to explain the survival of neoliberalism.[48] For example, almost every scholar agrees that ideas matter more during periods of crisis and uncertainty. Judith Goldstein and Robert Keohane talk about ideas functioning as road maps or focal points when there is a lack of clarity about what to do.[49] Mark Blyth refers to the problem of "Knightian uncertainty" during an economic crisis—the moment when actors look to ideas to explain both its causes and possible solutions.[50]

Uncertainty is a function of three factors: the depth of the shock, the linkage between the idea and the adverse outcome, and the depth of the preexisting consensus among policy elites for the privileged set of ideas. The bigger the shock, the bigger the uncertainty. A market crash or sustained recession clearly suggests that the status quo is not working, which creates a powerful incentive to search for new ideas. As the biggest global downturn since the Great Depression, the 2008 financial crisis definitely met this threshold criterion.

The connection between privileged ideas and bad outcomes also matters, however. If the link between an economic idea and an outcome is clear, simple, and direct, then it is easier for elites and publics to make the cognitive connection. For example, there has been considerable debate about the underlying causes of the 2008 financial crisis.[51] The misplaced faith in the efficient-market hypothesis seems to be directly related to the subprime mortgage crisis: deregulation permitted the creation of an asset bubble that, once popped, triggered the crisis. In finance, the causal logic connecting the privileged idea to negative outcomes was tightly coupled. On the other hand, few analysts blamed the Great Recession on low trade barriers. In trade, therefore, the causal logic was more loosely linked.

The strength of the expert consensus also affects uncertainty. One can argue that confidence in policy ideas mirrors the way Bayesian statisticians predict how people update their beliefs.[52] In Bayesian theory, expectations about the future are based on the strength of prior beliefs and the extent to which new data contradict those beliefs. In the world of economic ideas, the strength of that prior distribution is a function of the historical depth and current breadth of the consensus view among policy elites. The longer an ideational consensus has taken root, the more it takes on a "technical" rather than "ideological" cast—thereby making it harder to challenge. Deeply privileged ideas often possess an array of auxiliary arguments that can explain anomalous effects, making it less likely that these ideas will be usurped.[53] So in areas in which experts have been in agreement for quite some time, even severe shocks might not trigger a substantive reevaluation of beliefs. In public policy areas in which the consensus is shallower, however, such shocks might lead to large changes in policy attitudes.

Even during periods of high uncertainty, it is not enough for the privileged set of ideas to be discredited. There must also be a viable alternative. It is quite easy for discontented elites to criticize the privileged set of ideas; it is quite another for them to agree on another idea. For that to happen, there must be a substitute paradigm that provides a compelling explanation for the current negative outcome, offers a policy that reverses the status quo, and coalesces strong interests around the idea to supplant the existing ideational order.[54] This is a daunting intellectual task, particularly if there is no "off the shelf" idea available that can explain current events. It is also a daunting political task: the proposed alternative needs to be simple and clear, and compelling enough to serve as a focal point for a heterogeneous group of individuals opposed to the status quo.[55]

Given this checklist, the failure to dislodge the Washington Consensus begins to make more sense. To be sure, the Great Recession triggered genuine uncertainty, but that uncertainty varied across different areas of global public policy. Post-crisis surveys of leading economists suggest that a powerful consensus persisted on several key international policy dimensions. For example, the University of Chicago's business school has run surveys of the world's leading economists since the crisis started. On the one hand, the surveys show a strong consensus on the virtues of freer trade, as well as a rejection of returning to the gold standard to regulate international exchange rates. On the other hand, there is less consensus on monetary policy and the benefits of continued quantitative easing.[56]

To demonstrate the ways in which the relative strength of economic ideas affected the willingness of states to cooperate with global economic governance, the next two sections look at two areas where the outcomes differed. First, we examine why a Beijing Consensus failed to take root to challenge the Washington Consensus. In this case, the

necessary conditions to displace the ordering principles of neoliberalism were never in place. The depth of belief in the privileged set of
ideas was strong, and the alternative set of ideas was too inchoate to be
a plausible substitute. This explains, in part, why China proved to be a
supporter rather than a spoiler after 2008.

Then we examine the more contested debate about macroeconomic
policy coordination. In this case, the possibility of ideational change
found more fertile ground. The depth of the consensus on macroeconomic policy was newer and weaker. The existence of Keynesian ideas
enabled a global policy shift. Nevertheless, the shift turned out to be
only a transient deviation from the neoliberal paradigm. The tightly
coupled relationship between macroeconomic policy and the sovereign debt crisis enabled advocates of austerity to push back against
Keynesian ordering principles.

The Chimera of the Beijing Consensus

As previously noted, many Chinese officials and commentators took
great delight in criticizing the United States for some of the neoliberal
policies it espoused during and after the Great Recession. Numerous
Western commentators began to embrace China's development model
as a genuine challenger to the neoliberal model. There were certainly
some policy steps that could be equated with growing Chinese assertiveness in the global political economy. Chinese policymakers embraced
the openness of the WTO trading system while simultaneously arguing in the G20 and the IMF that exchange-rate questions were matters
of domestic sovereignty and should not be discussed.[57] China created
or joined new institutional structures that were outside America's
reach, including the Forum on China-Africa Cooperation, Asian Bond
Markets Initiative, and Chiang Mai Initiative.[58] China's response to the
2008 financial crisis was to double down on its investment-and-export
growth model. Massive fiscal and monetary stimulus benefited
state-owned sectors far more than it did private firms over the next
few years.[59] China's robust rate of economic growth during the Great
Recession seemed to vindicate its development path yet again.

Nevertheless, Chinese officials were not keen on proselytizing the
Beijing Consensus to other countries. Indeed, both boosters and

critics of the Beijing Consensus note that Chinese officials refrained from promoting such a discourse.[60] The Chinese Communist Party flatly refused to officially promote any formulation of a Beijing Consensus or China model. Chinese officials and commentators also abstained from espousing a China model of development as a pattern to be copied by other developing countries. Le Yucheng, the Ministry of Foreign Affairs' director of policy planning, stated, "There is no Beijing Consensus."[61] Miles Kahler notes that, "China's policy preferences might have created an even more serious challenge to the prevailing consensus at the World Bank and the IMF. During the Great Recession, however, China's policy preferences have hardly deviated from this revised [Washington] consensus."[62] This attitude mirrors a more general reluctance from the Chinese government to offer an alternative pole of leadership. David Shambaugh concludes that "China does not lead…It does not shape international diplomacy, drive other nations' policies, forge global consensus, or solve problems."[63] Another assessment comparing China with the other BRIC economies concluded that "China has yet to provide many major ideas or set many important norms pertaining to global governance."[64]

This lack of economic proselytizing is doubly puzzling when one considers that China acted more assertively vis-à-vis the security status quo following the 2008 financial crisis.[65] In early 2009, Chinese ships engaged in multiple skirmishes with US surveillance vessels in an effort to hinder American naval intelligence-gathering efforts.[66] China's 2010 Defense White Paper suggested that China viewed its own security situation as one of intense security competition.[67] At the 2010 ASEAN Regional Forum, Chinese foreign minister Yang Jiechi faced pushback from the United States and ASEAN over China's assertive actions in the South China Sea. Yang responded angrily, bluntly lecturing other participants that "China is a big country and other countries are small countries, and that's just a fact."[68] In November 2013 China announced a new air defense identification zone that contested Japanese and South Korean sovereignty claims in the East China Sea, ratcheting up security tensions across the region. Even scholars who generally downplay China's aggressive behavior acknowledge that Beijing acted in a bellicose fashion in the South China Sea.[69] While Chinese officialdom has been willing to act aggressively in the security sphere, this has not been the case in the economic sphere.

Why has China not been more outspoken about its economic model? In part, China's traditional foreign policy posture stresses noninterference in the affairs of other countries, making Beijing reluctant to proselytize to the rest of the world. However, there has also been a lack of clarity about exactly what constitutes its growth model. This is particularly true with respect to anything labeled the Beijing Consensus. As one scholarly assessment noted, "Whatever one may think about the impact and underpinning logic of the so-called 'Washington Consensus,' it did represent a fairly coherent set of policy proposals and implicit normative values. Few people are making similar arguments about the 'Beijing Consensus.'"[70]

A look at the authors who use the term "Beijing Consensus" reveals its heterogeneous meanings. Joshua Cooper Ramo coined the term, characterizing it as a combination of China's innovative capabilities, environmentally sustainable economic growth, and the preservation of economic equality.[71] This description invited derision from serious China watchers.[72] Innovation, for example, has played a marginal role in China's economic ascent to date.[73] As noted in previous chapters, China's contributions to the value-added of its manufacturing exports are extremely small, suggesting minimal high-tech input. Similarly, China's "indigenous innovation" policies have not yielded significant successes to date.[74] China's environmental degradation has been extensively documented.[75] No serious Chinese economic observer believes its current growth trajectory is environmentally sustainable. Nor has economic growth occurred without a rapid rise in inequality, to the point where China has one of the highest levels of income inequality in the world.[76] In fact, most of the planks that Ramo outlined in his definition of the Beijing Consensus were wildly off-base.

To other observers, such as Stefan Halper and Martin Jacques, the key element of the Beijing Consensus is the large number of state-owned enterprises, the authoritarian mode of governance, and official overseas investments. Backed by unlimited state finances, Chinese firms have been able to expand both their domestic and overseas operations. In particular, Halper argues that "what makes the model attractive is the simple, political equation behind it: the power of the market plus the stability of authoritarian rule."[77] A more careful examination of these claims, however, reveals reasons to be skeptical. China's state-owned enterprises are growth laggards rather than growth leaders. Between 1978 and 2007, China's private sector generated total factor productivity growth at three times the rate of its state-owned enterprises. The doubling down of investment in state-owned enterprises caused a massive misallocation of capital investment.[78] Furthermore, a majority of the state-owned firms' overseas mergers and investments have been unprofitable—making it unlikely that they are the source of China's economic successes.[79]

One thing the proponents of a Beijing Consensus have in common is that they come from outside of China. This may be a clue as to why Chinese authorities have been reluctant to proselytize—the big-gest boosters of a Beijing Consensus are not Chinese. As one Chinese academic joked to me, "The Washington Consensus and the Beijing Consensus have one thing in common: they were both invented in Washington." Chinese elites are understandably reluctant to embrace a model as framed by Westerners.[80] And, with this provenance, Chinese officials have been understandably reluctant to adopt the moniker.[81]

To be clear, there *has* been a debate among Chinese elites on the "China model" of economic growth, with some experts expressing enthusiasm about the virtues of China's development path. Even this debate, however, reveals the failure of Chinese policymakers to reach a consensus on an alternative to the Washington Consensus. There is considerable disagreement among Chinese commentators over what constitutes the China model. There are large elements of current China policy that actually reflect the Washington Consensus; some have argued that China followed most of its original dictates—particularly the lib-eralization of trade and foreign direct investment.[82] Nevertheless, it is the departures from the Washington Consensus that trigger the great-est internal debates between the New Left critics of neoliberalism and Chinese liberals critical of excessive state economic control. As Tsinghua University's Matt Ferchen observes, "the different ways in which the Beijing Consensus or the China Model are portrayed as alternatives to the Washington Consensus are in themselves part of the battle of ideas."[83] The heterogeneity of ideas suggests one reason Chinese author-ities have not proclaimed an alternative model—there is not enough consensus on which to base a proposal. Scott Kennedy concludes, "The word 'model' implies a coherence and guiding plan that likely does not square with the reality of China's path." Randall Schweller and Xiaoyu Pu concur, noting that "Chinese ideas about alternative world orders remain inchoate and contested within China itself. Accordingly, these visions have not yet gained traction within or beyond China."[84]

There is also considerable debate within China about whether its development has been an unqualified success. Chinese elites have been surprisingly candid in discussing the weaknesses of their own development path. In his 2007 press conference, Chinese prime minister Wen Jiabao stated unequivocally, "There are structural problems in China's economy, which cause unsteady, unbalanced, uncoordinated and unsustainable development." He would echo these remarks in his farewell address as prime minister.[85] Similarly, Li Keqiang, Wen's successor and then vice-premier, noted in 2010 that China's development had created an "irrational economic structure" and that "uncoordinated and unsustainable development is increasingly apparent."[86] Both internal and external observers of China's economy have argued that the post-2006 stage of Chinese development had numerous flaws—including environmental degradation, the misallocation of capital, low levels of personal consumption, and a bloated state sector.[87]

The trajectory of debate over the China model does suggest that a consensus may be emerging—but not one that will directly challenge neoliberalism. Until 2012, for example, two leading New Left advocates of creating a Chinese pathway for development chose as their exemplar the "Chongqing Model" of Communist Party boss Bo Xilai as their exemplar. These analysts praised Bo's housing policies, anticorruption campaigns, and quasi-Maoist sloganeering in Chongqing as the remedies to the worst ills of neoliberalism. But hitching their star to Bo, however, made their argument vulnerable to his downfall. Bo Xilai was arrested in early 2012; he was tried and convicted a year later. Subsequent media reports revealed that his success in Chongqing was predicated on bribery, corruption, extralegal forms of brutal coercion, and quite possibly, murder.[88] At a minimum, this made it much harder for advocates of the emerging Chongqing Model to portray their version of the China model as a roaring success.

As the New Left advocates lost their luster, other Chinese officials began to ratchet up their criticism of China's development model.

Perhaps the biggest signal that China was uninterested in articulating an alternative economic model was the China 2030 project. This was a joint study—the first of its kind—produced by researchers from the World Bank, China's Ministry of Finance, and the Development Research Center of the State Council, a top government think tank.[89] The China 2030 project had the official imprimatur of key organs of the Chinese central government, as well as the personal backing of president Xi Jinping and premier Li Keqiang, who took leadership positions in the party and government in 2012 and 2013.[90] With powerful patrons, the China 2030 project had an authority that other external assessments of the China model had lacked.

The official report, *China 2030: Building a Modern, Harmonious, and Creative High-Income Society,* made clear that whatever the virtues of the China model, they were fading fast. It stressed that unique factors had contributed to China's post-1978 economic growth, thereby rendering it not useful as a model to emulate.[91] The report went on to note the myriad problems facing China over the next two decades—environmental degradation, rising levels of income and asset inequality, a looming demographic crunch, and low rates of personal consumption—and concluded that "it is imperative that China adjusts its development strategy as it embarks on its next phase of economic growth." Most of the proposed adjustments push China's political economy in a direction that more closely resembles the advanced industrial democracies. For example, the report stressed that the government had to retreat from the commanding heights of the economy: "the government's continued dominance in key sectors of the economy, while earlier an advantage, is in the future likely to act as a constraint on productivity improvements, innovation and creativity."[92] With respect to China's approach to the rest of the world, the report concluded, "China's long-term interest lies in global free trade and a stable and efficient international financial and monetary system. China benefited enormously from entering the WTO and is now an important stakeholder in the existing global trading system. Similarly, it will want to see stable international financial markets and a well-regulated international monetary system supported by stable currencies and underpinned by sound monetary policies."[93]

As previously noted, China's "fifth generation" of leaders supported the drafting of the *China 2030* report as well as its conclusions. Since taking office they have credibly signaled that they are beginning to push for the core components of the *China 2030* recommendations. In a major speech in May 2013 outlining his plan for further economic reform, Prime Minister Li Keqiang stressed the need to "further develop the market's fundamental role in allocating resources." Among his recommendations were proposals to significantly scale back the central government's licensing requirements for new businesses, outsource public services to private enterprises where appropriate, boost intellectual property rights enforcement, and demonstrate greater adherence to the rule of law. Many of these proposals echoed kindred observations and recommendations from the *China 2030* report. Li noted, "If we excessively rely on government dominance and policy traction to stimulate the economy, it will be difficult to keep it going, and will even produce new contradictions and risks."[94]

Following Li's speech, the government issued new edicts that buttressed some of these recommendations, including proposals to liberalize interest rates, ease the credit boom, reduce barriers to FDI in China's service sector, and initiate steps toward the full convertibility of China's currency.[95] Chinese authorities also took measures to crack down on its shadow banking system and tighten credit, allowing economic growth to taper off in the short run. The *New York Times* concluded, "China's recent cooling has been engineered by the authorities in Beijing, who are trying to steer the economy from an increasingly outdated growth model toward expansion that is more productive and sustainable."[96] The government's summer 2013 "mini-stimulus," intended to counteract the effects of tightening credit, rewarded private small businesses and households rather than state-owned enterprises.[97] Beijing restarted negotiations with the United States over a bilateral investment treaty, demonstrating an unexpected willingness to liberalize most of its economy to FDI. China also renewed its intent to sign the WTO's Government Procurement Agreement.[98]

The most important signal came at the third plenum of the Communist Party's 18th National Congress in November 2013, Traditionally devoted to economic matters, this third plenum laid the groundwork for further liberalizing the market and constraining the state's role in the economy. The communiqué explicitly stated that the market must play a "decisive role" in the allocation of resources. This was stronger rhetoric than in previous third plenums, which had described the market's role as merely "basic."[99] Concrete policy pledges included a reform of the permit system that constrains labor mobility and an end to the one-child policy. Several additional planks of the plenum's concrete policy document were drawn from the *China 2030* report.[100] Both the tenor of the leadership's rhetoric and these announced reforms are consistent with the neoliberal economic ideas that still dominate the global economy. They also suggest that China sees itself as merely the latest Pacific Rim country to transition from a state-led economy to one with a greater emphasis on market forces.[101]

To be sure, these rhetorical and policy gestures may be more hype than reality. It is likely that China will continue to deviate from free-market orthodoxy in practice. Throughout his term as prime minister, Wen Jiabao made similar noises about the need for further economic and political reforms and produced little in the way of follow-through. China's ability to alter its growth model to boost domestic consumption is also far from clear.[102] Unless and until Chinese policymaking institutions are recast to permit consumption-friendly lobbies to thrive, substantial policy change is unlikely. Furthermore, nothing in the Third Plenum documents guarantees that neoliberal economic reforms will necessarily occur. Vows of reform in earlier third plenums did not necessarily lead to concrete policy actions, and nothing in the 2013 Third Plenum documents suggests state-owned companies will be reformed anytime soon.[103] The Chinese Communist Party's goal of maintaining political control will likely override any preference for comprehensive economic reform. The new leadership has made clear its intent to keep a grip on political power.[104] In summer 2013, the leadership published an ideological memo—Document No. 9—that listed seven perils to the party. One was free-market "neoliberalism."[105] These sentiments are hard to reconcile with a push toward greater economic liberalization.

A lack of clarity about China's intentions exists but is also beside the point. Skeptics of the Washington Consensus looked to China, as the fastest-growing great power in the post-2008 era, to articulate a coherent replacement. China's internal splits over the future of its economic model make it impossible for Chinese officials to do so. Indeed, China's response has been to reject any notion of a Beijing Consensus. Prime Minister Li Keqiang insisted in a *Financial Times* op-ed that China "can no longer afford to continue" its existing growth model.[106] China may not be rigidly adhering to its stated reform path, but neither is it articulating an alternative pathway. Even if the global financial crisis battered and bruised the Washington Consensus, it did not break it—in part because the most viable potential proponent of an alternative pathway acted more like a responsible stakeholder of the status quo.

The Fall and Rise and Fall of Keynesianism

Contrary to expectations in late 2008, there has been no serious challenge to neoliberalism as an ordering principle for global economic governance. Within the macroeconomic policy dimension, however, there was greater flux in both the state of economic ideas and the state of economic policymaking. The macroeconomic components of the Washington Consensus had stressed relatively conservative fiscal and monetary policies: keeping budgets close to balance and focusing on keeping rates of inflation low.[107] During the initial stages of the financial crisis, however, there was consensus among policymakers on pursuing Keynesian macroeconomic policies. As noted earlier, by 2010 this consensus had fallen apart as European economies began to favor policies of fiscal austerity and monetary tightening. Over the next two years, adherence to austerity wavered in the countries that tried it. At the same time, faith in Keynesian stimulus waned somewhat in the United States. What explains the gyrations in macroeconomic policy during the post-crisis years?

For one thing, the depth of the macroeconomic policy consensus was never as strong as that surrounding trade liberalization. The dominant belief on macroeconomic policy before the crisis was known as the Great Moderation. The Great Moderation was based on the argument that monetary policy had been refined to such a degree that it could displace the blunt tool of fiscal policy in managing the business cycle.[108] The reduction of business cycle volatility in the United States seemed to buttress this belief. This relegated Keynesian ideas about fiscal policy to the margins. That said, the Great Moderation rested on weaker foundations than did the microeconomic roots of neoliberalism. The macroeconomic policy consensus was of a more recent vintage—it emerged only in the 1980s. Furthermore, there were still prominent experts that did not reject the utility of Keynesian fiscal policies in case of emergencies.[109]

The 2008 financial crisis prompted a search for new macroeconomic ideas.[110] In short order there was a dramatic ideational shift toward the Keynesian position that expansionary fiscal and monetary policies would have to be pursued while the private sector recovered.[111] Leading economists such as Lawrence Summers were calling for fiscal stimulus in September 2008.[112] The consensus grew stronger as prominent conservative economists—including Martin Feldstein, Lawrence Lindsey, and Kenneth Rogoff—began to publicly call for deficit spending and looser monetary policy.[113] Robert Lucas praised Federal Reserve chairman Benjamin Bernanke for turning to quantitative easing as the economy worsened.[114] Advocates of Keynesian policies took advantage of their online prominence to loudly and publicly advocate their positions.[115] Traditional critics of Keynesian spending had little in the way of positive policy alternatives to recommend, making it harder for them to politically counter the emerging consensus. In November 2008, N. Gregory Mankiw, a skeptic of greater spending, nevertheless acknowledged, "If you were going to turn to only one economist to understand the problems facing the economy, there is little doubt that the economist would be John Maynard Keynes....His insights go a long way toward explaining the challenges we now confront."[116]

Global economic governance structures also played a role. In fall 2008, IMF officials, including managing director Dominique Strauss-Kahn, called for governments to achieve deficit spending equal to 2 percent of global output.[117] Given the IMF's traditional association with fiscal conservatism, such a pronouncement sent a powerful signal. The consensus around a Keynesian macroeconomic response coalesced quickly in the United States and in the international financial institutions. Because of the hegemonic position of US-based economists within the profession, this consensus quickly became a global one.[118] It was therefore not surprising that policymakers in the G20 economies received similar advice from their national economists. UK chancellor of the exchequer Alistair Darling noted in his memoirs, "In late 2008, I was influenced hugely by Keynes's thinking, as indeed were most other governments dealing with the fallout from the crisis."[119] By December 2008, many of these economies were announcing their own emergency fiscal measures designed to prop up the global economy.

Not all policymakers embraced the switch to expansionary fiscal policy. As noted earlier, Germany fiercely resisted the Keynesian turn. Germany's initial spending proposal was meager, consisting of little beyond accelerating previously planned spending.[120] When asked about the global shift to expansionary fiscal policy, the German finance minister Peer Steinbrück blasted it, proclaiming, "The same people who would never touch deficit spending are now tossing around billions. The switch from decades of supply-side politics all the way to a crass Keynesianism is breathtaking."[121] This statement was revealing in two ways. First, Steinbrück was admitting that a Keynesian consensus had formed and, second, emphatically not agreeing with it. Similarly, Angela Merkel viewed both quantitative easing and greater stimulus spending as "treating a junky with massive doses of heroin," according to one of her advisors.[122] An allied pole of opposition was the European Central Bank. In a December 2008 interview with the *Financial Times*, European Central Bank president Jean-Claude Trichet stressed the need for member governments to adhere to the Growth and Stability Pact, which restricted eurozone members from running fiscal budget deficits larger than 3 percent of GDP.[123] Nevertheless, bank officials were largely silent during the debates about fiscal policy in late 2008 and early 2009.[124]

German politicians from across the political spectrum resisted external pressure for more government spending.[125] Deficit spending was anathema in Germany for numerous reasons. The country's principal economic trauma in the twentieth century—the hyperinflation of the 1920s—had long conditioned Germans to be wary of deficit spending. German ordoliberalism stressed a minimal state role in managing the business cycle. The high rate of German household savings also raised valid questions about whether tax cuts would have had the same stimulative effects in Berlin that they were projected to have in London or Washington. The prominent role of manufacturing exports in the

German economy meant that Germany was less dependent on domestic consumption as a driver for the domestic economy. Finally, one of Angela Merkel's signature political achievements was bringing the federal budget closer to balance, and pushing through a constitutional amendment designed to limit deficit spending. Even before the crisis, Merkel compared herself to a thrifty "Swabian housewife" to whom money saved is money earned.[126] Keynesian spending flew in the face of entrenched German ideas and interests.

In the end, however, Germany enacted the third-largest fiscal stimulus in the world in 2009.[127] There were three sources of pressure on German policymakers. First, as the German economy encountered the effects of the Great Recession, Merkel felt greater domestic political pressure to do something.[128] Second, global governance structures began to pressure Germany to follow their lead. In January 2009, IMF managing director Dominique Strauss-Kahn said that Western European governments were "behind the curve" on fiscal stimulus and were "underestimating the needs" of more expansionary policy.[129] Germany found itself isolated from its G20 peers. Great Britain's Gordon Brown and other G20 leaders also called on Merkel to pledge greater government spending or be accused of freeriding off the fiscal stimulus of others. Responding to Steinbrück's interview, British officials said that there was "a broad international consensus that a fiscal stimulus is now the right step for the economy."[130] Third, most German economists agreed with the notion of a temporary stimulus program.[131] Merkel consulted regularly with private-sector economists as the crisis unfolded. Germany's influential Council of Economic Experts, which had traditionally been anti-Keynesian, changed its tune and recommended a bigger stimulus in late 2008. Critics of the volte-face blamed the change in German attitudes on the "social contagion" of American economists.[132] Nevertheless, there was little depth of conviction behind this conversion. As one German economist explained in early 2009, "We are only doing all this for symbolic reasons; we don't believe it will affect the current crisis."[133] This is consistent with the theory that Germany's compliance with global norms and ideas was superficial and due to fear of ostracism, rather than the internalization of such ideas.[134]

The Keynesian consensus on macroeconomic policy did not last long. Changes in both outcomes and ideas altered the policy landscape dramatically. The beginnings of the eurozone debt crisis in Greece in late 2009 gave critics of Keynesian deficit spending a useful hook for attacking sustained deficit spending. This hook was based on a valid connection to a policy outcome; even staunch advocates of Keynesian policies agreed that Greek fiscal profligacy had precipitated its sovereign debt crisis.[135] However, Keynesians emphasized that Greece was a sui generis situation; whereas advocates of fiscal austerity argued that the prognosis was the same for other countries running large fiscal deficits.[136] In the United States, Alan Greenspan and other opponents of deficit spending warned that the United States would soon become "another Greece."[137] In Europe, the reluctance of the European Central Bank and Germany to help Greece led to a feedback loop. The bank's foot-dragging exacerbated the sovereign debt crisis, which worsened the fiscal balance sheets of the affected countries and, in turn, allowed opponents of Keynesian policies to harp even more about skyrocketing budget deficits.

Two economic papers added intellectual heft to pro-austerity policies and demonstrated the end of any consensus among economists for continued Keynesianism. In October 2009, Alberto Alesina and Silvia Ardagna published a National Bureau of Economic Research (NBER) paper in which they made multiple pro-austerity arguments. The opening of the paper framed the problem: "After the large reduction in government deficits of the nineties and early new century, public finances in the OECD are back in the deep red."[138] Alesina and Ardagna suggested that fiscal consolidation could boost economic growth by bolstering private actors' confidence in the stability of public finances. They concluded that the superior way to exit from deficit spending was through reducing government spending rather than increasing taxes.

In January 2010, Carmen Reinhart and Kenneth Rogoff also published an NBER paper, "Growth in a Time of Debt," that buttressed the argument for fiscal austerity from a different angle. Their main result: "whereas the link between growth and debt seems relatively weak at 'normal' debt levels, median growth rates for countries with public debt over 90 percent of GDP are roughly one percent lower than otherwise; average (mean) growth rates are several percent lower."[139] In other words, the 90 percent level was deemed to be a tipping point, after which debt could have nonlinear and negative effects on economic growth. As Reinhart and Rogoff's paper was being published, the debt-to-GDP ratios of several advanced industrialized countries, including the United States, were about to exceed that 90 percent threshold.[140]

Both papers framed Europe's sovereign debt crisis and America's tepid economic recovery as a failure of Keynesianism. Key policymakers in the developed world imbibed their pro-austerity arguments. In April 2010, Alesina presented a similar paper to European finance ministers that was based on his previous work with Ardagna. It opened with the assertion that "many OECD countries now need to reduce large public sector deficits and debts." Alesina further argued that "large, credible and decisive" spending cuts could boost economic growth and bolster the political fortunes of incumbent governments.[141] Christina Romer, then the chair of the Council of Economic Advisers in the United States, complained publicly that everyone was citing Alesina and Ardagna's paper.[142] The IMF noted in fall 2010 that Alesina and Ardagna's research had been "extremely influential in the debate regarding the consequences of fiscal adjustment."[143]

Reinhart and Rogoff's paper made similar waves.[144] Reinhart presented her findings to the bipartisan Simpson-Bowles Commission on Fiscal Responsibility and Reform.[145] Other senior policymakers, including the European Union's economic commissioner Olli Rehn, began to quote the Reinhart and Rogoff finding.[146] Paul Krugman went so far as to assert, "Reinhart-Rogoff may have had more immediate influence on public debate than any previous paper in the history of economics."[147] Furthermore, these economists went beyond their scholarly findings in delivering policy recommendations. Alesina stated in mid-2010 that he agreed with the German position on austerity, concluding, "I don't see how anyone can argue that we should push even more on the fiscal accelerator." Similarly, when Reinhart presented her findings to the bipartisan fiscal commission, she said, "I have no positive news to give. Fiscal austerity is something nobody wants, but it is a fact."[148]

Foreign affairs commentators in the United States made a parallel intellectual case for deficit reduction based on misguided geopolitical considerations.[149] In *Foreign Affairs*, Niall Ferguson compared the United States to other empires that had collapsed suddenly. He suggested that a sudden shift in expectations could destroy America's ability to recover from the crisis: "Neither interest rates at zero nor fiscal stimulus can achieve a sustainable recovery if people in the United States and abroad collectively decide, overnight, that such measures will lead to much higher inflation rates or outright default."[150] Commentators at the Council on Foreign Relations, concerned about the spike in developed-country debt, warned about the ways foreign indebtedness threatened to constrain the power of the West.[151] The council's director of international economics went further, arguing that Keynesian macroeconomic policies were perpetuating the bubbles and imbalances of the pre-crisis economy.[152]

As 2010 progressed, the Keynesian consensus disintegrated within official policy circles. The G7 rejected any lingering American enthusiasm for expansionary fiscal policies at the February 2010 finance ministers summit in Iqaluit.[153] The OECD began to urge fiscal consolidation and tighter monetary policy. In the run-up to the June 2010 Toronto G20 summit, key policymakers penned op-eds in the *Financial Times* to make their case, echoing points made by Alesina and Ardagna and Reinhart and Rogoff. German finance minister Wolfgang Schäuble opened his piece by blasting the "excessive budget deficits" in European countries, and pledging a German exit to deficit spending.[154] While the Obama administration retained the support of some developing countries, such as Brazil, a coalition that included Germany, Britain, Canada, France, Germany, and China advocated shifting to austerity. Canadian prime minister Stephen Harper proposed that governments pledge to cut their budget deficits as a percentage of GDP in half over the next three years.[155]

Following the summit, the European Central Bank's then president Jean-Claude Trichet encapsulated the views of fiscal austerity advocates in a *Financial Times* op-ed in which he declared, "Now is the time to restore fiscal sustainability."[156]

[G]iven the magnitude of annual budget deficits and the ballooning of outstanding public debt, the standard linear economic models used to project the impact of fiscal restraint or fiscal stimuli may no longer be reliable. In extraordinary times, the economy may be close to non-linear phenomena such as a rapid deterioration of confidence among broad constituencies of households, enterprises, savers and investors. My understanding is that an overwhelming majority of industrial countries are now in those uncharted waters, where confidence is potentially at stake. Consolidation is a must in such circumstances. . . .

With hindsight, we see how unfortunate was the oversimplified message of fiscal stimulus given to all industrial economies under the motto: "stimulate," "activate," "spend"! A large number fortunately had room for manoeuvre; others had little room; and some had no room at all and should have already started to consolidate. Specific strategies should always be tailored to individual economies. But there is little doubt that the need to implement a credible medium-term fiscal consolidation strategy is valid for all countries now.

Trichet's logic encapsulates both the "expectations" mechanism that Alesina and Ardagna stressed in their work and the notion of threshold effects that Reinhart and Rogoff posited in their work.

The ensuing macroeconomic policies in Europe and the United States soon shifted toward austerity. In the United Kingdom, the coalition government led by conservative David Cameron quickly implemented an austerity budget. On the continent, Germany followed through on its austerity pledge. The European Central Bank, led by Trichet, began raising interest rates in early 2011, despite mounting evidence of a double-dip recession. The sovereign debt crisis forced the Southern European economies to implement austere budgets. The United States continued to pursue relatively expansionary policies throughout 2010, including a December deal to extend tax cuts for another two years. The GOP's victory in the congressional midterm elections acted as an inflection point, however. From January 2011 onward, the House GOP majority acted as a hard political constraint on further Keynesianism. The 2011 Budget Control Act—and its effects on the fiscal cliff and sequestration eighteen months later—meant that by 2013, the US federal government was effectively pursuing austerity policies. Indeed, after 2009, the US budget deficit as a percentage of GDP fell at the fastest rate in postwar history.

Mark Blyth has argued that policymakers pushed austerity policies to benefit particular interest groups. The proposed budget cuts to social safety nets, entitlement spending, and government jobs and salaries would have distributional and deflationary effects that benefit the wealthy more than the median voter.[157] It buttressed Blyth's argument that conservative parties were the biggest boosters of reining in government spending in the United States and the United Kingdom.

This thesis is plausible, but it is worth considering that the pro-austerity position resonated beyond conservative quarters. In part, this was because left-leaning economists—including, most prominently, Paul Krugman—had sounded warnings about the perils of rising debt well before the 2008 financial crisis. In a February 2006 column, for example, Krugman bemoaned the mounting levels of government and personal debt, concluding, "serious analysts know that America's borrowing binge is unsustainable. Sooner or later the trade deficit will have to come down, the housing boom will have to end, and both American consumers and the U.S. government will have to start living within their means."[158] In January 2009, noted Keynes biographer Robert Skidelsky argued that "the crisis also represents a moral failure: that of a system built on debt."[159] To be sure, there are differences between amassing large deficits during a boom and amassing them during a bust. There are also profound differences between when households and firms accumulate debt and when national governments engage in deficit spending. Nevertheless, it was a challenging rhetorical task for Keynesians to explain why ballooning private debt was bad before the Great Recession, but ballooning public debt after the 2008 crisis was a good idea.

As Skidelsky's observation suggests, the desire for austerity had a moral resonance as well. For example, Krugman notes, "When applied to macroeconomics, this urge to find moral meaning creates in all of us a predisposition toward believing stories that attribute the pain of a slump to the excesses of the boom that precedes it—and, perhaps, also makes it natural to see the pain as necessary, part of an inevitable cleansing process."[160] Advocates for austerity repeatedly compared public finances to personal finances, arguing that governments should balance their budgets just like households. This gave their ideas a moral and personal dimension that was intuitively plausible to citizens, even if the comparison of households to governments was fatally flawed. Furthermore, in contrast to the challenges to the Washington Consensus, the austerity argument was coherent, simple, and connected with preexisting ideas in economic and moral theory.[161]

The moral resonance of austerity helps to explain the reaction to the intellectual and policy failures of austerity. Three years after it gained intellectual traction, the outcomes of austerity policies seem clear cut. The economies that had vigorously embraced austerity experienced stagnant rates of economic growth.[162] Low growth rates reduced tax receipts, which in turn increased the budget deficits that were supposed to fall. In 2013, the Red Cross issued a report blasting European policy-makers for "obsolete austerity-based policies that were increasing poverty rates—and suicide rates."[163] In contrast, the United States—the primary developed country that enacted the largest stimulus and was the last to turn to austerity—found that its fiscal picture had brightened considerably by 2013. The Congressional Budget Office projected the federal budget deficit to fall to 2.1 percent of GDP by 2015—an astonishing turnaround from the 10.1 percent figure in 2009.[164]

At the same time, the intellectual underpinnings of the austerity argument encountered some significant reversals from global governance structures. In October 2010, the IMF critiqued Alesina and Ardagna's methodology and findings. It concluded that fiscal retrenchment equivalent to 1 percent of GDP led to a reduction in growth by 0.5 percent and raised unemployment by 0.3 percentage points.[165] That finding also received media play.[166] In April 2013, three researchers from the University of Massachusetts revealed significant methodological problems with Reinhart and Rogoff's coding and data selection—including an embarrassing Excel spreadsheet error.[167] This also generated considerable negative publicity for the pro-austerity argument.[168] IMF managing director Christine Lagarde criticized US efforts to cut the budget deficit too steeply, as the cuts would threaten the economic recovery.[169]

It is therefore intriguing to note that public support for austerity policies in the developed world remained robust—even in many of the most hard-hit countries. When the Pew Global Attitudes Project surveyed eight European countries in March 2013 about the best way to stimulate economic growth, 59 percent of respondents preferred reducing public debt over providing fiscal stimulus. In France and Germany, the support for austerity policies was at 81 percent and 67 percent, respectively. In Spain and Italy—the two countries that have borne the brunt of austerity policies—support for austerity was at 67 and 59 percent, respectively.[170] Similarly, political support for fiscal retrenchment in the

United States remained strong. News coverage focused far more on deficits than unemployment. US public opinion polls in 2013 revealed that only 6 percent of Americans believed that the budget deficit was, in fact, shrinking.[171] One February 2013 poll showed that more than 73 percent of Americans wanted the government to cut spending to boost the economy; whereas less than 15 percent wanted spending to increase. This poll also showed that 60 percent of Americans believed that the 2009 fiscal stimulus had not worked.[172]

As the continental economy sagged, European policymakers did soften the edges of their austerity programs. On the monetary side, European Central Bank president Mario Draghi's summer 2012 declaration that he would do "whatever it takes" to save the euro angered the Bundesbank but calmed financial markets, lowering borrowing rates for distressed eurozone economies.[173] By the summer of 2013, both the European Central Bank and the Bank of England indicated that they would continue quantitative easing measures indefinitely. On the fiscal side, German policymakers demonstrated more flexibility in delaying the deadline for France, Portugal, Italy, and Spain to reduce their deficits to the European Union target.[174] This permitted these nations to continue pursuing expansionary fiscal policies in the short term. At home, Chancellor Merkel hinted at a more expansionary fiscal policy following the fall 2013 elections.[175] In the United States, Democrats seized on the errors in the Reinhart and Rogoff paper to push back against those calling for further austerity.[176]

Yet despite this softening, policymaking and political elites on both sides of the Atlantic continued to push for austerity. In the United States, prominent foreign affairs commentators, such as Council on Foreign Relations president Richard Haass, former chairman of the Joint Chiefs of Staff Michael Mullen, MSNBC host Joe Scarborough, and *Washington Post* columnist Charles Krauthammer, advocated for rapid deficit reduction, labeling rising levels of US debt as the biggest threat to national security.[177] Congressional Republicans continued to lobby fiercely for severe budget cuts, leading to the budget sequester and government shutdown in 2013. European Commission president José Manuel Barroso noted in a June 2013 interview: "Let's not forget why we came to this situation: in many cases because of high levels of public debt, and we have seen that growth fueled by debt is simply not sustainable."[178] The faith in austerity policies among large swaths of elites and the public remained powerful on both sides of the Atlantic.

While not dispositive, the contrast in the positions of global economic governance structures on the merits of China's economic model and on the merits of austerity policies should be noted. On the former, the international financial institutions acknowledged the fallibility of some Washington Consensus policies but nevertheless remained uniformly critical of the future of the China model, as the *China 2030* report demonstrates. On the subject of austerity policies, however, global governance structures were sharply divided. IMF authorities were skeptical of the merits of austerity programs, whereas OECD officials supported austerity measures and tight monetary policies. BIS officials were equally emphatic on the need to implement austerity policies. Indeed, in their 2012 and 2013 annual reports, the BIS urged central bank officials to taper off quantitative easing sooner rather than later.[179] BIS's 2013 report called repeatedly for greater fiscal consolidation and argued that quantitative easing was enabling fiscal profligacy: "Cheap money makes it easier to borrow than to save, easier to spend than to tax, easier to remain the same than to change."[180] Given these divisions at the global level, it is not surprising that the state of global macroeconomic policy is more unsettled.

Conclusion

This chapter has considered the role of ideas in affecting the performance of global economic governance. The distribution of economic ideas clearly affected actor preferences as the crisis unfolded. The ideational depth of neoliberalism, for example, was a formidable barrier for any actor wanting to challenge its ideas, even after the shock of the 2008 crisis. China was best placed to challenge the Washington Consensus, but policy elites never converged around a coherent alternative. On the other hand, the state of macroeconomic thinking was in flux. This heterogeneity allowed a brief Keynesian consensus from late 2008 to early 2010. The sovereign debt crisis, however, led quickly to battles over the virtues of austerity. Paradoxically, even though China was perceived as more powerful, it was Europe that proved more capable at producing influential economic ideas. This is why China proved to be cooperative on questions of microeconomic policy coordination, whereas the European Union members proved to be far more resilient in advocating austerity.

The contrast between the state of economic ideas post-2008 and in the Depression era is worthy of note. As the Great Depression worsened during the 1930s, there was no expert consensus about the best way to resuscitate the global economy.[181] Prominent economists, such as John Maynard Keynes, who had been staunch advocates of free trade a decade earlier reversed their ideas as the Depression worsened. There was little agreement on the proper policy responses to the downturn, particularly with respect to trade or exchange rates. In contrast, the post-2008 state of economic ideas remains relatively cohesive.[182] While there remained areas of discord, a strong post-crisis consensus among economists constrained the search for alternative paradigms. After more than a half century of laying the intellectual groundwork for an open global economy and an increase in laissez-faire domestic economic policies, the ideas animating the Washington Consensus have proved to be more resilient than expected.[183] As one intellectual history of free-market thought recently concluded, "The hold of market advocacy on the popular imagination has remained far stronger than in the early 1930s.... Capitalism may be in crisis, but the horizon of alternatives has narrowed."[184]

7

Where Do We Go from Here?

TO UNDERSTAND THE MISMATCH between perception and reality about what global economic governance has accomplished since 2008, it is worth thinking about the role that the Troubled Assets Relief Program played in addressing the financial crisis in the United States.[1] In September 2008, global financial markets were reeling and the US economy was approaching freefall. The Federal Reserve and US Treasury Department had tried an array of conventional and unconventional tools to prop up the US economy, to little avail. Concerned about eroding political legitimacy, Fed chairman Benjamin Bernanke and Treasury secretary Henry Paulson decided their only option was to go to Congress to seek authorization for a massive sum of money to purchase mortgage-backed securities. Paulson requested $700 billion for TARP. Paulson's initial proposal amounted to three pages that provided few details and absolutely no judicial or legislative oversight. The first attempt to pass the bill failed in the House of Representatives. The negative vote took the markets by surprise. The Dow Jones Industrial Average experienced its largest single-day loss in history; the S&P 500 and NASDAQ both lost approximately 9 percent of their value.

A week later, the House passed a revised bill. By that point, however, much of the damage had been done. Washington's initial inability to act as expected rattled investors.[2] The failure of financial markets to rally after the creation of TARP seemed to vindicate its critics. Paulson's subsequent decision to use TARP to make direct capital injections into big banks, rather than purchase toxic assets as originally announced, generated even more political controversy. When TARP money was used to assist the automobile companies as well, the program became even more unpopular. Although the American people initially favored TARP, this public support soon ebbed.[3] The program was quickly framed as a bank bailout, rendering it anathema to the American people and to members of Congress. TARP and a panoply of other emergency Federal Reserve measures to provide liquidity seemed to many little more than budget-busting exercises in crony capitalism.

Yet as time has passed, two facts have become manifestly clear about TARP and the related Federal Reserve programs. First, on policy grounds, these measures were huge successes. The econometric evidence strongly suggests that TARP and the actions taken by the Fed greatly eased the credit crunch faced by banks.[4] According to one bipartisan analysis, without TARP and the Fed's actions, US GDP would have shrunk by an additional $800 billion, unemployment would have been three percentage points higher, and the federal budget deficit would have been even bigger because of reduced tax revenue.[5] A strong majority of leading economists agreed that the benefits of the bank bailouts exceeded the costs.[6] In the end, TARP was a bargain. Because almost all the bailed-out financial institutions recovered relatively quickly, they were able to pay back the US government ahead of schedule. The final estimates of TARP's cost range between $21 billion and $47 billion—a small price to pay for saving the US financial system.

Second, TARP has remained political poison. A July 2010 Bloomberg poll revealed that 58 percent of Americans believed, in retrospect, that TARP was an "unneeded bailout." By October of that year, 46 percent of respondents in a Pew poll said they were less likely to vote for a member of Congress who had voted for TARP.[7] Politicians who voted for the bill abstained from speaking publicly in favor of it. As Ben Smith reported in *Politico*, "[TARP] is widely seen as the tipping point for disgust with elites and insiders of all kinds—though it could also be seen as those insiders' finest moment, a successful attempt to at least partially fix their own mistakes."[8] Another assessment concluded that TARP was "one of the most hated, misunderstood, and effective policies in modern economic history."[9] John F. Kennedy famously said that in politics, victory has a thousand fathers but defeat is an orphan.

TARP highlights a post-2008 political phenomenon: the policy victory that remains a political orphan.

The most salient explanation for TARP's unpopularity is that it requires counterfactual reasoning to appreciate its success. The argument in favor of TARP and the related Federal Reserve programs is that even though the US economy has struggled since 2008, it could have been far, far worse. This is true of global economic governance as well. There is no denying that, in the wake of the crisis, the global economy shrunk, protectionism rose, cross-border financial flows dried up, and governments squabbled over macroeconomic policies. Nevertheless, the system worked. In the presence of functioning global economic governance, the global economy suffered only a temporary downturn. In its absence, the world would have likely experienced an explosion of trade and investor protectionism, an evaporation of liquidity, and a second Great Depression.

What about the future? It is one thing to say that the system has worked in the first few post-crisis years. It is another thing entirely to assert that current global governance structures will endure. It is worth remembering that genuine efforts were made to provide global public goods in 1929 as well but eventually fizzled out.[10] The failure of the major economies to assist the Austrian government after the CreditaAnstalt bank failed in 1931 led to a cascade of bank failures across Europe and the United States. The collapse of the 1933 London conference guaranteed an absence of global policy coordination for the next several years. The start of the Great Depression was bad, but international policy coordination failures made it worse.

Such a scenario could play out again. The system has worked by preventing a major reversal of globalization. There is no denying, however, that the momentum of economic openness has slowed considerably.[11] This could just be the beginning of the end of the system as we know it. It is not hard to identify fragility and instability in the current world economy. The international system averted a second Great Depression, but can it continue to do so? Can current global economic governance structures help the world economy survive and thrive going forward?

This concluding chapter summarizes the argument made in the previous chapters, reviews the evidence that the system worked, and then considers the significance of these findings for future scholarship. It speculates about why global economic governance might go downhill from here—and, finally, explains why it will not.

THE ARGUMENT REDUX

In the fall of 2008, the global economy suffered a bigger and deeper shock than it did in the fall of 1929. Despite that shock, the global economy rebounded. Given the depth of the financial damage, and given how the global economy had previously responded to similar shocks, the post-2008 performance was remarkable. Cross-border flows in trade, FDI, and remittances suffered temporary downturns but soon exceeded or approximated pre-crisis averages. Despite the biggest financial crash in seventy years and the ensuing sovereign debt crises in Europe, the global economy demonstrated remarkable resilience.

How did the global economy recover so quickly? Global economic governance did what it had to do. During a systemic crisis, markets need to stay open and liquidity needs to be provided. International institutions, supported by the great powers, ensured that this happened. The data on trade restrictions show that although levels of protectionism did increase after the crisis, those increases were small; the number of restrictions eventually fell to historic lows. The United States, the European Union, and China adhered to their WTO obligations, ensuring that the rest of the world could export to them. Despite a lot of loose talk about currency wars, actual exchange-rate volatility subsided and was never a serious concern for business executives. The world's major central banks coordinated interest-rate cuts and swap lines to revive the global economy and avert a liquidity crisis. Quantitative easing and other monetary policy actions also helped to avert the worst-case scenario. Between 2008 and 2010, the G20 economies also coordinated expansionary fiscal policies to make up for the shortfall in private-sector activity. These economies also bolstered the ability of the World Bank and the IMF to help the smaller and less-developed economies. Global economic governance structures aided and abetted exactly the policies that Charles Kindleberger would have advocated to prevent a depression.

The standard narrative about post-2008 international institutions is that though they might functiioned acted during the depths of the crisis, sclerosis soon set in. The evidence suggests otherwise. The IMF orchestrated negotiations between capital importers and exporters over a voluntary regime to govern sovereign wealth fund investments, which successfully defused brewing political firestorms in the developed world. The Basel Committee on Banking Supervision negotiated Basel III in two years—far more rapidly than it negotiated its predecessor. In taking steps to comply with Basel III, the big banks in Europe and the United States have gone far in recapitalizing themselves. Even though the consensus on macroeconomic policy fell apart in the G20, that body still served its purpose as a focal point for great-power negotiations. In response to a spike in piracy on the high seas, a coalition of states quickly adopted a successful antipiracy strategy. The WTO successfully completed a trade facilitation agreement and expanded its geographic scope to include Russia. G20 pressure nudged China to let its currency slowly appreciate after June 2010. All the major multilateral economic institutions—including the WTO, the IMF, and the OECD—stepped up their monitoring activities to notify G20 economies of incipient trends toward economic closure. Furthermore, recognizing shifts in the distribution of power, key global governance structures reformed their operations. The IMF and the World Bank reformed their quota allocations to reflect the growing economic clout of the developing world. The G20 supplanted the G8 as the premier economic forum for the major economies. Other economic clubs, such as the Financial Stability Board and the Basel Committee on Banking Supervision, expanded their memberships to include the developing-country members of the G20. To be sure, there are a lot of areas in which global governance failed to function as hoped. Against the odds, however, the system worked.

This is not, however, the conclusion that one would derive from most assessments of international institutions after 2008. Why are perceptions about global economic governance so at variance with reality? To be fair, there are examples that made it seem that the system was broken. Despite the longest trade negotiations in history, the Doha Round of trade talks remains unfinished at best and deadlocked at worst. Despite overwhelming scientific evidence that climate change represents a global threat, progress toward meaningful global action on this issue has been feeble. Despite the existence of the strongest, most robust supranational institutions in history, the European Union let difficulties in Greece—a place less populous than Cuba—metastasize into the greatest economic threat to the continent in seventy years.

These problems hint at one major source of misperception—a nostalgia for a mythical Golden Age of global economic governance when everything worked properly. As demonstrated in chapter 3, this yearning is misplaced. Even in the best of times, the proper expectation for international institutions is that they will be "good enough." There is also a mismatch between the center of gravity for global economic growth and the center of gravity for studying the global political economy. The latter is located in the advanced industrialized economies—precisely the regions that have taken the longest to recover from the Great Recession. It is not surprising that pessimism about one's national situation translates into pessimism about the global economy. This, in turn, leads to another source of misperception—the conflation of national and global governance. National governments are responsible for most of the egregious policy errors that have taken place since 2008. In some instances, these national governments failed to heed the advice of international institutions. In most instances, these policy errors were own-goals unrelated to events at the global level.

Why did the system work? The answer provided here is analytically eclectic. There is no doubt that globalization transformed an array of sectoral interests to favor sustained economic openness. The development of the global supply chain enlarged the number of factors and actors that would lobby for an open global economy even during hard times. That said, an interest-based answer is insufficient to explain what happened after 2008. There are too many examples of powerful actors making concessions that hurt concentrated interests for this logic to be completely persuasive. The history of the Basel III negotiations shows that even the systemically important financial institutions—presumably the most powerful interest group in the world—failed to get their way. Indeed, it is in the financial realm—where sectoral interests have been at their most concentrated—that the greatest limits have been placed on pre-2008 openness. The absence of concentrated interest-group opposition was a permissive condition for the system working—but an open economy politics story cannot explain much more than that.

A closer look at the post-2008 distribution of power and ideas reveals a more surprising two-part explanation for why the system worked.

First, the United States was still able to exercise effective leadership. Contrary to public perceptions, the United States remained the most powerful actor in the world. On a host of issues, such as antipiracy and financial regulation, the United States continued to wield the preponderance of power. In other issue areas, the United States was still first among equals, and therefore able to signal its preference that the status quo be preserved.

While the global financial crisis did not fundamentally alter the power of the United States, it did fundamentally weaken its traditional supporters in Europe and Japan. The European Union was still powerful enough to act as a significant supporter, but Japan fell from the first tier of great powers. Furthermore, the crisis enabled China to ascend to that top tier. This leads to the second, even more surprising, part of the explanation. Despite concerns that it would be a revisionist actor as it acquired more power, China largely supported the rules of global economic governance that had enabled the country to rise so quickly. China contributed to global antipiracy operations. China complied with its WTO obligations—indeed, its track record was superior to that of any other advanced industrialized country on that front. Beginning in 2010, China allowed its currency to appreciate slowly against the dollar and its major trading partners, permitting macroeconomic imbalances to subside. China contributed significant resources to bolster the IMF's reserves.

Perhaps the most important thing is what China did *not* do. In the wake of the Great Recession, there was a clamoring for new ways of thinking about the global economy. With the Washington Consensus seemingly discredited, a number of elites looked to the People's Republic of China as the only country that could point another way forward. Western commentators proclaimed the rise of a Beijing Consensus, and Chinese commentators talked about the existence of a China model that might supplant the preexisting ordering principles. In the end, however, Chinese authorities opted not to follow that path—in no small part because there was no consensus about the precise content of the China model. Without a clear set of ordering principles, authorities in Beijing refrained from proselytizing their development path to others. Chinese authorities were keenly aware of the flaws in their development model. Indeed, if anything, by 2013 China was taking concrete steps toward, not away from, the Washington Consensus. To be sure, some elements of neoliberalism, such as unfettered capital mobility, are no longer accepted as gospel. On the whole, however, neoliberalism remains the privileged set of economic ideas in the global political economy. By maintaining an open global economy, these ideas likely helped to prevent another Great Depression. When they privileged fiscal and monetary conservatism, they likely caused more harm than help.

Charles Kindleberger noted that the problem of the Great Depression was that Great Britain was willing but unable and the United States was able but unwilling to provide global public goods. There wasn't a second Great Depression in 2008 because the United States and China were both able and willing to help—and because they agreed far more than they disagreed about how to make the system work.

The Implications for Theory

As the initial stages of the financial crisis were unfolding, Robert Keohane challenged global political economy scholars to "spend more of their time pondering the big questions about change." He noted the rise of BRIC economies—China in particular—and the increased volatility of global markets. He also acknowledged, "We have taken for granted certain power structures that are in fact changeable."[12] Keohane's provocative challenge was one of the inspirations for this book. It seems appropriate at this point to consider what my tentative answers mean for the future study of international political economy.

Perhaps the most surprising conclusion to draw is that none of Keohane's "big changes" dramatically affected post-2008 global economic governance. As discussed in chapter 5, China's rise is undeniable. That said, the other BRIC economies—India, Russia, and Brazil—have not seen their relative power increase at all since Lehman Brothers collapsed. Any decent assessment of economic power reveals that the other BRIC actors are not in the same league as the United States, the European Union, or China. The 2008 crisis likely accelerated the shift from a world in which there were two great powers to one in which there are three, but the "hegemonic coalition" is unlikely to increase more than that anytime soon. This is particularly true given the demographic, economic, and political constraints that will hamper many of the advanced developing countries over the next few decades.[13] Despite the best efforts to turn a Goldman Sachs marketing term into an actual multilateral grouping, Ruchir Sharma is likely correct when he concludes that "no idea has done more to muddle thinking about the global economy than that of the BRICs."[14] Indeed, even Goldman Sachs officials now lament their overhyping of the phenomenon.[15]

Furthermore, what's surprising is how little China's rise affected either the outputs or outcomes of global economic governance. To be sure, in some areas, such as currency manipulation, China's concessions have been grudging. Beijing also engaged in a hedging strategy at the regional level.[16] Nevertheless, across a host of issue areas, China acted much more like a responsible stakeholder than as a spoiler. This is particularly true when one compares China's approach to the global economy to its approach to security issues in the Pacific Rim. At a minimum, the findings in this book offer a strong data point to support John Ikenberry's contention that the liberal international order can survive China's rise, and a data point against John Mearsheimer's contention that a conflict between China and the United States is inevitable.[17] Indeed, the performance of post-2008 global governance suggests the resiliency, rather than the fragility, of the liberal international order.

Another conclusion to draw is that there are hard limits to what open economy politics can explain during times of crisis and uncertainty.[18] It is not a coincidence that the rise of open economy politics occurred at a time when the distribution of power and ideas in the global political economy seemed stable. So long as systemic factors can be held constant, an open economy politics approach can explain significant amounts of variation in the global political economy. When the global financial order is stable, observers can take as given the established rules of thumb, without overtly acknowledging the underlying processes of social construction and power that reproduce that stability on a daily basis. With a crisis, however, the underpinnings of the system become visible, questioned, and potentially up for grabs. This does not mean that the system will necessarily change—merely that what had been invisible becomes visible.

The post-crisis global political economy also revealed the deep structural roots of American power.[19] The relative influence of the United States declined on some dimensions after 2008, but what is striking are the areas in which US power was resilient. If one looks at financial metrics, one sees that the United States retains considerable capabilities. Washington controls the global reserve currency, and there is no short-term alternative to it. Its capital markets are the largest, most liquid, and most networked in the world. The United States retains a commanding position in terms of asset ownership. Washington still controls the world's largest military. US reservoirs of soft power are still formidable, especially when compared to China's.[20] In other words, five years after precipitating the biggest economic crisis in seventy years, the United States still has the most guns and the most butter, and of all the great powers, is the most liked. Contrary to the predictions of some,[21] the crisis barely dented American power, especially when compared to the other OECD economies. China is a rising power in terms of material capabilities but not in the realm of ideas.

The Future of Global Economic Governance

This book has painted a relatively rosy picture of global economic governance for the past five years. Nevertheless, there are valid reasons to be concerned about the future. For one thing, considerable amounts of fragility remain in the global economy. The eurozone has still not found a viable way to fix the internal imbalances between Germany and Southern Europe.[22] A renewed slump would increase the probability of a global recession. As central banks in the developed economies try to navigate exits from quantitative easing, and as the BRIC economies try to contain their own emergent asset bubbles, a double-dip Great Recession is possible. In the summer of 2013 the Federal Reserve tried to map out an end to its quantitative easing program at the same time that China clamped down on credit. The uncoordinated actions roiled global markets.[23]

Another issue is the state of economic ideas going forward. As chapter 6 demonstrated, neoliberalism has persisted since 2008. In the case of keeping borders open to international trade and investment, this is all for the better. On macroeconomic policy, however, the neoliberal consensus has preached the importance of low inflation and fiscal austerity *über alles*. During boom times, these policy prescriptions made sense. They were wildly misplaced, however, during the depths of the biggest economic downturn in seventy years. Despite the lessons of the Great Depression, and despite the ephemeral victory of Keynesianism in 2008 and 2009, neoliberal ideas remained privileged after the 2008 financial crisis. One can plausibly argue that in the developed world, the economic damage wreaked by austerity policies negated much of the economic benefit derived from global economic openness.

Misperceptions about power and governance continue to fester as well. Perceptions in the global political economy can generate self-fulfilling prophecies. If countries are viewed as powerful, they will be treated as if they are powerful. This can exacerbate conflict in world politics.[24] Misperceptions are particularly problematic if they lead to mutual misunderstandings about the responsibilities governments have to preserve the open global economy.[25] There is a similar problem with misperceptions about global economic governance. Despite an abundance of evidence that the system worked, economics columnists, such as Clive Crook, continue to write that the Great Recession "tested the world's economic policy institutions and found them wanting." Similarly, George Soros concluded that "the absence of global governance may continue indefinitely."[26] If elites continue to insist that the system did not work, they will devote time and effort to figuring out how to fix something that was not necessarily broken. This is scarce political capital that can best be devoted to more pressing policy problems. An even worse possibility is that policies that actually worked will, after the fact, still be framed as political failures—like TARP.

A paradoxical problem is that the successful reforms of global economic governance structures will increase the likelihood of policy sclerosis. The case of the WTO is instructive here. It was the earliest multilateral economic institution to recognize shifts in the global distribution of power. When the Doha Round was initiated in 2001, the old negotiation "Quad" of the United States, the European Union, Canada, and Japan that had traditionally hammered out trade concessions was no more. India, Brazil, and eventually China joined the "green room" as well. Even the smaller West African countries had an influential voice on cotton subsidies. The result has been the longest and most fruitless negotiating round in the history of GATT/WTO. Arvind Subramanian argues that the WTO has acquired too much legitimacy at the expense of negotiating efficiency, and therefore needs to be "de-democratized."[27]

The WTO could be merely the harbinger of changes in other global governance structures. As noted in chapter 2, every significant club governance structure increased its membership, creating a greater potential for disagreement among members and policy stalemates.[28] Given that the status quo bias in many of these institutions favors economic openness, this might not be an altogether bad outcome. Nevertheless, stalemates allow bad equilibria to persist as well. As noted above, the consensus about austerity seems likely to continue. This has brought economic growth in the European Union to a screeching halt. If Europe's troubles infect the rest of the global economy, then the failure of global economic governance on this issue might tarnish the reputation of the entire system.

Rising security tensions could also transform global governance. China has acted like a responsible stakeholder in the economic dimension, but matters are more muddled in the security realm. If China and the United States were to decide that their security rivalry trumped the economic benefits of the open global economy, then both great powers would carry that security rivalry into the economic sphere. As expectations of future conflict rise, states become far more willing to disrupt economic relationships as a tool of coercion.[29] This would echo the economic statecraft being practiced in the run-up to the First World War, when cooperation on the gold standard broke down a few years before Archduke Ferdinand was assassinated.[30] A century after the start of the Great War, historians started drawing parallels to 1914 in their prognostications.[31]

Either policy stalemates or geopolitical rivalries could lead to the fragmentation of global governance. When preeminent international institutions fail to take necessary actions, great powers can choose to create alternative structures to implement their preferred policies. On the trade front, for example, the United States is currently negotiating a Trans-Pacific Partnership with Pacific Rim allies, and a Transatlantic Trade and Investment Partnership with the European Union. China, in turn, has engaged in its own hedging strategy. Beijing negotiated a network of preferential trade agreements with ASEAN and other regional actors such as Taiwan and New Zealand.[32] In 2013, China launched talks on a trilateral free-trade agreement with Japan and South Korea. Beijing was also been a leading proponent of the East Asia Summit, Chiang Mai Initiative, and Asian Bond Markets Initiative. None of these structures necessarily conflict with global economic governance, but they have the capacity to do so.[33]

In a truly multipolar world, institutional proliferation can shift global governance from a world of binding rules to a world of forum-shopping. Institutional proliferation could erode the legitimacy of the Bretton Woods institutions.[34] Jagdish Bhagwati has complained about the "spaghetti bowl" of overlapping trade agreements weakening the coherence of the WTO.[35] Even if these challenges are currently at nascent levels, over time forum-shopping has the capacity to erode the cohesion of global economic governance. As more and more institutions are created, each will find its legitimacy devalued when forum-shopping occurs. With each state willing to walk away from global governance structures that fail to advance its interests, all these structures will experience a decline in both legitimacy and effectiveness. In the long run, it appears that an institutionally thick world bears more than a passing resemblance to the Hobbesian world of anarchy. Paradoxically, the proliferation of governance structures could lead to a tragedy of the global institutional commons.

There is one last pessimistic note: it is possible that the global economic challenges of the twenth-first century might be so different from any experienced in the past that existing institutions will simply be incapable of addressing them. Climate change is one example. This will be a growing concern moving forward, but international cooperation on this issue has been woeful to date; none of the traditional institutions have established a sustainable governance structure. Another, more unorthodox possibility would be a toxic combination of rising inequality and slower growth. Economic inequality has skyrocketed in almost every major economy. Globalization has generated an economics of superstars, which in turn has produced an explosion of plutocrats.[36] If the distribution of benefits from the global economy skews more toward the superrich, a disturbing feedback of rent-seeking behavior perpetuating further inequality could ensue. At the same time, some economists predict a future of slower economic growth.[37] Rising inequality combined with slower growth translates to a world economy in which the losers massively outnumber the winners. Neither national governments nor global institutions will necessarily be well equipped to cope with the policy externalities and political resentments of that future.

The More Things Change...

So it is clear that there are a lot of ways in which things could go wrong. But, given what has happened since 2008, it is safer to conclude that they won't. Based on the performance of global economic governance—and the causes of that performance—there are reasons to be optimistic going forward. First, it would appear that post-crisis, the resilience of the system actually increased. As noted in chapter 2, the current character of cross-border financial exchange rests on more-durable flows such as FDI and remittances. This suggests that another negative shock would have less of an impact on these markets. Furthermore, more recent financial scares have not had the same contagion effects. The 2013 Cyprus crisis, for example, led to significant financial repression in that country. Despite those repressive actions, it failed to trigger the same continentwide financial panic as happened in prior eurozone episodes. Paradoxically, the very centrality of American finance to the global economy increases overall stability. The only way a shock could have the same contagion effects as occurred in 2008 would be if the crisis started in the United States.[38] The improved health of the US financial sector suggests that this scenario is highly unlikely for the foreseeable future.

There are also reasons to believe that oft-predicted Sino-American security tensions will not escalate. The distribution of power is unlikely to change as radically as many predicted in 2008. In 2011, Michael Beckley compared China to the United States across a wide range of comprehensive power measures and concluded that "the trends favor continued US dominance." Robert Kagan has reached a similar conclusion: "The American system, for all its often stultifying qualities, has also shown a greater capacity to adapt and recover from difficulties than many other nations, including its geopolitical competitors."[39] Even previous skeptics of US power have begun to acknowledge this fact. Arvind Subramanian's book *Eclipse: Living in the Shadow of*

China's Economic Dominance came out in 2011. Just two years later, Subramanian wrote that "reports of the decline in American economic power appear to have been exaggerated."[40]

The enduring strengths of the United States—healthy demographics; geographic security; a syncretic, dynamic popular culture; and excellence in higher education and innovation—remain unchanged. As in previous eras of stagnation, a combination of private-sector and public-sector adjustments have triggered a revival in American capabilities. In areas such as manufacturing and energy production, the trend lines point to a renaissance in US capabilities. In a sharp contrast to pre-crisis projections, the International Energy Agency predicts that the United States will become the world's leading oil producer sometime before 2020. Lower energy costs in the United States will ease energy bottlenecks everywhere while increasing the competitiveness of the US economy.[41] America's political economy is far from perfect, but the United States responded to the shock of the 2008 financial crisis more adroitly than its rivals. Meanwhile, China's leaders are taking steps to reform the country's development model so that its domestic economy more closely resembles that of the United States.

Institutional fragmentation is possible, but continued open regionalism seems more likely. The desire of each major economy to deepen economic ties with strategic partners has spurred other great powers to sign integration agreements with the same countries. The US endorsement of the Trans-Pacific Partnership, for example, has caused China to accelerate its strategy of signing regional free-trade agreements.[42] The United States has joined the East Asia Summit, and China has joined the Inter-American Development Bank. The result is a world of deeper integration, rather than fragmentation. The international investment regime demonstrates the ability of bilateral and regional agreements to sustain an international regime without fragmenting.[43]

Just as open regionalism appears to be sustainable, so do current multilateral economic institutions. The legitimacy of global economic governance can have a path-dependent quality. If existing structures establish a reputation for reasonably effective governance, the gains from coordination increase while the costs decline.[44] National policymakers have an incentive to correct misperceptions and bolster existing regimes' reputations for competency. If successful, they can use these international regimes to bypass domestic political roadblocks. In other words, the more that people realize the system worked after 2008, the more likely they are to believe the system will continue to work in the future—which, in turn, increases the actual probability of the system continuing to work.

LAST WORDS...

In the world of international affairs punditry, pessimism sells. Professionally, it is less risky to predict doom and gloom than to predict that things will work out fine. Warning about a disaster that never happens carries less cost to one's credibility than asserting that all is well just before a calamity. History has stigmatized optimistic prognosticators who turned out to be wrong. Beginning with Norman Angell's errant prediction a century ago that war would soon become obsolete, to Francis Fukuyama's proclamation that history has ended, errant optimists have been derided for their naiveté. Policymakers prematurely declaring "mission accomplished" have suffered even more embarrassment.

In saying that the system has worked reasonably well since 2008, I risk joining that ignominious list—but it is a risk worth taking. Despite considerable economic turmoil, global economic governance reinforced preexisting norms of economic openness. The intersection of material interests, enduring American power, European and Chinese support, and adherence to market-friendly ideas allowed the system to function better than expected. If past financial crises are any guide, the global economy should be primed for more-robust economic growth for quite some time.[45] There has been excessive pessimism about the state of global economic governance over the past few years, and this pessimism has spread just as widely as financial contagion did in 2008. It is wrong and needs to be corrected. After looking at the evidence, it is clear that the distribution of material interests, state power, and economic ideas combined to make the system work. Going forward, a healthy dollop of optimism is in order.

NOTES

Chapter 1

1. In the popular memory, the global financial crisis started with the collapse of Lehman Brothers in September 2008. In actuality, the crisis had started thirteen months earlier, in August 2007, when the market for subprime mortgage securities evaporated. See Irwin 2013, p. 1-4, and Blinder 2013, chapter 4, on how the subprime mortgage crisis metastasized into the Great Recession.
2. On comparisons with the Great Depression, see Eichengreen and O'Rourke 2010. On financial losses, see International Monetary Fund 2009, p. xi.
3. Roxburgh, Lund, and Piotrowski 2011, p. 2. An Asian Development Bank report estimates the 2008 decline in asset values to have been twice as large. See Loser 2009, p. 7.
4. International Labour Organization, 2010, p. 9.
5. See, for example, Cole 2012.
6. For a recent archaeology of the term "global governance," see Weiss and Wilkinson 2013. The overwhelming focus of this literature has been on the noneconomic components of global governance.
7. See the discussion in chapter 2.
8. Wendt 1999; Johnston 2001.
9. For example, policies pushing trade and capital account liberalization are consistent with the animating ideas of free-market capitalism. See chapter 6 for more on the role of ideas.
10. Chinn and Frieden 2011, p. xvi. See also James 2001.

11. Claessens, Kose, and Terrones 2011, p. 18.

12. BBC World Service Poll, "Governments Misspend More Than Half of Our Taxes: Global Poll," September 27, 2010, available on WorldPublicOpinion.org, http://www.worldpublicopinion.org/pipa/pdf/sep10/BBCEcon_Sep10_rpt.pdf.

13. BBC World Service Poll, "U.N. Continues to Get Positive, though Lower, Ratings with World Public," January 24, 2006, available on WorldPublicOpinion.org, http://www.worldpublicopinion.org/pipa/articles/btunitednationsra/163.php.

14. See, for example, Stiglitz 2002.

15. See, for example, Bolton 2007.

16. Mason, Thibault, and Misener 2006.

17. Kieran Daley, "IOC Report Shows 'Decades of Bribery,'" *Independent* (London), January 21, 1999; Duncan Mackay, "Samaranch's Expensive Tastes Revealed as IOC Opens Its Books," *Guardian*, March 19, 1999; Jules Boykoff and Alan Tomlinson, "Olympian Arrogance," *New York Times*, July 4, 2012.

18. Forster 2006. See also Doreen Carvajal, "For FIFA Executives, Luxury and Favors," *New York Times*, July 17, 2011.

19. According to the *Guardian*, twelve of the twenty-four members have been accused of corruption since 2009. Owen Gibson, "Sepp Blatter: How FIFA's Great Survivor Has Stayed on Top," *Guardian*, May 30, 2013.

20. Leander Schaerlaeckens, "FIFA Acts Like It's above the Law," *Leander Schaerlaeckens blog*, ESPN.com, http://espn.go.com/sports/soccer/blog/_/name/schaerlaeckens_leander/id/6611552/fifa-acts-the-law. See also Associated Press, "Blatter Poised for Re-election," June 1, 2011, Associated Press, ESPN online, http://espn.go.com/sports/soccer/news/_/id/6614357/sepp-blatter-poised-re-election-fifa-vote-take-place-planned.

21. Roger Blitz and Stanley Pignal, "Battered Blatter Admits Fifa 'Unstable.'" *Financial Times*, May 31, 2011; Dorveen Carvajal and Stephen Castle, "European Soccer Clubs Challenging FIFA," *New York Times*, July 29, 2011.

22. "FIFA Corruption Probe 'Being Resisted,'" ESPN, September 21, 2012, http://m.espn.go.com/soccer/story?storyId=1166102; Associated Press, "President: FIFA 'Not Corrupt or a Mafia Organization,'" *USA Today*, September 28, 2012, http://www.usatoday.com/story/sports/soccer/world/2012/09/28/sepp-blatter-tells-fifa-advisers-to-curb-criticism-corruption/1600285/.

23. Rob Hughes, "Skeletons in Blatter's Closet Return to Haunt Him," *New York Times*, December 2, 2011.

24. James Montague, "Sympathy for the 'Devil': In Defense of Sepp Blatter," CNN online, January 8, 2013, http://edition.cnn.com/2013/01/08/sport/football/blatter-racism-fifa-football.

25. Roger Blitz, "FIFA's Tense Relations with Brazil on Show as Protests Rock Nation," *Financial Times*, June 20, 2013.

26. See Hepeng Ja, "Closer Ties Urged between China and IEA," *Chemistry World*, August 6, 2008; Eberhard Rhein, "China, India and Russia Should Join IEA," *BlogActiv.eu*, August 6, 2008, http://rhein.blogactiv. eu/2008/06/08/china-india-and-russia-should-join-iea/; Henry Kissinger, "The Future Role of the IEA" (speech, 35th anniversary of the International Energy Agency, Paris, France, October 14, 2009), HenryKissinger.com, http://www.henryakissinger.com/speeches/101409. html.

27. Shai Oster, "U.S. Asks China to Join Global Energy Group," *Wall Street Journal*, May 21, 2008; *Press Trust of India*, "US Keen on India to Join IEA,"May 22, 2008, http://www.business-standard.com/article/ economy-policy/us-keen-on-india-to-join-iea-108052200029_1.html.

28. International Energy Agency website, "About us," "FAQs," http://www. iea.org/aboutus/faqs/membership/#d.en.20933, accessed June 2013.

29. Carola Hoyos, "China Invited to Join IEA as Oil Demand Shifts," *Financial Times*, March 30, 2010.

30. On IEA member apprehension, see Patrick 2010, p. 49. On Chinese apprehension about joining, see Gao Xiaohui, "Time Not Yet Ripe for China's IEA Membership," *Global Times*, April 1, 2010.

31. Nick Butler, "It's Time for the IEA to Get Real," *Financial Times*, January 8, 2013.

32. Bernanke 2005; Gagnon 2012; Pettis 2013.

33. Alan Beattie, "IMF in Discord over Renminbi," *Financial Times*, January 26, 2009.

34. Associated Press, "IMF Approves Huge Eventual Gold Sale," *USA Today*, July 7, 2008, http://usatoday30.usatoday.com/news/washington/2008-04-07-3860859895_x.htm.

35. Crotty 2009; Levinson 2010; Bair 2012, pp. 27–40; Zaring 2009/10, p. 483.

36. Drezner 2006, p. 94.

37. The G7 members are Canada, France, Germany, Great Britain, Italy, Japan, and the United States.

38. Martin 2006; Sobel and Stedman 2006.

39. Martin 2008, p. 358; Cammack 2012, fn. 7.

40. Irwin 2013, pp. 1–4.

41. Paulson 2010, pp. 160–61.

42. Alison Smale, " 'Magic Is Over' for U.S., Says French Foreign Minister," *International Herald-Tribune*, March 12, 2008; Bertrand Benoit, "US 'Will Lose Financial Superpower Status,' " *Financial Times*, September 25, 2008.

43. See Irwin 2013, chapter 10.

44. Barma, Ratner, and Weber 2007; Cammack 2012.

45. Mahbubani 2008.

46. Paulson 2010, pp. 210–11. See also Sorkin 2009, pp. 343–50; and Blinder 2013, p. 124.

47. See also Darling 2011; Irwin 2013, pp. 142–43.
48. National Intelligence Council 2008; Abdelal and Segal 2007; Drezner 2007a; Alexandroff 2008.
49. See BBC World Service Poll, "Economic System Needs 'Major Changes,'" March 31, 2009, available on World Public Opinion.org, http://www.worldpublicopinion.org/pipa/articles/btglobalizationtradera/596.php; Program on International Policy Attitudes, "Publics Want More Aggressive Government Action on Economic Crisis," July 21, 2009, available on World Public Opinion.org, http://www.worldpublicopinion.org/pipa/articles/btglobalizationtradera/626.php.
50. Pew Research Center, "Pervasive Gloom about the World Economy," Pew Research Global Attitudes Project survey, Pew Research online, July 12, 2012, http://www.pewglobal.org/2012/07/12/pervasive-gloom-about-the-world-economy/
51. Samans, Schwab, and Malloch-Brown 2011, p. 80. See also Lee Howell, "The Failure of Governance in a Hyperconnected World," *New York Times*, January 10, 2012.
52. World Economic Forum 2012.
53. Bremmer and Roubini 2011, p. 4.
54. Ian Bremmer, "Decline of Global Institutions Means We Best Embrace Regionalism," *The A-List* blog, *Financial Times*, January 27, 2012, http://blogs.ft.com/the-a-list/2012/01/27/decline-of-global-institutions-means-we-best-embrace-regionalism/. See, more generally, Bremmer 2012.
55. Rothkopf quote from June 3, 2012 tweet at https://twitter.com/djrothkopf/status/209257908553261056. Patrick 2014, p. 73.
56. Beattie 2012, p. 18. For other pessimistic books by *Financial Times* authors, see Rachman 2011 and Luce 2012.
57. See Mark Leonard, "In 2013, the Great Global Unraveling," December 30, 2012, Reuters.com, http://blogs.reuters.com/mark-leonard/2012/12/30/in-2013-the-great-global-unraveling/; Martin Indyk and Robert Kagan, "A 'Plastic Juncture' in World Politics," *New York Times*, January 20, 2013.
58. There are notable exceptions. See, for example, Kahler 2013 and Jones 2014.
59. Hale, Held, and Young 2013, p. 2; Frieden, Pettis, Rodrik, and Zedillo 2012, p. 2; Mazower 2012, p. 424; Zaring 2009/10, p. 475; Barma, Ratner, and Weber 2013, p. 56. See also, more generally, Patrick 2014.
60. See, for example, Mastanduno 2009; Cohen and DeLong 2009; Chinn and Frieden 2011; Temin and Vines 2013.
61. Kindleberger 1973, p. 292.
62. Feis 1966; James 2001; Ahamed 2009.
63. Altman 2009, pp. 8, 10.
64. Friedman and Mandelbaum 2011.
65. Zakaria 2008.

66. Layne 2012, p. 211. See also, more generally, Reich and Lebow 2014.
67. Mastanduno 2009, p. 152; Kupchan 2012, p. 7.
68. Jacques 2009; Bremmer 2009; Halper 2010; Kurlantzick 2013.
69. Liu Chang, "U.S. Fiscal Failure Warrants a De-Americanized World," October 13, 2013, Xinhua online, http://news.xinhuanet.com/english/indepth/2013-10/13/c_132794246.htm; David Li, "Beijing Should Cut Back Its Lending to Washington," *Financial Times*, October 15, 2013.
70. Ferguson 2004; Haass 2008.
71. Naim 2013, p. 158; Fabius quoted in Steven Erlanger, "Saudi Prince Criticizes Obama Administration, Citing Indecision in Mideast," *New York Times*, December 15, 2013; Jentleson 2012, pp. 140–41; Schweller 2011, p. 287.
72. Cooper 2010, p. 742. This is an extension of the concept of "good enough" governance developed by Grindle (2004).
73. Rodrik 2011a.
74. Bremmer 2012, p. 4. See also Patrick 2014. [ALSO, I THINK THIS ENDNOTE NEEDS TO BE PUT BACK IN SEQUENCE]
75. See Davis and Pelc 2013 on learning in the context of trade policy.
76. I am grateful to Walter Mattli for making this point clear to me.
77. Zoellick 2005.
78. For an excellent discussion of this issue, see Gutner and Thompson 2010.
79. On embedded liberalism, see Ruggie 1982. On the new international economic order, see Cox 1979.
80. Wolf 2004; Bhagwati 2004; Dreher 2006; Subramanian and Kessler 2013.
81. Kindleberger 1978; Minsky 1986; Galbraith 1993; Reinhart and Rogoff 2009.
82. Webb 1995; Rodrik 2011.
83. See the discussion in chapter 6.
84. See King, Keohane, and Verba 1994 on the distinction between descriptive inference and causal inference.
85. On analytic eclecticism, see Katzenstein and Sil 2010.
86. See Lake 2009 for a summary of the open economy politics paradigm.
87. Pinker 2011; Goldstein 2011.
88. Burrows and Harris 2009, p. 35. See also Gelb 2010.

Chapter 2

1. Goldsmith and Posner 2005, pp. 38 and 86.
2. Krasner 1983, p. 2.
3. Keohane and Martin 1995, p. 45.
4. Martin 1992b; Drezner 2000.
5. Cooper 2010.
6. Keohane 1984; Axelrod and Keohane 1985; Martin 1992a, 1992b.
7. Snidal and Abbott 2000; Goldstein and Martin 2000.
8. Goldstein and Martin 2000, p. 619.

9. Or, to use the language of March and Olsen 1998, constuctivists rely more on the logic of appropriateness than the logic of consequences.
10. Drezner 2007b, chapters 3 and 5. See also Irwin 2013.
11. Finnemore and Sikkink 1998.
12. Hurd 1999; Johnston 2001.
13. Steffek 2003.
14. Haas 1992.
15. Goldstein 1996; Cortell and Davis 1996; Drezner 2003.
16. Simmons 2009.
17. Mansfield and Milner 2013.
18. In that sense, this effort is consistent with the "analytical eclecticism" of Katzenstein and Sil 2010.
19. By no means are these the only facts mentioned when critics talk about the failure of global economic governance. Other examples include the PBoC chairman's March 2009 call for a "super-sovereign currency" to replace the dollar; the failure of the Copenhagen climate-change summit in December 2009; and the ongoing dispute between China, the United States, and the European Union over solar-panel dumping. Very often, general fecklessness of the United Nations is also cited as evidence of the failure of global governance.
20. Gamberoni and Newfarmer 2009.
21. Schwab 2011.
22. Rickards 2011; Dadush and Eidelman 2011.
23. Irwin 2013, pp. 204–5.
24. Andrew Ward, "EU in cold as climate deal redefines relations," *Financial Times*, December 29, 2009. See also James Kanter, "E.U. Blames Others for 'Great Failure' on Climate," *New York Times*, December 22, 2009; Mark Lynas, "How Do I Know China Wrecked the Copenhagen Deal? I Was in the Room," *Guardian*, December 22, 2009.
25. Gutner and Thompson 2010, pp. 234–37.
26. Keohane 1984; Downs, Rocke, and Barsoom 1996.
27. Reinhart and Rogoff 2009, chapter 14; Claessens, Kose, and Terrones 2011; Reinhart and Reinhart 2010; Eichengreen 2011b; Jorda, Schularick, and Taylor 2012.
28. One example is the Scandinavian countries that experienced severe banking crises in the early 1990s.
29. Eichengreen and O'Rourke 2010, 2012.
30. Based on calculations from the Maddison Project Database presented in Bolt and Van Zanden 2013, http://www.ggdc.net/maddison/maddison-project/data.htm.
31. Shaochua Chen and Martin Ravallion, "An Update to the World Bank's Estimate of Consumption Poverty in the Developing World," March 1, 2012 ; Annie Lowrey, "Dire Poverty Falls Despite Global Slump, Report Finds," *New York Times*, March 6, 2012.
32. United Nations Development Programme 2013, pp. 75–77.

33. For more on the KOF index, see Dreher, Gaston, and Martens 2008.
34. The mean globalization score was 56.36 in 2007 and 56.6 in 2010, a modest increase of 0.4 percent.
35. For the overall globalization index, the mean G20 score was 69.52 in 2007 and 68.98 in 2010.
36. Dinah Walker, "Quarterly Update: The U.S. Economic Recovery in Historical Context," Report released August 22, 2013, Council of Foreign Relations online, http://www.cfr.org/geoeconomics/quarterly-update-economic-recovery-historical-context/p25774. Accessed July 2012.
37. Ip 2013, p. 4.
38. Lund et al. 2013, p. 14; TheCityUK, *Fund Management Report*, November 2012, p. 1.
39. Lund et al. 2013, pp. 2 and 17.
40. Hills and Hoggarth 2013, p. 126.
41. Ip 2013, pp. 5 and 9.
42. United Nations Conference on Trade and Development 2013, p. xvi.
43. For FDI data, see OECD/UNCTAD 2012, 2013. For foreign investment assets, see Lund et al. 2013. For remittance flows, see World Bank 2013, p. 3.
44. See, for example, Rogers 2008; Joshua Kurlantzick, "The World Is Bumpy," *The New Republic*, July 15, 2009; Brubaker 2011, p. 93.
45. Ponticelli and Voth 2011.
46. Institute for Economics and Peace 2013.
47. Data in this paragraph comes from ICC International Maritime Bureau 2013.
48. Thom Shanker, "U.S. Reports That Piracy Off Africa Has Plunged," *New York Times*, August 28, 2012.
49. Institute for Economics and Peace 2012, p. 37.
50. Themnér and Wallensteen 2012, p. 566. See also Human Security Report Project 2010.
51. Brubaker 2011, p. 94.
52. Reinhart and Rogoff 2009, p. 273.
53. O'Rourke and Williamson 1999.
54. Krugman 2012; Stiglitz 2012.
55. Kindleberger 1973, p. 292.
56. "The Return of Economic Nationalism," *Economist,* February 5, 2009; Kurlantzick, "The World Is Bumpy"; Michael Sesit, "Smoot-Hawley's Ghost Appears as Economy Tanks," *Bloomberg News*, February 19, 2009; Rawi Abdelal and Adam Segal, "Yes, Globalization Has Passed Its Peak," http://www.foreignaffairs.com/articles/64856/rawi-abdelal-and-adam-segal/yes-globalization-passed-its-peak, March 17, 2009.
57. Evenett 2013.
58. Ip 2013.

59. The Simon Fraser Insititute reports can be accessed on the website Freetheworld.com, http://www.freetheworld.com/. The Heritage Foundation data can be accessed at http://www.heritage.org/index/visualize.
60. Hoekman 2012, p. 18.
61. Dadush, Ali, and Odell 2011.
62. European Central Bank 2013; Bown 2012; Siles-Brügge 2014.
63. World Trade Organization 2013; See also Henn and McDonald 2011; Siles-Brügge 2014.
64. Rose 2012, p. 4. See also Kee, Neagu, and Nicita 2013; Kim 2013, p. 7.
65. Ruddy 2010, p. 477; Madsen 2001, p. 849.
66. Dadush, Ali, and Odell 2011. See also Bussière et al. 2011.
67. Bown and Crowley 2013.
68. Ibid. See also Davis and Pelc 2013; Siles-Brügge 2014.
69. Gawande, Hoekman, and Cui 2011; Baccini and Kim 2012; Kee, Neagu, and Nicita 2011.
70. Bown 2012; Kee, Neagu, and Nicita 2013; Bown and Crowley 2013.
71. Ruddy 2010, pp. 492–93.
72. On pre-2008 compliance, see Wilson 2007. On Chinese compliance in particular, see He and Sappideen 2009; Zhang and Li 2013.
73. Alan Beattie, "Decommission the Weapons of Trade Warfare." *Financial Times*, August 8, 2012.
74. Bhagwati was the great popularizer of the term (1988, p. 41).
75. Between May 2011 and November 2013, a maximum of 13 percent of business executives cited trade protectionism as a serious concern. The surveys can be accessed at http://ig.ft.com/barometer/.
76. Dadush, Ali, and Odell 2011, p. 3. See also Bown 2010.
77. Schwab 2011, p. 112.
78. Beattie 2012, pp. 10–11; Bremmer 2012, p. 4; Frieden, Pettis, Rodrik, and Zedillo 2012, p. 2.
79. Recounted in Irwin 2013, pp. 127–32.
80. Ibid., p. 161.
81. Bank of International Settlements 2012, p. 39.
82. Ibid., p. 41.
83. "IMF Creates Short-Term Liquidity Facility for Market-Access Countries," IMF Press Release No. 08/262, October 29, 2008.
84. Joyce 2013, p. 170.
85. Ibid. p. 168.
86. Kindleberger 1988, p. xi.
87. Prasad and Sorkin 2009.
88. Coenen et al. 2010, fig. 92.
89. Ibid.
90. Organization for Economic Cooperation and Development 2008, p. 6.

91. Bob Davis, "Foreign Funds Agree to Set of Guiding Principles," *Wall Street Journal*, September 3, 2008.

92. Das 2009, pp. 99–100; Cohen and DeLong 2009, p. 89; Truman 2010, pp. 124–33; Bagnall and Truman 2013. See also Robin Wigglesworth, Andrew England, and Simeon Kerr, "Sovereign Wealth Funds Open Up Books," *Financial Times*, March 17, 2010.

93. OECD/UNCTAD 2012.

94. OECD/UNCTAD 2013, p. 3. The report went on to note, however, that these governments might still be blocking some investment deals through more informal measures.

95. See, for example, Tom Braithwaite, "Enforcement of Basel III Should Be Focus," *Financial Times*, October 1, 2012.

96. Chinn and Frieden 2011, p. 214; Véron 2012.

97. Chalk 2012, p. 555.

98. Naval patrols were not the only explanatory factor. The posting of armed guards on commercial ships as well as political developments in Somalia proper also played a role. See, for example, "Pirates Face a New Foe: A Private Navy," *Economist*, January 12, 2013.

99. Peter Finn, "Somali Pirates Will Face Death Penalty in Federal Trial in Virginia," *Washington Post*, June 02, 2013.

100. ICC International Maritime Bureau 2013, p. 20.

101. G20 Leaders Statement, September 25, 2009, G20 Information Centre, http://www.g20.utoronto.ca/2009/2009communique0925.html. Accessed December 2013.

102. Martin 2006; Sobel and Stedman 2006; Drezner 2007a.

103. Garrett 2010, p. 29. See also Cooper 2010, p. 749.

104. See, for example, Hale, Held, and Young 2013, p. 167.

105. Beattie 2012; Bremmer 2012; Patrick 2014.

106. Butler 2012.

107. G20 Information Centre 2013.

108. Downs, Rocke, and Barsoom 1996; Gutner and Thompson 2010.

109. See Irwin 2013, pp. 344–48.

110. Davis and Pelc 2013.

111. Statement of Treasury Secretary Geithner on the Report to Congress on International Economic and Exchange Rate Policies, April 3, 2010, http://www.treasury.gov/press-center/press-releases/Pages/tg627.aspx.

112. Jamil Anderlini and Alan Beattie, "China Hints at Currency Accord," *Financial Times*, April 3, 2010.

113. Rickards 2011, p. 113.

114. Keith Bradsher, "On China Currency, Hot Topic in Debate, Truth Is Nuanced," *New York Times*, October 17, 2012; Simon Rabinovitch, "Renminbi Hits 19-Year High against the Dollar," *Financial Times*, October 12, 2012; Lingling Wei and Bob Davis, "China's Zhu

Changhong Helps Steer Nation's Currency Reserves," *Wall Street Journal*, July 16, 2013.

115. Lund et al. 2013, p. 6.
116. "Less Skewed," *Economist*, September 28, 2013.
117. Drezner 2007b, chapter 5.
118. Kahler 2013, p. 49.
119. The IMF/World Bank Development Committee report, from September 30, 2010, can be accessed at at http://siteresources.worldbank.org/DEVCOMMINT/Documentation/22723851/DC2010-0014(E)Reform.pdf.
120. Council on Foreign Relations, "Global Finance Report Card," New York: CFR, April 2013. http://www.cfr.org/thinktank/iigg/reportcard/PDFs/CFR%20Finance%20Report%20Card%20Backgrounder.pdf,
121. Subramanian 2013, p. 4.
122. Ostry et al. 2010.
123. Dani Rodrik, "The End of An Era in Finance," Project Syndicate, March 10, 2010, http://www.project-syndicate.org/commentary/the-end-of-an-era-in-finance#dkuJB92AvW6Fckoy.99.
124. International Monetary Fund 2012, p. 1.
125. Wolfe 2012, pp. 787–79; Kim 2013; Kahler 2013.
126. Wolfe 2012; Kim 2013. See also Ruddy 2010, fn. 38l, and European Central Bank 2013, p. 93.
127. Doug Palmer, "US, trade allies push for international services talks," Reuters, http://www.reuters.com/article/2012/09/19/wto-services-idUSL1E8KJ8Q520120919, September 19, 2012.
128. Data from the WTO's Regional Trade Agreements Information System at http://rtais.wto.org/UI/PublicPreDefRepByEIF.aspx. Accessed July 2012.
129. Lazer 1999.
130. See Drezner 2006, pp. 71–92 for more on this dynamic.
131. Dadush, Ali, and Odell 2011, pp. 8–9.
132. There are also growing concerns about the arbitration process used to settle disputes between states and investors in BITs. See United Nations Conference on Trade and Development 2013, chapter 3.
133. James Politi, "US Revises Investment Treaty Approach," *Financial Times*, April 20, 2012.
134. Ikenberry 2011, p. 6.

Chapter 3

1. Exceptions include Kahler 2013 and Jones 2014.
2. Eric Pfanner, "U.S. Rejects Telecommunications Treaty," *New York Times*, December 13, 2012; Ellen Nakashima, "U.S. Refuses to Back U.N. Treaty, Saying It Endorses Restricting the Internet," *Washington Post*, December 13, 2012.

3. Deibert 2013.

4. Nyhan and Reifler 2010.

5. Alan Beattie, "IMF Chief Warns on Exchange Rate Wars," *Financial Times*, October 5, 2010.

6. Irwin 2013, pp. 273–74.

7. Eichengreen 2011a.

8. Matthew Brown, "Currency Swings Show Faith in G-20 Pledges Fading," Bloomberg, November 1, 2010.

9. Sebastian Mallaby, "The Fed's Foreign Policy Misstep," November 4, 2010, First Take, Council on Foreign Relations, http://www.cfr.org/monetary-policy/feds-foreign-policy-misstep/p23314.

10. Dadush and Eidelman 2011, pp. 17–21.

11. Ibid., pp. 13 and 21.

12. Hood 2012.

13. Bloomberg Global Poll, September 22, 2010, http://media.bloomberg.com/bb/avfile/rDd_07fmjdxc.

14. Bloomberg Global Poll, January 25, 2011, http://media.bloomberg.com/bb/avfile/rv_TLKsI_zGc.

15. "How to Stop a Currency War," *Economist*, October 14, 2010.

16. Jim O'Neill, "Time to End the Myth of Currency Wars," *Financial Times*, November 21, 2010; Eichengreen 2011a; Dadush and Eidelman 2011.

17. Google Trends, http://www.google.com/trends/explore#q=currency%20war. Accessed July 2013.

18. Aaron Back and In-Soo Nam, "Beijing, Seoul Blast Fed Push," *Wall Street Journal*, September 27, 2012.

19. Reuters, "ECB's Weidmann: Pressure on Central Banks Risks FX Competition," January 21, 2013, Reuters Editorial online, http://www.reuters.com/article/2013/01/21/ecb-weidmann-currency-idUSL6N0AQCMF20130121; Simon Kennedy and Scott Rose, "Russia Says World Is Nearing Currency War as Europe Joins," January 16, 2013, Bloomberg, http://www.bloomberg.com/news/2013-01-16/russia-says-world-is-nearing-currency-war-as-europe-joins.html.

20. Mohammed El-Erian, "Beggar Thy Currency or Thy Self?" Project Syndicate, January 22, 2013, http://www.project-syndicate.org/commentary/the-logic-of-today-s-brewing-currency-wars-by-mohamed-a—el-erian; Transcript of Fareed Zakaria's interview with Bill Gates, February 3, 2013, CNN online, http://transcripts.cnn.com/TRANSCRIPTS/1302/03/fzgps.01.html. See also Stephen King, "Era of Independent Central Banks Is Over," *Financial Times*, January 10, 2013; Felipe Larrain, "QE Takes a Toll on Emerging Economies," *Financial Times*, February 4, 2013; Komal Sri-Komar, "Fix Exchange Rates to Revive Growth," *Financial Times*, February 11, 2013; and Rickards 2012.

21. Philipp Hildebrand, "No Such Thing as a Global Currency War," *Financial Times*, February 11, 2013. See also Jeffrey Frankel, "All Quiet on the Currency Front," June 11, 2013, Project Syndicate, http://www.project-syndicate.org/commentary/a-currency-war-without-warriors-by-jeffrey-frankel.

22. Communiqué of Meeting of G20 Finance Ministers and Central Bank Governors, Moscow, Russia, February 16, 2013, University of Toronto, G20 Information Centre, http://www.g20.utoronto.ca/2013/2013-0216-finance.html.

23. See, for example, Victor Mallet, "Sing Demands 'Orderly Exit' from Global Easing Policies," *Financial Times*, September 4, 2013.

24. Eichengreen 2013a.

25. Jim O'Neill, "Currency Warriors!" January 20, 2013, Goldman Sachs.

26. Joe Weisenthal, "Facebook Is to Blame for the Outbreak of 'Currency Wars.'" Business Insider, January 26, 2013, http://www.businessinsider.com/goldmans-jim-oneill-facebook-is-to-blame-for-the-outbreak-of-global-currency-wars-2013-1.

27. Frieden 2006, p. 17.

28. Nathan Lewis, "Would a Gold Standard Have Worsened the 2008 Financial Crisis?" *Forbes*, August 30, 2012; Will Weissert, "Ron Paul Gives New Life to Gold Standard Issue," Associated Press, January 18, 2012, HuffingtonPost.com, http://www.huffingtonpost.com/2012/01/18/ron-paul-gold-standard_n_1212651.html.

29. Ikenberry 2011; Drezner 2007a.

30. Scowcroft 2012, p. 8.

31. Frieden 2006, pp. 261–71.

32. Barnett and Finnemore 2004, chapter 3; Foot and Walter 2011, chapter 3.

33. Gowa 1984.

34. Keohane 1980.

35. Putnam and Bayne 1987; Andrews 2005.

36. Eichengreen 2008, p. 30.

37. Flandreau et al. 1998.

38. Dominguez 2006.

39. Webb 1994; Willett 1999.

40. This parallels the recent argument by Robert Kagan that many people exaggerate the effectiveness of American hegemony in the past as well. Kagan 2012, pp. 109–22.

41. Reinhart and Rogoff 2009.

42. Author's calculation based on a survey of research abstracts and author identification. The journals were *International Organization, International Studies Quarterly, World Politics, Review of International Studies,* and *Review of International Political Economy,* which were the top five international relations journals that published International Political Economy work according to Maliniak, Peterson and Tierney 2012.

43. For example, a few years into the financial crisis, the *Review of International Political Economy* published a reading list that included books, special issues of journals, and popular articles written about the crisis. Of the forty-five suggested readings, only two contained material written by non-Western authors. See RIPE Editors 2009.

44. See, for example, Zhu 2001.

45. Chanley, Rudolph, and Rahm 2000.

46. See "2012 Edelman Trust Barometer Global Results," Edelman Trust Barometer 2012 Annual Global Study, Edelman online, http://trust. edelman.com/trust-download/global-results/.

47. Inglehart 1997.

48. Mahbubani 2013; Arvind Subramanian, "This Is a Golden Age of Growth (Yes, You Read That Right)," *Financial Times*, April 7, 2013.

49. Frieden, Pettis, Rodrik, and Zedillo 2011; Rodrik 2011a.

50. For a recent primer, see Akram 2012.

51. William Pesek, "Abenomics Races against the Clock," June 17, 2013, Bloomberg online, http://www.bloomberg.com/news/2013-06-17/ abenomics-races-against-clock-as-stocks-seesaw-william-pesek.html.

52. Eberstadt 2012.

53. See "2012 Edelman Trust Barometer Global Results," Edelman Trust Barometer 2012 Annual Global Study, Edelman online, http://trust. edelman.com/trust-download/global-results/.

54. Data available from "Senate Action on Cloture Motions" table, website of the US Senate, http://www.senate.gov/pagelayout/reference/cloture_ motions/clotureCounts.htm.

55. See Ezra Klein, "14 Reasons Why This Is the Worst Congress Ever," *Washington Post*, July 13, 2012; Klein, "Goodbye and Good Riddance, 112th Congress," *Washington Post*, January 4, 2013; Stephen Dinan, "Capitol Hill Least Productive Congress Ever: 112th Fought 'about Everything,'" *Washington Times*, January 9, 2013.

56. On the degree of policy uncertainty, see Baker, Bloom, and Davis 2013. On the macroeconomic effects of uncertainty, see Haddow et al. 2013.

57. "Debt Limit Analysis," report of the Bipartisan Policy Center, Bipartisanpolicycenter.org, November 27, 2012, http://bipartisanpolicy. org/sites/default/files/files/Debt%20Limit%20Analysis%20Slides. pdf ; Betsey Stevenson, and Justin Wolfers, "Debt-Ceiling Déjà Vu Could Sink Economy," Bloomberg online, May 28, 2012, http:// www.bloomberg.com/news/2012-05-28/debt-ceiling-deja-vu- could-sink-economy.html.

58. Standard and Poor, "United States of America Long-Term Rating Lowered to 'AA+' Due to Political Risks, Rising Debt Burden; Outlook Negative," August 5, 2011. http://www.standardandpoors.com/ratings/ articles/en/us/?assetID=1245316529563. Accessed December 2013.

59. See, for example, Nelson D. Schwartz, "Fearing an Impasse in Congress, Industry Cuts Spending," *New York Times*, August 5, 2012.

60. U.S. Council of Economic Advisers 2013; Macroeconomic Advisers 2013.
61. See the discussion of austerity in chapter 6.
62. Macroeconomic Advisers 2013.
63. Gallup poll, "Trust in Government," Gallup online, 2013, http://www.gallup.com/poll/5392/trust-government.aspx. Accessed March 2013; Pew Research Center, "Public Trust in Government, 1958-2013." Pew Research Center for the People and the Press online, October 19, 2013, http://www.people-press.org/2013/01/31/trust-in-government-interactive/. Accessed March 2013.
64. Thomas Mann, and Norman Ornstein, "Let's Just Say It: The Republicans Are the Problem," *Washington Post*, April 27, 2012. See, more generally, Mann and Ornstein 2012.
65. Irwin 2013, pp. 227–29.
66. Ibid., p. 226.
67. Blyth 2013.
68. Reinhart and Rogoff 2009; Roxburgh et al. 2012.
69. Peter Doyle, letter to IMF Executive Board, June 18, 2012, available at http://cnnibusiness.files.wordpress.com/2012/07/doyle.pdf.
70. Alan Beattie, and Chris Giles, "IMF and Eurozone Clash over Estimates," *Financial Times*, August 31, 2011; James Kanter, "IMF Urges Europe's Strongest to Shoulder Burdens of Currency Bloc," *New York Times*, June 21, 2012.
71. Edwards and Senger 2013.
72. Pepinsky 2012.
73. Dadush and Eidelman 2011, p. 8.

Chapter 4

1. Gourevitch 1986.
2. Mansfield and Mutz 2009; Naoi and Kume 2011.
3. Rose 2012; Bown and Crowley 2013.
4. Hirschman 1970.
5. Drezner 2007b, chapter 2.
6. Simmons 1994; James 2001; Frieden 2006, chapters 8 and 9.
7. Yergin and Stanislaw 1997; Blyth 2002.
8. Erixon and Sally 2010.
9. Ikenberry 2011, p. 340.
10. Lake 2009, p. 225.
11. Examples of effects that would be neglected under OEP are ideational factors, second-image reversed factors, and systemic complexity. See Oatley 2011; Drezner and McNamara 2013; and Katzenstein and Nelson 2013 for a fuller critique.
12. Xing and Detert 2010.
13. Ibid.

14. This data set can be accessed at http://www.wto.org/miwi. The data in this paragraph comes from "OECD-WTO Database on Trade in Value-Added: Preliminary results," at https://www.wto.org/english/res_e/statis_e/miwi_e/tradedataday13_e/oecdbrochurejanv13_e.pdf, accessed January 2013.
15. Briand et al. 2012; Ip 2013.
16. Mishkin 2010.
17. Obstfeld 2012, fig. 2.
18. Palmer and Maher 2010. See also Clive Cookson, Gillian Tett, and Chris Cook, "Organic Mechanics," *Financial Times*, November 26, 2009.
19. Kinderman 2008.
20. See, for example, Farrell and Newman 2010.
21. Ibid., p. 618. See also Pierson 2004.
22. Rogowski 1989; Hathaway 1998.
23. Chwieroth 2009.
24. Philippon and Reshef 2013.
25. Figures from Rajan 2010.
26. Baker 2010, p. 655.
27. Johnson and Kwak 2010.
28. Philippon and Reshef 2013.
29. Gawande, Hoekman, and Cui 2011.
30. Bown and Crowley 2013; Davis and Pelc 2013.
31. The KOF data can be accessed at the KOF Index of Globalization website, http://globalization.kof.ethz.ch/. The G20 compliance data can be found at the University of Toronto's G20 Information Centre, http://www.g20.utoronto.ca/analysis/. The correlation coefficient between the two indices for the nineteen countries (minus the European Union) was approximately 0.3.
32. For example, even though the United States was the epicenter of the financial crisis, it had not truly implemented Basel II prior to the collapse of Lehman Brothers.
33. Crotty 2009; Levinson 2010. See Bair 2012, pp. 27–40 and Zaring 2009/10, p. 483, for more pointed critiques.
34. Eichengreen 2009.
35. Financial Stability Forum 2008.
36. There is another reason that this would seem to be an ideal issue to test the strength of sectoral interests: because the regulatory debate was so arcane, it should have been easier for the banks to make their preferences clear without a fear of public backlash. See Kono 2006 on how standards can be used by sectoral groups to more readily advance material interests.
37. Thirkell-White 2009.
38. See BBC World Service, "Economic System Needs 'Major Changes,'" March 31, 2009, available on WorldPublicOpinion.org, http://www.worldpublicopinion.org/pipa/articles/btglobalizationtradera/596.php,

accessed December 2012; and PIPA, BBC World Service, "Publics Want More Aggressive Government Action on Economic Crisis," July 21, 2009, available on WorldPublicOpinion.org, http://www. worldpublicopinion.org/pipa/articles/btglobalizationtradera/626.php, accessed December 2012.

39. See Singer 2007; Schirm 2009; and Lyngen 2012 for more on the preferences of national financial sectors.

40. Quoted in Robert Kaiser, "'Act of Congress': How Barney Frank Foiled the Banking Lobby to Form a New Financial Watchdog," *Washington Post*, May 5, 2013. Indeed, even during the depths of the 2008 crisis, the IIF's primary recommendation to regulators was the "full and consistent implementation of the Basel II accord." See IIF letter to George W. Bush, November 7, 2008.

41. Interview with Timothy Geithner, *Wall Street Journal*, January 17, 2013.

42. Vitali, Glattfelder, and Battiston 2011.

43. Johnson and Kwak 2010, p. 5.

44. Makkai and Braithwaite 1992; Seabrooke and Tsingou 2009; Baker 2010, pp. 652–53.

45. Underhill and Zhang 2008; Helleiner and Porter 2009; Ozgercin 2012.

46. "Declaration of the Summit on Financial Markets and the World Economy," Washington, DC, November 15, 2008, University of Toronto G20 Information Centre, http://www.g20.utoronto. ca/2008/2008declaration1115.html, accessed January 2013.

47. See, for example, "Global Plan Annex: Declaration on Strengthening the Financial System," London, UK, April 2, 2009. Accessed at the University of Toronto's G20 Information Centre, http://www.g20. utoronto.ca/2009/2009ifi.html, July 2013.

48. Paulson 2010, p. 451.

49. Basel Committee on Banking Supervision 2009a.

50. "G20 Leaders Statement: The Pittsburgh Summit," Pittsburgh, PA, September 25, 2009. Accessed at the University of Toronto's G20 Informaton Centre, http://www.g20.utoronto. ca/2009/2009communique0925.html, July 2013. For the BIS press release see http://www.bis.org/press/p090907.htm. For a chronology of key moments in Basel III negotiations, see Bair 2012 and Wilf 2013.

51. Basel Committee on Banking Supervision 2009b, p. 1.

52. Ibid.

53. Baker 2013a, 2013b; Lyngen 2012, p. 527.

54. Young 2013, table 2.

55. All comments can be accessed at the BIS website, http://www.bis.org/ publ/bcbs165/cacomments.htm.

56. Lall 2012, pp. 628–29; Chris Bryant and Brooke Masters, "Bankers Fear Effect of Basel Rules," *Financial Times*, June 10, 2010.

57. Quoted in Binyamin Appelbaum, "Regulators Push for Global Rule on Bank Capital," *New York Times*, May 25, 2010.

58. Although the IIF was the principal lobbying group for banks, it was far from the only one. Other groupings, such as the Financial Services Roundtable and the European Financial Services Roundtable (EFSR), also weighed in on Basel III. See, for example, their responses to the draft Basel III accord at http://www.bis.org/publ/bcbs165/fsrl.pdf and http://www.bis.org/publ/bcbs165/efsr.pdf.

59. "Basel 3: The Banks Battle Back," *Economist*, May 27, 2010.

60. Bair 2012, p. 259.

61. Sara Schaefer Munoz, "Capital Idea, Say Regulators," *Wall Street Journal*, October 11, 2011.

62. Institute for International Finance 2010.

63. Elliot 2010, p. 11.

64. KPMG 2010, p. 3.

65. For an excellent primer on terms and terminology, see Auer and von Pfoesti 2012.

66. Lyngen 2012, p. 520.

67. See Jean Eagelsham and Chris Giles, "UK Change of Heart on Banking Tax Plan," *Financial Times*, November 8, 2009.

68. See the IIF's December 2010 assessments at http://www.iif.com/regulatory/article+936.php.

69. Felix Salmon, "The Quiet Victory of Basel III" (blog), Reuters.com September 14, 2010, http://blogs.reuters.com/felix-salmon/2010/09/14/the-quiet-victory-of-basel-iii/.

70. Schaefer Munoz, "Capital Idea."

71. See, for example, Credit Suisse equity research note, "Basel 3," September 13, 2010, accessed at https://doc.research-and-analytics.csfb.com/docView w?language=ENG&source=ulg&format=PDF&document_id=86021334 1&serialid=5TD%2BZIhEE1vif6roIyrWYDDQO11dSKPlTfrmZDpg8B4 %3D.

72. Chinn and Frieden 2011, p. 214; Véron 2012.

73. Wilf 2013, p. 29.

74. See Bach and Newman 2007 on this causal mechanism.

75. Elliott 2010, p. 11.

76. Basel Committee on Banking Supervision 2011.

77. Interviews with Basel Committee on Banking Supervision officials, Basel, Switzerland, February 2011.

78. Young 2013.

79. Trichet 2010, p. 1.

80. Freeland 2012, pp. 252–55.

81. Rachelle Youngrai and Philipp Halstrick, "Aggressive Style of JP Morgan Boss May Hurt Bank Cause," September 29, 2011, Reuters.com, http://www.reuters.com/article/2011/09/29/financial-regulation-dimon-idUSS1E78S1MW20110929,

82. Young 2012, p. 682.

83. Bair 2012, p. 260.

84. Interviews with BCBS officials, February 2011. On press coverage, see Felix Salmon, "The Politics of Basel III" (blog), Reuters.com, April 3, 2010, http://blogs.reuters.com/felix-salmon/2010/04/03/the-politics-of-basel-iii/, and Brooke Masters, "Fears for German banks Under New Rules," *Financial Times*, September 9, 2010.

85. Interviews with BCBS officials.

86. On the significance of banks in determining varieties of capitalism, see Soskice and Hall 2001.

87. Blyth 2013, pp. 82–83.

88. Oatley and Nabors 1998.

89. Lall 2012. It is true that US banks protested the increases in capital adequacy less vehemently than they protested the introduction of liquidity and leverage ratios. Still, this is very weak support for this hypothesis.

90. Tom Braithwaite and Patrick Jenkins, "JPMorgan Chief Says Bank Rules 'Anti-US,'" *Financial Times*, September 12, 2011. See also Freeland 2012, p. 253.

91. Wilf 2013.

92. Young 2013, p. 13.

93. Baker 2010; Culpepper 2010.

94. Interviews with BCBS officials, February 2011; Bair 2012.

95. See, for example, Brooke Masters, "US Banks Call for Easing of Basel III," *Financial Times*, December 16, 2012.

96. It should be noted that only 15 percent of the Level 2 assets could be held in equities or mortgage-backed securities. See Annex 1 at http://www.bis.org/press/p130106a.pdf.

97. Brooke Masters, "Banks Win More Flexible Basel Rules," *Financial Times*, January 6, 2013.

98. Bair 2012.

99. See, for example, Felix Salmon, "Why the Basel Change Was a Bad Idea" (blog), Reuters.com, January 9, 2013, http://blogs.reuters.com/felix-salmon/2013/01/09/why-the-basel-change-was-a-bad-idea/; and Howard Schneider and Danielle Douglas, "Post-Lehman, the Push for Global Financial Protections Stalls," *Washington Post*, January 29, 2013.

100. Simon Johnson, "Betrayed by Basel," *Economix* (blog), *New York Times*, January 10, 2013, http://economix.blogs.nytimes.com/2013/01/10/betrayed-by-basel/.

101. Interviews with BCBS officials, February 2011.

102. Brooke Masters, "Basel Tries Fluid Position on Liquidity," *Financial Times,* January 7, 2013.

103. Quoted in Baker 2013a, p. 129.

104. Young 2012. See Milner 1997 for the general argument about the role interest groups play in the provision of information.

105. van Rixtel and Vause 2012, p. 11.
106. An additional assumption that proved to be wrong was that the European economy would be in better shape by January 2013. See Salmon, "Why the Basel Change Was a Bad Idea."
107. Ralph Atkins and Keith Fray, "Global Pool of Triple A Status Shrinks 60%," *Financial Times*, March 26, 2013. See, more generally, Ralph Atkins, Philip Stafford, and Brooke Masters, "Regulation: Collateral Damage," *Financial Times*, October 24, 2012.
108. International Monetary Fund 2012, chapter 3. See also Davies and Ng 2011.
109. Andrews and Ng 2011; see also Liam Vaughn and Gavin Finch, "Basel Rules Face Change with No-Risk Sovereign Debt a Focus," *Business Week*, December 7, 2011.
110. International Monetary Fund 2012a, pp. 83 and 101.
111. Quoted in Andrew Ross Sorkin, "Easing of Rules for Banks Acknowledges Reality," Dealbook, *New York Times*, January 7, 2013, http://dealbook.nytimes.com/2013/01/07/easing-of-rules-for-banks-ackno wledges-reality/. See also Masters, "Basel Tries Fluid Position."
112. Basel Committee on Banking Supervision 2013.
113. European Banking Authority 2013; Masters, "US Banks Call for Easing." For a cautionary tale about the numbers produced by banks, however, see Frank Portnoy and Jesse Eisinger, "What's Inside America's Banks?" *Atlantic*, January/February 2013.
114. Jenkins and Shäfer, "Europe's Banks Turn to Capital Raising to Meet Basel III," *Financial Times*, May 13, 2013.
115. The banks built up these capital reserves largely through the accumulation of retained earnings. See Cohen 2013.
116. Baker 2010.
117. Peter Evans, "Big Banks, Flooded in Profits, Fear Flurry of New Safeguards," *New York Times*, July 19, 2013.
118. Krasner 1991; Drezner 2007b.
119. See, for example, Chwieroth 2009.
120. Stiglitz 2002.
121. Ostry et al. 2010.
122. Dani Rodrik, "The End of an Era in Finance," Project Syndicate, March 10, 2010, http://www.project-syndicate.org/commentary/ the-end-of-an-era-in-finance#dkuJB92AvW6Fckoy.99.
123. International Monetary Fund 2012b, p. 1.
124. Baker 2012, p. 131. It should be noted that BCBS officials did not endorse the linkage between macroprudential supervision and capital controls.
125. Ip 2013, p. 10.
126. Rodrik, "End of an Era in Finance."

Chapter 5

1. Indeed, as the *New York Times* noted at the time, "The measures did little to overcome widespread doubts that they—or even the additional steps pledged by American and European officials—would accomplish the Council's long-standing goal: halting Iran's production of nuclear fuel." Neil MacFarquhar, "U.N. Approves New Sanctions to Deter Iran," *New York Times*, June 9, 2010.
2. Quoted in Maloney 2010, p. 142.
3. See Tehran Bureau, "China Floods Iran with Cheap Consumer Goods in Exchange for Oil," *Guardian*, February 20, 2013.
4. US Government Accountability Office 2013.
5. See, for example, Thomas Erdbrink, "Iran Staggers as Sanctions Hit Economy," *New York Times*, September 30, 2013.
6. Gourevitch 1986, p. 17.
7. Kindleberger 1973; Krasner 1976; Gilpin 1975, 1981; Lake 1993; Ikenberry 2000; Norrlof 2010; Keohane 2012.
8. McKeown 1983; Keohane 1984, 2012; Axelrod and Keohane 1985; Snidal 1985.
9. Lake 1983; Stein 1984; Eichengreen 1989; Lazer 1999; Nye 2007; Mastanduno 2009.
10. Lazer 1999; Hafner-Burton and Montgomery 2009.
11. Ibid.
12. Mastanduno 2009.
13. Krasner 1976; Lake 1983; Stein 1984; Mansfield 1992, 1994.
14. Krasner's initial periodization was 1820–1879 (rising UK hegemony, more openness); 1880–1900 (fading UK hegemony, modest closure); 1900–1913 (fading UK hegemony, modest opening); 1919–1939 (US hegemony, closure); 1945–1960 (US hegemony, openness); and 1960–1975 (fading US hegemony, openness). Forty years later, the natural periodization would be identical to Krasner's for the first four, but the last three would be 1945–1971 (US hegemony, openness); 1971–1991 (fading US hegemony, modest closure); and 1991–2008 (US hegemony, strong opening). Hegemonic stability theory would only fail to explain the pre–World War I and interwar eras.
15. For "k-group," see Snidal 1985 and Lake 1993. For "hegemonic coalition," see Foot and Walter 2011.
16. Snidal 1985; Lake 1993.
17. Drezner 2007b.
18. Morrow 1994.
19. Axelrod and Keohane 1985; Koremenos, Lipson, and Snidal 2001; Drezner 2007b.
20. Nye 2006; Drezner 2007b; McNamara 2008.
21. Wilson and Purushothaman 2003; Bergheim 2005; Zakaria 2008; Khanna 2009; Alexandroff and Cooper 2010.
22. Eichengreen 2011b, pp. 142–45.

23. See Khanna 2009 for the Second World; Alexandroff and Cooper 2010 for BRICSAM; and Buiter and Rahbari 2011 on Global Growth Generators.

24. National Intelligence Council 2010.

25. Subramanian 2011.

26. Fogel 2010; Dadush and Stancil 2010.

27. Reilly 2012.

28. Drezner 2009.

29. Burrows and Harris 2009, p. 30.

30. On Clinton's remarks, see Ewen MacAskill, "Hillary Clinton's Question: How Can We Stand Up to Beijing?" *Guardian*, December 4, 2010. More generally, see Evan Osnos, "China and the State of the Union," *New Yorker*, January 25, 2012.

31. Wang 2012, p. 11.

32. Pew Research Center, "America's Global Image Remains More Positive than China's," Pew Research Global Attitudes Project, July 18, 2013, http://www.pewglobal.org/2013/07/18/americas-global-image-remains-more-positive-than-chinas/.

33. The UN Human Development Index indicators can be accessed at the UN Development Programme's Human Development Reports website,http://hdr.undp.org/en/. The Legatum Prosperity Index can be accessed at the Legatum Institute's website: http://www.prosperity.com/Ranking.aspx.

34. Eichengreen, Park, and Shin 2011; Pettis 2013.

35. Lasswell and Kaplan 1950; Dahl 1957; Bachrach and Baratz 1962; Lukes 1974; Baldwin 1979; Baldwin 1989; Cohen 2008; Grewal 2008; Nye 2011.

36. Gilpin 1981.

37. Strange 1987. See also Schwartz 2009.

38. Nye 1990, 2004, 2011.

39. Nadelmann 1990 is an early example. See Barnett and Duvall 2005 for a more recent discussion.

40. Kahler 2009. See also Grewal 2008; Slaughter 2009.

41. Schweller 2011; Jentleson 2012; Naim 2013.

42. Drezner 2007b.

43. Bach and Newman 2007; Newman and Posner 2011.

44. Wohlforth, 1999, pp. 32–34; Callen 2007; Brooks and Wohlforth 2008, pp. 40–42; Lieber 2011.

45. See, for example, Moravcsik 2009; Nye 2011, chapter 6.

46. A time series of the past decade would show the exact same distribution.

47. Older data is not usable because of the complications of excluding intra-European trade.

48. Drezner 1999, 2007.

49. Cao 2012, pp. 379–80; Gray and Potter 2012, p. 796.

50. Because possessing a common medium of exchange matters in assessing the size of capital markets, I have disaggregated EU financial markets by currency.

51. Oatley, Winecoff, Pennock, and Danzmann 2013, p. 148.

52. Rey 2013.

53. All data accessed from http://stats.oecd.org/Index. aspx?DataSetCode=TIVA_OECD_WTO, July 2013. No other BRIC economy approaches these actors. Japan does somewhat better, but is still responsible for only 6.2 percent of global value-added exports.

54. Quotations from Starrs 2013, p. 2, data from p. 9.

55. For firms, see Vitali, Glattfelder, and Battiston 2011; Nolan 2012. For private wealth, see Schwartz 2009; Davies, Sandström, Shorrocks, and Wolff 2011.

56. For concerns, see Helleiner and Kirshner 2009. For claims, see World Bank 2011 and Subramanian 2011. For both, see Kirshner 2013, 2014.

57. Data from Cohen and Benney 2014; and Jeffrey Frankel, "The Dollar and Its Rivals," Project Syndicate, November 21, 2013, http:// www.project-syndicate.org/commentary/jeffrey-frankel-argues-t hat-the-dollar-s-status-as-the-world-s-top-international-currency-is-not-in-jeopardy. The percentages are out of a possible 200 percent.

58. Cohen and Benney 2014. See also Bracke and Bunda 2011; Stokes 2014.

59. See Drezner 2010; McNally 2012; and Eichengreen 2013b on the difficulties China will have trying to internationalize its currency. For more positive assessments of Chinese efforts to "internationalize" the renminbi, see Subramanian 2001 and Kirshner 2013, 2014.

60. Stokes 2014, p. 11 (italics in the original). See also Drezner 2010; Cohen and Benney 2014; Eichengreen 2013b; Prasad 2014.

61. Goldberg 2010, p. 7. More generally on the structural significance of the dollar's reserve currency status, see Strange 1987; and Schwartz 2009.

62. See Norrlof 2010; Brooks, Ikenberry, and Wohlforth 2012; and Drezner 2013b for the contours of this debate.

63. Strange 1987; Ikenberry 2011, p. 57.

64. Stockholm International Peace Research Institute data from Sam Perlo-Freeman, Elisabeth Sköns, Carina Somilrano and Helén Wilandh, "Trends in World Military Expenditure, 2012," SIPRI Fact Sheet, April 2013, http://books.sipri.org/files/FS/SIPRIFS1304.pdf, accessed April 15, 2013.

65. Brooks and Wohforth 2008, p. 30; Ikenberry 2011, p. 42.

66. Nye 2011, p. 189.

67. Layne 2012, p. 210.

68. Simon Rabinovitch, "China's Forex Reserves Reach $3.4tn," *Financial Times*, April 11, 2013. These figures likely understate the size of China's reserve assets, because of the PRC's efforts to conceal the magnitude of its foreign reserve position.

69. Data from IMF, "Data Template on International Reserves and Foreign Currency Liquidity," July 2013, http://www.imf.org/external/np/sta/ir/IRProcessWeb/colist.aspx.

70. See Drezner 2009, pp. 42–43.

71. Geoff Dyer, Jamil Anderlini, and Henny Sender, "China's Lending Hits New Heights," *Financial Times*, January 17, 2011.

72. "Chinese Loans to Latin America Top World Bank, IDB Combined," Bloomberg News, February 17, 2012, http://www.bloomberg.com/news/2012-02-17/chinese-loans-to-latin-america-top-world-bank-idb-combined.html.

73. Drezner 2009.

74. Tony Capaccio and Daniel Kruger, "China's U.S. Debt Holdings Aren't Threat, Pentagon Says," Bloomberg, September 10, 2012, http://www.bloomberg.com/news/2012-09-11/china-s-u-s-debt-holdings-aren-t-threat-pentagon-says.html.

75. See United Nations Conference on Trade and Development 2013 for further discussion.

76. William Wan, "China's Economic Data Draw Sharp Scrutiny from Experts Analyzing Global Trends," *Washington Post*, February 4, 2013. See also Wallace 2011 and IMF 2012b.

77. Standard and Poor's, "United States of America Long-Term Rating Lowered to 'AA+' Due to Political Risks, Rising Debt Burden; Outlook Negative, August 5, 2011, http://www.standardandpoors.com/ratings/articles/en/us/?assetID=1245316529563.

78. Porter and Rivkin 2012.

79. Mike Dorning, John Detrixhe, and Ian Katz, "Downgrade Anniversary Shows Investors Gained Buying U.S." Bloomberg, July 16, 2012, http://www.bloomberg.com/news/2012-07-16/downgrade-anniversary-shows-investors-gained-buying-u-s-.html.

80. See also Carvalho, Eusepi, and Grisse 2012.

81. Roxburgh et al. 2012; Brown et al. 2013; Gillian Tett, "Europe and US Lines Cross on Household Debt Ratio," *Financial Times*, May 9, 2013.

82. Congressional Budget Office 2013.

83. Standard and Poor's, "United States of America 'AA+/A-1+' Ratings Affirmed; Outlook Revised to Stable on Receding Fiscal Risks," June 10, 2013, https://www.globalcreditportal.com/ratingsdirect/renderArticle.do?articleId=1142712&SctArtId=161026&from=CM&nsl_code=LIME.

84. A. T. Kearney 2013.

85. Kupchan 2002; Leonard 2005; Chinn and Frankel 2007; McNamara 2008.

86. For an intriguing exception, see Moravcsik 2009.

87. Cohen and Benney 2014; Stokes 2014; Prasad 2014.

88. Portugal, Ireland, Italy, Spain, and Greece.

89. World Economic Forum 2013.

90. David Barboza, "Contrarian Investor Sees Economic Crash in China," *New York Times*, January 7, 2010. See also Edward Wong, "China's Growth Slows, and Its Political Model Shows Limits," *New York Times*, May 10, 2012.

91. Josh Noble and Simon Rabinovitch, "Fitch Downgrades China's Credit Rating," *Financial Times*, April 9, 2013.

92. The United States was fourth. The data can be accessed at the World Bank's Ease of Doing Business index, archived at World Development Indicators at http://data.worldbank.org/indicator/IC.BUS.EASE.XQ.

93. A. T. Kearney 2012.

94. Dobbs et al. 2010; Moe, Maasry, and Tang 2010; Bain Capital 2012.

95. Slaughter 2009.

96. Acharya 2011, p. 859.

97. Wang and French 2013. See also Kahler 2010; Shambaugh 2013, pp. 45–46. The capacity of the other BRIC economies to engage with established international institutions is also open to question. See Miller 2013 and Jones 2014 on this point.

98. Schweller and Pu 2011, p. 69. See also Besson 2013; and Breslin 2013.

99. Foot and Walter 2011.

100. McNally 2012, p. 754.

101. "Chinese Infighting: Secrets of a Succession War," *Financial Times*, March 4, 2012; John Garnault, "Rotting from Within," *Foreign Policy*, April 19, 2012, http://www.foreignpolicy.com/articles/2012/04/16/rotting_from_within#sthash.iT3wVZIJ.dpbs; and David Barboza, "Billions in Hidden Riches for Family of Chinese Leader," *New York Times*, October 25, 2012.

102. Political instability is also a problem in a tripolar system. See Schweller 1998.

103. Khanna 2008; Gelb 2009; National Intelligence Council 2010; Naim 2013.

104. Patrick 2010.

105. Drezner 2007b.

106. Helleiner 2010.

107. For the list of contributors, see International Monetary Fund, "IMF Managing Director Christine Lagarde Welcomes Additional Pledges to Increase IMF Resources, Bringing Total Commitments to US$456 B," IMF press release 12/231, June 19, 2012, http://www.imf.org/external/np/sec/pr/2012/pr12231.htm.

108. Those who have stressed the resilience of American power include Norrlof 2010; Ikenberry 2011; Lieber 2011; and Beckley 2011/12.

109. Ploch et al. 2011.

110. Jones 2014, p. 85.

111. Oatley, Winecoff, Pennock, and Danzmann 2013, p. 135, fn. 12.

112. Irwin 2013, p. 154.

113. See Mishkin 2010; Aït-Sahalia et al. 2012; and Irwin 2013.

114. Roy 2013, p. 19.

115. Truman 2013.

116. Keith Bradhser, "China Uses Rules on Global Trade to Its Advantage," *New York Times*, March 14, 2010.

117. Chris Giles and Alan Beattie, "China Reprimanded by G20 Leaders," *Financial Times*, March 30, 2010.

118. See People's Bank of China, "Further Reform the RMB Exchange Rate Regime and Enhance the RMB Exchange Rate Flexibility," news release, June 19, 2010, available at http://www.pbc.gov.cn/publish/english/955/2010/20100622144059351137121/20100622144059351137121_.html.

119. Coastas Paris and Kanga Kong, "India, Brazil to Press China on Yuan," *Wall Street Journal*, February 18, 2011.

120. Lowery 2007.

121. Bob Davis, "U.S. Pushes Sovereign Funds to Open to Outside Scrutiny," *Wall Street Journal*, February 26, 2008. Policy principles can be accessed at the International Working Group on Sovereign Wealth Funds, "Generally Accepted Principles and Practices," http://www.iwg-swf.org/pubs/gapplist.htm, accessed December 2013.

122. Truman 2010.

123. Peter Thal Larsen and Martin Dickson, "Singapore Fund Pledges Greater Transparency," *Financial Times*, January 27, 2008.

124. Yousef al Otaiba, "Our Sovereign Wealth Plans," *Wall Street Journal*, March 19, 2008.

125. Nadim Kawach, "SWFs Still Face Risk of Western Curbs," *Emirates Business 24/7*, August 1, 2008. The Inter-Arab Investment Guarantee Corporation issued the report.

126. Norton Rose 2008.

127. Gao interviewed by Leslie Stahl, "Chinese Investment: An Open Book?" *60 Minutes*, April 4, 2008, http://www.cbsnews.com/news/china-investment-an-open-book/; Jamil Anderlini, "China Fund Shuns Guns and Gambling," *Financial Times*, June 13, 2008.

128. Krishna Guha, "Sovereign Funds Back Code," *Financial Times*, September 3, 2008.

129. Halper 2010; Bremmer 2010; Sanderson and Forsythe 2013.

130. Lanteigne 2013.

131. "NATO Chief Praises China's Participation in Anti-Piracy Campaign off Somalia," *China Daily*, January 19, 2009; "U.S. Praises China Anti-Piracy Role Off Somalia," Associated Press, *USA Today*, February 28, 2009, http://usatoday30.usatoday.com/news/world/2009-02-28-somalia-pirates_N.htm; "U.S., Chinese Navies in Joint Anti-Piracy Drills Off Somalia," Reuters, September 18, 2012, http://www.reuters.com/article/2012/09/18/us-china-usa-piracy-idUSBRE88H0PY20120918.

132. Prasad and Sorkin 2009. Chinese officials stress this fiscal stimulus as their greatest contribution to stabilizing the global economy following the collapse of Lehman Brothers.
133. Gallagher 2014.
134. Cline and Williamson 2012; Lund et al. 2013.
135. Gagnon 2012, 2013. See also Keith Bradsher, "China Uses Rules on Global Trade to Its Advantage," *New York Times*, March 14, 2010.
136. "China's Decade in the WTO," Reuters, November 29, 2011.
137. Gawande, Hoekman, and Cui 2011, p. 25. More generally, see Baccini and Kim 2012.
138. Bown 2012.
139. Kennedy 2010; Zhang and Li 2014.
140. McNally 2012, p. 758. See also He and Sappideen 2009; Kennedy 2010; Kahler 2010.
141. Breslin 2013.
142. Jane Perlez, "Rebuffed by China, Pakistan May Seek I.M.F. Aid," *New York Times*, October 18, 2008.
143. Irwin 2013, chapter 20.
144. Jones 2014.
145. Steinfeld 2010; Foot and Walter 2011; Shambaugh 2013; Breslin 2013.
146. Johnston 2013, pp. 32–33.
147. Frieden 2006, chapter 8; Ahamed 2009.

Chapter 6

1. Prasad and Sorkin 2009; Corsetti and Müller 2011, p. 8.
2. Yergin and Stanislaw 1997; Frieden 2006, chapter 17.
3. Burgin 2012. Though I use "neoliberalism" and "Washington Consensus" as synonymous terms in this chapter, it should be noted that the content of the Washington Consensus has evolved over time. See Hale, Held, and Young 2013, pp. 138–44.
4. Greenspan 2007; Fox 2009; Quiggin 2010.
5. Fukuyama 1992.
6. Jeffrey M. Jones, "Americans Shift to More Positive View of Foreign Trade," Gallup Economy, February 28, 2013, http://www.gallup.com/poll/160748/americans-shift-positive-view-foreign-trade.aspx.
7. Drezner 2006; Broz 2010; Hufbauer and Woollacott 2012.
8. Kahler 2010, p. 187.
9. Pearson 2001.
10. Committee of 100, "Hope and Fear: American and Chinese Attitudes toward Each Other," C-100 2007 Survey Report, /Committee of 100, New York, NY, December 2007, p. 27, http://survey.committee100.org/2007/EN/2007_C-100_EN_Survey.pdf.
11. See Ferchen 2013, pp. 402–3.

12. Jamil Anderlini, "China Rebukes West's Lack of Regulation," *Financial Times*, May 27, 2008; Edward Wong, "Booming, China Faults U.S. Policy on the Economy," *New York Times*, June 17, 2008.

13. Edmund Andrews, "Greenspan Concedes Error on Regulation," *New York Times*, October 23, 2008.

14. Quoted in Babb 2013, p. 285.

15. Alan Beattie, "Washington's Waning Way: How Bail-Outs Poison a Free Market Recipe for the World," *Financial Times*, September 28, 2008; Christopher Hayes, "Free Traitors," *New Republic*, October 8, 2008; Barrett Sheridan, "Why Barriers Don't Matter," *Newsweek*, December 8, 2008.

16. For a sampling, see Posner 2009; Lewis 2010; Rajan 2010; Quiggin 2010; Roubini and Mihm 2010; Chinn and Frieden 2010; and Johnson and Kwak 2010. For an authoritative review, see Lo 2012.

17. See, for example, Peter Beinart, "How the Financial Crisis Has Undermined U.S. Power," *Time*, June 21, 2010.

18. Katrin Beinhold, "As China Rises, Conflict with West Rises Too," *New York Times*, January 26, 2010.

19. The seven sectors were defense, electricity generation and distribution, petroleum and petrochemicals, telecommunications, coal, civil aviation, and waterway transport.

20. Yu 2014, p. 168. See also Woolridge 2012.

21. Halper 2010; Jacques 2009, pp. 227–30.

22. For the most prominent versions of this argument, see Gat 2007 and Bremmer 2010.

23. Halper 2010, p. 104.

24. Jacques 2009, p. 230. See also McNally 2012, p. 745.

25. Francis Fukuyama, "US Democracy Has Little to Teach China," *Financial Times*, January 17, 2011; Thomas Friedman, "Our One-Party Democracy," *New York Times*, September 8, 2009; see also Williamson 2012, Kurlantzick 2013.

26. Rodrik 2011a; Kurlantzick 2013, chapter 7.

27. Nathan and Scobell 2012, p. 35.

28. Wang 2012, p. 10. See also Kurlantzick 2013, chapter 7.

29. Committee of 100, "US-China Public Perceptions: Opinion Survey 2012," New York Report, New York, April 19, 2012, http://survey. committee100.org/2012/EN/C100_2012Survey.pdf, accessed July 2013.

30. In 2010, Chinese attitudes toward the U.S. were 58% to 37% favorable/ unfavorable; in 2013, the numbers shifted to 40% to 53%. Pew Research, Global Attitudes Project, Global Indicators Database, "Opinion of the United Sates," http://www.pewglobal.org/database/indicator/1/survey/all/ response/Unfavorable/, accessed July 2013.

31. See Drezner 2009.

32. OECD/UNCTAD 2012, 2013.

33. "G20 Leaders Statement: The Pittsburgh Summit," Pittsburgh, PA, September 25, 2009. Accessed at University of Toronto's G20 Information Centre, http://www.g20.utoronto. ca/2009/2009communique0925.html, July 2013.

34. From 2008 to 2010, these were BRIC summits. South Africa official joined the group in December 2010.

35. "Brazil, Russia, India and China Finance Ministers Joint Communiqué," São Paulo, November 7, 2008. Accessed at the University of Toronto's BRICS Information Centre, http://www.brics. utoronto.ca/docs/081107-finance.html, July 2013.

36. All communiqués can be accessed at the University of Toronto's BRICS Information Centre, http://www.brics.utoronto.ca/.

37. "2nd BRIC Summit of Heads of State and Government: Joint Statement," Brasília, Brazil, April 15, 2010. Accessed at the University of Toronto's BRICS Information Centre, July 2013, http:// www.brics.utoronto.ca/docs/100415-leaders.html.

38. "Statement by BRICS Leaders on the establishment of the BRICS-LED Development Bank," Fifth BRICS Summit, Ethekwini, South Africa, March 27, 2013, http://www.thepresidency.gov.za/pebble.asp?relid=15128, accessed July 2013.

39. Jones 2014, p. 107.

40. See, for example, BBC World Service, "Wide Dissatisfaction with Capitalism:Twenty Years after Fall of Berlin Wall," November 9, 2009, available on WorldPublicOpinion.org, http:// worldpublicopinion.org/pipa/articles/btglobalizationtradera/644. php?lb=btgl&pnt=644&nid=&id=, accessed July 2013.

41. Respondents were asked to agree or disagree with the statements: "What do you think about the growing trade and business ties between (survey country) and other countries—do you think it is a very good thing, somewhat good, somewhat bad or a very bad thing for our country?"

42. The full question was "Please tell me whether you completely agree, mostly agree, mostly disagree or completely disagree with the following statements: Most people are better off in a free market economy, even though some people are rich and some are poor."

43. Data accessed from Pew Research Global Attitudes Project, Global Indicators Database, July 2012, http://www.pewglobal.org/database/ ?indicator=16&survey=13&response=Good%20thing&mode=table.

44. Jeffrey M. Jones, "Americans Shift to More Positive View of Foreign Trade," Gallup Economy, February 28, 2013, http://www.gallup.com/ poll/160748/americans-shift-positive-view-foreign-trade.aspx.

45. Kahler 2013, pp. 40–41. See also Nel 2010, p. 952.

46. Babb 2013, p. 285. See also Kahler 2013.

47. Quiggin 2010, p. 2; Crouch 2011, p. viii.

48. See Hall 1989, 1993; Jacobsen 1995; Rodrik 2014.

49. Goldstein and Keohane 1993.
50. Blyth 2002 See also Rodrik 2014.
51. Lo 2012.
52. I am indebted to Noah Smith for making this point clear to me.
53. Drezner and McNamara 2013.
54. Legro 2005.
55. Ibid. See Kreps 1990 on simplicity.
56. On free trade and the gold standard, see "Gold Standard," Chicago Booth School of Business IGM Forum, January 12, 2012, http://www.igmchicago.org/igm-economic-experts-panel/poll-results?SurveyID=SV_cw1nNUYOXSAKwrq; and "Free Trade," Chicago Booth School of Business IGM Forum, March 13, 2012, http://www.igmchicago.org/igm-economic-experts-panel/poll-results?SurveyID=SV_0dfr9yjnDcLh17m. On monetary policy, see "Monetary Policy," Chicago Booth School of Business IGM Forum, September 29, 2011, http://www.igmchicago.org/igm-economic-experts-panel/poll-results?SurveyID=SV_9yFWHquReQZjC6w; and "QE3," Chicago Booth School of Business IGM Forum, September 25, 2012, http://www.igmchicago.org/igm-economic-experts-panel/poll-results?SurveyID=SV_02pBtPuOkYPP9bv. On the degree of consensus, see Gordon and Dahl 2013. On the absence of consensus on monetary policy, compare Martin Wolf, "We Still Have That Sinking Feeling," *Financial Times*, July 10, 2012, and Mohamed El-Erian, "Central Bankers Can't Save the World," *Bloomberg View*, August 2, 2012, http://www.bloomberg.com/news/2012-08-02/central-banks-can-t-save-the-world.html?cmpid=BVrelated. See also Joe Weisenthal, "The Biggest Tragedy in Economics," *Business Insider*, September 7, 2012, http://www.businessinsider.com/the-biggest-tragedy-in-economics-2012-9.
57. Gagnon 2012. See also Keith Bradsher, "China Uses Rules on Global Trade to Its Advantage," *New York Times*, March 14, 2010
58. Barma, Ratner, and Weber 2007.
59. Roach 2009; Yu 2014, p. 168.
60. See, for example, Halper 2010, p. 127; Jacques 2009, p. 427; Ferchen 2013; Wang and French 2013, p. 98.
61. Daniel W. Drezner, "The Sounds of Chinese Boilerplate," *Foreign Policy*, June 13, 2011, http://www.foreignpolicy.com/posts/2011/06/13/the_sounds_of_chinese_boilerplate#sthash.q94TIm7i.dpbs.
62. Kahler 2010, pp. 187–88.
63. Shambaugh 2013, pp. 45–46. See also Acharya 2011; Breslin 2013.
64. Wang and French 2013, p. 97.
65. Beeson 2013, p. 244.
66. "Naked Aggression," *Economist*, March 12, 2009.
67. "China's National Defense in 2010," Information Office of the State Council, People's Republic of China, March 2011, Beijing, http://news.

xinhuanet.com/english2010/china/2011-03/31/c_13806851.htm, accessed July 2013.

68. Quoted in Joshua Kurlantzick, "The Belligerents: Meet the Hardliners Who Now Run China's Foreign Policy," *New Republic*, January 27, 2011.
69. Johnston 2013, p. 19.
70. Beeson 2013, p. 239.
71. Ramo 2004.
72. Kennedy 2010; Naughton 2010; Ferchen 2013.
73. Kennedy 2010; Shambaugh 2013.
74. Kennedy 2010, p. 469.
75. Economy 2010.
76. Shen Hu, "China's Gini Index at 0.61, University Report Says," Caixin Online, December 10, 2012, http://english.caixin.com/2012-12-10/100470648.html.
77. Halper 2010, p. 126. See also Jacques 2009, chapter 6.
78. Brandt and Zhu 2010.
79. Shambaugh 2013, chapter 5.
80. Kennedy 2010, p. 476.
81. A related issue is that Chinese officials are wary of advertising the term "Beijing Consensus" because it needlessly roils the United States: "[Chinese officials] are acutely aware of American sensitivity to any talk suggesting the emergence of a rival power and ideology—and conflict with America could wreck China's economic growth." See "The Beijing Consensus Is to Keep Quiet," *Economist*, May 6, 2010.
82. Kennedy 2010, p. 470. See also McNally 2012, p. 756.
83. Ferchen 2013, p. 410.
84. Kennedy 2010, p. 468; Schweller and Pu 2011, p. 52. See also Breslin 2013.
85. Tania Branigan, "China's Wen Jiabao Signs Off with Growth Warning," *Guardian*, March 5, 2013.
86. Quoted in Pettis 2011.
87. For internal critiques, see Yu Yongding, "A Different Road Forward," *China Daily*, December 23, 2010; Yao Yang, "The End of the Beijing Consensus," *Foreign Affairs,* February 2, 2010, http://www.foreignaffairs.com/articles/65947/the-end-of-the-beijing-consensus. For external critiques, see Roach 2009; Eurasia Group 2011; Pettis 2013.
88. "Chinese Infighting: Secrets of a Succession War," *Financial Times*, March 4, 2012.
89. Development Research Center and World Bank 2013.
90. See Robert Zoellick's comments at http://www.worldbank.org/en/news/speech/2012/02/27/world-bank-president-zoellick-opening—remarks; Ambrose Evans Pritchard, "China May Not Overtake America This Century After All," *Daily Telegraph*, May 8, 2013. Li Keqiang in particular provided unwavering political support for the project.

91. Development Research Center and World Bank 2013, p. 4. See also Kahler 2010; McNally 2013, fn. 136.
92. Development Research Center and World Bank 2013, p. 25.
93. Ibid., p. 60.
94. Li Keqiang, speech, State Council Videophone Conference on Mobilizing the Efforts to Change Government Organizations' Functions, May 13, 2013.
95. David Barboza and Chris Buckley, "China Plans to Reduce the State's Role in the Economy," *New York Times*, May 24, 2013; "Chinese Govt Says Financial System Must Support Economy," Bloomberg, June 19, 2013, http://www.bloomberg.com/news/2013-06-19/china-says-financial-system-must-support-economy-as-rates-rise.html.
96. Bettina Wassener and Chris Buckley, "China's G.D.P. Growth Slows as Government Changes Gears," *New York Times*, July 14, 2013.
97. Simon Rabinovitch, "China Unveils Measures to Boost Economy," *Financial Times*, July 24, 2013.
98. Geoff Dyer, "Sino-US investment Deal Sought," *Financial Times*, July 12, 2013.
99. Tom Mitchell and Lucy Hornby, "China's Pledge of Big Reforms Cements Era of Market Forces," *Financial Times*, November 12, 2013; Carlos Tejada, "China Endorses 'Decisive Role' for Markets as Plenum Concludes," *Wall Street Journal*, November 12, 2013.
100. Christian Murck, "The Third Plenum: Prospects for Reform in China," National Bureau of Asian Research Commentary, December 4, 2013, http://www.nbr.org/research/activity.aspx?id=376#.UtBEovRDtw4.
101. Steinfeld 2010.
102. Roach 2009; Woetzel et al. 2009.
103. On prior third plenum promises coming to naught, see Keith Bradsher, "China's Leaders Confront Economic Fissures," *New York Times*, November 6, 2013. On state-owned enterprises, see Bob Davis and Brian Spegele, "State Companies Emerge as Winners Following Top China Meeting," *Wall Street Journal*, November 13, 2013.
104. See, for example, Jamil Anderlini, "How Long Can the Communist Party Survive in China?" *Financial Times*, September 20, 2013; Simon Denyer, "China's Leader, Xi Jinping, Consolidates Power with Crackdowns on Corruption, Internet," *Washington Post*, October 3, 2013.
105. Chris Buckley, "China Takes Aim at Western Ideas," *New York Times*, August 19, 2013.
106. Li Keqiang, "China Will Stay the Course on Sustainable Growth," op-ed, *Financial Times*, September 8, 2013.
107. Williamson 1990; Quiggin 2010.
108. Quiggin 2010; Irwin 2013, chapter 8.
109. Farrell and Quiggin 2013, pp. 19–20.
110. Kotios and Galamos 2012, p. 870.

111. Farrell and Quiggin 2013, p. 20.
112. Lawrence Summers, "The $700bn Bail-Out and the Budget," *Financial Times*, September 28, 2008.
113. Martin Feldstein, "The Stimulus Plan We Need Now," *Washington Post*, October 30, 2008. Rogoff, quoted in Rich Miller and Matt Benjamin, "Calls for $1 Trillion Stimulus Package Grow as Economy Tumbles," Bloomberg, December 4, 2008, http://www.bloomberg.com/apps/news?p id=newsarchive&sid=afWnxP9DzvoM. For Lindsey, see Jim Kuhnhenn, "Obama Looking at $850 Billion Jolt to the Economy," Associated Press, December 17, 2008, http://www.foxnews.com/printer_friendly_wires/200 8Dec17/0,4675,ObamaStimulus,00.html.
114. Robert Lucas, "Bernanke Is the Best Stimulus Right Now," *Wall Street Journal*, December 23, 2008.
115. See, for example, Baldwin and Eichengreen 2008; or Paul Krugman, "The Keynesian moment," *The Conscience of a Liberal* (blog), *New York Times*, November 29, 2008, http://krugman.blogs.nytimes.com/2008/11/29/the-keynesian-moment/.
116. N. Gregory Mankiw, "What Would Keynes Have Done?" *New York Times*, November 28, 2008.
117. "Transcript of a Press Briefing by Dominique Strauss-Kahn," IMF, Washington DC, November 15, 2008, https://www.imf.org/external/np/tr/2008/tr081115.htm.
118. On the US dominance in the economics profession, see Fourcade 2006; Chwieroth 2009; and Farrell and Quiggin 2013, pp. 15–17.
119. Darling 2011, p. 177.
120. Bertrand Benoit, "Berlin's Next Stimulus Awaits Obama," *Financial Times*, December 14, 2008.
121. Steinbrück, interview with Stefan Theil, *Newsweek*, December 15, 2008.
122. Bertrand Benoit, "Woman in the News: Angela Merkel," *Financial Times*, January 16, 2009.
123. Jean-Claude Trichet interview with the *Financial Times*, December 15, 2008.
124. Farrell and Quiggin 2013, pp. 24–25; Irwin 2013, pp. 157–60.
125. Schieritz 2013.
126. Benoit, "Angela Merkel."
127. Prasad and Sorkin 2009.
128. Bruce Stokes, "Europe: Go Ahead and Spend, Please," *National Journal*, January 31, 2009.
129. Brian Parkin and Rainer Burgin, "Merkel's Coalition Forges Extra $66 Billion Stimulus," Bloomberg, January 13, 2009.
130. Farrell and Quiggin 2013, p. 33. See also Schieritz 2013.
131. Farrell and Quiggin 2013.
132. Ibid., p. 31.

133. Quoted in Bruce Stokes, "Berlin-Washington Tensions," *National Journal*, April 11, 2009.
134. See Hurd 1999; Johnston 2001.
135. See, for example, Krugman 2013, and Blyth 2013, pp. 62–64.
136. Irwin 2013, chapter 13; Farrell and Quiggin 2013; Blyth 2013.
137. Alan Greenspan, "U.S. Debt and the Greece Analogy," *Wall Street Journal*, June 18, 2010.
138. Alesina and Ardagna 2009, p. 2.
139. Reinhart and Rogoff 2010, p. 2.
140. "Not So Risk Free," *Economist*, February 11, 2010.
141. Alesina 2010, pp. 1 and 3.
142. Islam and Choudhury 2012.
143. International Monetary Fund 2010, p. 94.
144. A fact they themselves documented at http://www.reinhartandrogoff. com/related-research/growth-in-a-time-of-debt-featured-in.
145. Walter Alarkon, "U.S. Debt Reaches Level at Which Economic Growth Begins to Slow," *The Hill*, May 26, 2010.
146. For a plethora of examples of Reinhart and Rogoff's influence, see Tim Fernholz, "How Influential Was the Rogoff-Reinhart Study Warning That High Debt Kills Growth?" *Quartz*, April 16, 2013.
147. Krugman 2013.
148. Alesina quoted in Peter Coy, "Keynes vs. Alesina. Alesina Who?" *Business Week*, June 29, 2010.
149. See, for example, David Ignatius, "How Debt Imperils National Security," *Washington Post*, May 23, 2010.
150. Ferguson 2010, p. 27.
151. See, for example, Altman and Haass 2010; Roya Wolverson interview with Sebastian Mallaby, "The Sovereign Debt Dilemma," February 5, 2010, http://www.cfr.org/economics/sovereign-debt-dilemma/p21381; Benn Steil and Paul Swartz, "Dangers of U.S. Debt in Foreign Hands," *Financial News*, June 14, 2010.
152. Steil 2010.
153. Irwin 2013, pp. 208–9.
154. Wolfgang Scháuble, "Maligned Germany Is Right to Cut Spending," *Financial Times*, June 23, 2010.
155. Jackie Calmes and Sewell Chan, "Leaders at Summit Turn Their Attention to Deficit Cuts," *New York Times*, June 26, 2010.
156. Jean-Claude Trichet, "Stimulate No More—It Is Now Time for All to Tighten," *Financial Times*, July 22, 2010.
157. Blyth 2013.
158. Paul Krugman, "Debt and Denial," *New York Times*, February 13, 2006. See also Krugman, "Another Bogus Budget," *New York Times*, February 3, 2004.

159. Skidelsky 2009.
160. Krugman 2013. For another example, see Whitehead 2008.
161. Blyth 2013; Farrell and Quiggin 2013; Krugman 2013.
162. De Grauwe and Li 2013. Se also Martin Wolf, "The Sad Record of Fiscal Austerity," *Financial Times*, February 26, 2013; John Quiggin, "Austerity Has Been Tested, and It Failed," *Chronicle of Higher Education*, May 20, 2013.
163. International Federation of the Red Cross and Red Crescent 2013.
164. Congressional Budget Office 2013.
165. International Monetary Fund 2010, chapter 3.
166. See, for example, "Cutting Edge," *Economist*, September 30, 2010.
167. Herndon, Ash, and Pollin 2013.
168. See, for example, Brenda Cronin, "Seminal Economic Paper on Debt Draws Criticism," *Wall Street Journal*, April 16, 2013.
169. Lagarde, quoted in "Ease Off Spending Cuts to Boost U.S. Recovery," *IMF Survey, Magazine*, June 14, 2013, http://www.imf.org/external/pubs/ft/survey/so/2013/car061413a.htm.
170. Pew Research Global Attitudes Project, "The New Sick Man of Europe: the European Union," May 13, 2013, http://www.pewglobal.org/2013/05/13/the-new-sick-man-of-europe-the-european-union/.
171. Clifford Marks, "In Media Coverage, Deficit Eclipses Unemployment," *National Journal*, May 16, 2011; Dylan Byers, "Epic Media Fail, Deficit Edition," *Politico*, February 27, 2013, http://www.politico.com/blogs/media/2013/02/epic-media-fail-deficit-edition-158044.html.
172. Dana Blanton, "Fox News Poll: Voters Back Spending Cuts to Boost Economy by Huge Margins," Fox News, http://www.foxnews.com/politics/2013/02/08/voters-say-government-should-cut-spending-rather-than-increase-it-as-way-to/.
173. Michael Steen and Ralph Atkins, "Draghi's 'Dirty Harry' Act Keeps Euro Crisis at Bay," *Financial Times*, July 22, 2013.
174. Peter Spiegel and Peter Ehrlich, "Eurozone Anti-Austerity Camp on the Rise," *Financial Times*, April 21, 2013.
175. Alison Smale, "A Fiscal Scold, Merkel, Softens Tone at Home," *New York Times*, November 1, 2013.
176. Ben White and Tarini Parti, "Democrats Ask: What Debt Crisis?" *Politico*, April 28, 2013, http://www.politico.com/story/2013/04/democrats-debt-crisis-90717.html.
177. For the contours of this debate, see Charles Krauthammer, "Obama Unbound," *Washington Post*, January 24, 2013; Joe Scarborough, "Paul Krugman vs. the World," *Politico*, January 28, 2013, http://www.politico.com/story/2013/01/paul-krugman-vs-the-world-86822.html; and Haass 2013, pp. 123–28.
178. Andrew Higgins, "Europe Facing More Pressure to Reconsider Cuts as a Cure," *New York Times*, April 26, 2013; Jackie Calmes, "Lines Blur in U.S.-Europe Debate on Austerity," *New York Times*, June 16, 2013.
179. Bank for International Settlements 2012, 2013.

180. Bank for International Settlements 2013, p. 5.
181. James 2001.
182. Gordon and Dahl 2013.
183. On the development and spread of these ideas, see Yergin and Stanislaw 1997; Frieden 2006; Burgin 2012.
184. Burgin 2012, p. 216. See also Babb 2013, p. 286.

Chapter 7

1. Data in this paragraph comes from Sorkin 2009, chapter 19.
2. See Mishkin 2010, pp. 6–12.
3. Bowman and Rugg 2010.
4. Mishkin 2010; Aït-Sahalia et al. 2012.
5. Blinder and Zandi 2010.
6. See "Bailouts: Banks and Automakers," Chicago Booth School of Business IGM Survey, November 13, 2012, http://www.igmchicago.org/igm-economic-experts-panel/poll-results?SurveyID=SV_oqeKwxLWkDyiwjX.
7. Rich Miller, "Wall Street Fix Seen Ineffectual by Four of Five in U.S." Bloomberg, July 13, 2010; "Possible Negatives for Candidates: Vote for Bank Bailout, Palin Support," Pew Research Center, October 6, 2010, http://www.people-press.org/2010/10/06/possible-negatives-for-candidates-vote-for-bank-bailout-palin-support/.
8. Ben Smith, "TARP: A Success None Dare Mention," *Politico*, September 14, 2010, http://www.politico.com/news/stories/0910/42135.html.
9. Hoffman 2012, p. 3.
10. Frieden 2006; James 2001.
11. Ip 2013.
12. Keohane 2009, pp. 42 and 39.
13. Rodrik 2011b; Eichengreen, Park, and Shin 2011; Sharma 2012.
14. Sharma 2012, p. 4. See also Ruchir Sharma, "How Emerging Markets Lost Their Mojo," *Wall Street Journal*, June 26, 2013.
15. Sinead Cruise and Chris Vellacott, "Emerging Markets Mania Was a Costly Mistake: Goldman Executive," Reuters, July 4, 2013, http://www.reuters.com/article/2013/07/04/goldman-emerging-investment-idUSL5N0F138620130704; Luciana Megalhanes, "China Only BRIC Country Worthy of the Title—O'Neill," *Wall Street Journal*, August 23, 2013; Jim O'Neill, "Who You Calling a BRIC?" Bloomberg, November 12, 2013, http://www.bloomberg.com/news/2013-11-12/who-you-calling-a-bric-.html.
16. Grimes 2009; Sohn 2013.
17. Ikenberry 2011; Mearsheimer 2010.
18. See Oatley 2011 and Drezner and McNamara 2013 for fuller critiques.
19. Strange 1987; Schwartz 2009.
20. Meunier 2013; Huang 2013.

21. Zakaria 2008; Mastanduno 2009.
22. See, for example, Wolfgang Münchau, "Optimism about an End to the Euro Crisis Is Wrong," *Financial Times*, October 27, 2013.
23. Nathaniel Popper, "Global Sell-Off Shows Fed Reach beyond the U.S." *New York Times,* June 21, 2013; Alex Frangos and Eric Bellman, "China Slump Ripples Globally," *Wall Street Journal*, July 15, 2013.
24. Drezner 2013b, pp. 73–77.
25. Patrick 2010.
26. Clive Crook, "Broken Systems Plus Bad Ideas Equals Lame Recovery," Bloomberg, July 10, 2013, http://www.bloomberg.com/news/2013-07-10/broken-systems-plus-bad-ideas-equals-lame-recovery.html; George Soros, "The World Economy's Shifting Challenges," Project Syndicate, January 2, 2014, http://www.project-syndicate.org/commentary/george-soros-maps-the-terrain-of-a-global-economy-that-is-increasingly-shaped-by-china.
27. Arvind Subramanian, "Too Much Legitimacy Can Hurt Global Trade," *Financial Times*, January 13, 2013.
28. Hale, Held, and Young 2013.
29. Drezner 1999.
30. Ahamed 2009, pp. 43–44.
31. MacMillan 2013.
32. Song and Yuan 2012, p. 112.
33. Sohn 2013; Patrick 2014.
34. This paragraph draws from Drezner 2013a. See also Patrick 2014.
35. Bhagwati 2004.
36. Freeland 2012.
37. Cowen 2011; Gordon 2012.
38. Oatley, Winecoff, Pennock, and Danzman 2013.
39. Beckley 2011/12, p. 78; Kagan 2012, p. 131.
40. Subramanian 2013, p. 4. For other examples of this genre, see Ian Bremmer and David F. Gordon, "Powers on the Mend," *New York Times,* April 10, 2013; Ely Ratner and Thomas Wright, "America's Not in Decline—It's on the Rise," *Washington Post*, October 18, 2013.
41. Daniel Yergin, "The Global Impact of US Shale," Project Syndicate, January 8, 2014, http://www.project-syndicate.org/commentary/daniel-yergin-traces-the-effects-of-america-s-shale-energy-revolution-on-the-balance-of-global-economic-and-political-power.
42. Song and Yuan 2012.
43. Johnston and Trebilcock 2013.
44. Willett 1999; Beeson and Bell 2009.
45. Reinhart and Rogoff 2009.

REFERENCES

Abdelal, Rawi, and Adam Segal. 2007. "Has Globalization Passed Its Peak?" *Foreign Affairs* 86, no. 1: 103–14.

Acharya, Amitav. 2011. "Can Asia Lead? Power Ambitions and Global Governance in the Twenty-first Century." *International Affairs* 87, no. 4: 851–69.

Ahamed, Liaquat 2009. *Lords of Finance: The Bankers Who Broke the World*. New York: Penguin.

Aït-Sahalia, Yacine, Jochen Andritzky, Andreas Jobst, Sylwia Nowak, and Natalia Tamirisa. 2012. "Market Response to Policy Initiatives during the Global Financial Crisis." *Journal of International Economics* 87, no. 5: 162–77.

Akram, Tanweer. 2012. "The Economics of Japan's Lost Decades." ING White Paper, December. http://www.inginvestment.com/idc/groups/commentary/ documents/investor_education/064554.pdf, accessed July 2013.

Alesina, Alberto. 2010. "Fiscal Adjustments: Lessons from Recent History." Paper presented at the EcoFin meeting, Madrid, Spain, April. http://scholar. harvard.edu/files/alesina/files/fiscaladjustments_lessons-1.pdf. Accessed July 2013.

Alesina, Alberto, and Silvia Ardagna. 2009. "Large Changes in Fiscal Policy: Taxes Versus Spending," National Bureau of Economic Research (NBER) Working Paper No. 15438, Cambridge, MA, October.

Alexandroff, Alan, ed. 2008. *Can the World Be Governed? Possibilities for Effective Multilateralism*. Waterloo, ON: Wilfred Laurier University Press.

Alexandroff, Alan, and Andrew Cooper, eds. 2010. *Rising States, Rising Institutions: Challenges for Global Governance*. Washington, DC: Brookings Institution Press.

Altman, Roger C. 2009. "The Great Crash, 2008: A Geopolitical Setback for the West." *Foreign Affairs* 88, no. 1: 2–14.

Altman, Roger C., and Richard Haass. 2010. "American Profligacy and American Power." *Foreign Affairs* 89, no. 6: 25–34.

Andrews, David, ed. 2005. *International Monetary Power*. Ithaca, NY: Cornell University Press.

A. T. Kearney. 2013. "Back to Business: Optimism Amid Uncertainty." Report. A. T. Kearny online. "Ideas and Insights." June. http://www.atkearney.com/research-studies/foreign-direct-investment-confidence-index/full-report/-/asset_publisher/PHesJ9DLURrR/content/back-to-business-optimism-amid-uncertainty/10192. Accessed July 3, 2013.

Auer, Michael, and Georg von Pfoesti. 2012. *Basel III Handbook*. Washington, DC: Accenture.

Axelrod, Robert, and Robert Keohane. 1985. "Achieving Cooperation under Anarchy: Strategies and Institutions." *World Politics* 38, no. 1: 226–54.

Babb, Sarah. 2013. "The Washington Consensus as Transnational Policy Paradigm: Its Origins, Trajectory and Likely Successor." *Review of International Political Economy* 20, no. 2: 268–97.

Baccini, Leonardo, and Soo Yeon Kim. 2012. "Preventing Protectionism: International Institutions and Trade Policy." *Review of International Organizations* 7, no. 4: 369–98.

Bach, David, and Abraham Newman. 2007. "The European Regulatory State and Global Public Policy: Micro-Institutions, Macro-Influence." *Journal of European Public Policy* 14, no. 4: 827–46.

Bachrach, Peter, and Morton S. Baratz. 1962. "Two Faces of Power." *American Political Science Review* 56, no. 4: 947–52.

Bagnall, Allie, and Edwin Truman. 2013. "Progress on Sovereign Wealth Fund Transparency and Accountability: An Updated SWF Scorecard." Peterson Institute for International Economics Policy Brief PB13-19, Washington, DC, September.

Bain and Company. 2012. "A World Awash in Money: Capital Trends through 2020." http://www.bain.com/Images/BAIN_REPORT_A_world_awash_in_money.pdf. Accessed September 15, 2013.

Bair, Sheila. 2012. *Bull by the Horns*. New York: Free Press.

Baker, Andrew. 2010. "Restraining Regulatory Capture? Anglo-America, Crisis Politics and Trajectories of Change in Global Financial Governance." *International Affairs* 86, no. 3: 647–63.

———. 2013a. "The New Political Economy of the Macroprudential Ideational Shift." *New Political Economy* 18, no. 1: 112–39.

———. 2013b. "The Gradual Transformation? The Incremental Dynamics of Macroprudential Regulation." *Regulation & Governance* 7, no. 4: 417–34.

Baker, Scott R., Nicholas Bloom, and Steven J. Davis. 2013. "Measuring Economic Policy Uncertainty." Unpublished manuscript, Stanford University, April.

Baldwin, David A. 1979. "Power Analysis and World Politics: New Trends versus Old Tendencies." *World Politics* 31, no. 2: 161–94.

———. 1989. *Paradoxes of Power*. London: Basil Blackwell.

Baldwin, Richard, and Barry Eichengreen, eds. 2008. "Rescuing Our Jobs and Savings: What G7/8 Leaders Can Do to Solve the Global Credit Crisis." VoxEU.org. October. http://www.voxeu.org/pages/rescuing-our-jobs-and-savings-what-g78-leaders-can-do-solve-global-credit-crisis. Accessed July 2013.

Bank of International Settlements. 2012. "82nd BIS Annual Report 2011/2012." BIS online. June 24. http://www.bis.org/publ/arpdf/ar2012e.htm. Accessed July 3, 2012.

———. 2013. 83rd BIS Annual Report 2012/2013. June 24. BIS online.http://www.bis.org/publ/arpdf/ar2013e1.pdf. Accessed July 3, 2013.

Barma, Naazneen, Ely Ratner, and Steven Weber. 2007. "A World without the West." *National Interest*, no. 90: 23–35.

———. 2013. "The Mythical Liberal Order." *National Interest*, no. 124: 56–68.

Barnett, Michael, and Raymond Duvall. 2005. "Power in International Politics." *International Organization* 59, no. 1: 39–75.

Barnett, Michael, and Martha Finnemore. 2004. *Rules for the World*. Ithaca, NY: Cornell University Press.

Basel Committee on Banking Supervision. 2009a. *Enhancements to the Basel II Framework*. Bank of International Settlements. Basel: Switzerland. July. http://www.bis.org/publ/bcbs157.pdf. Accessed July 2013.

———. 2009b. *Strengthening the Resilience of the Banking Sector*. December. http://www.bis.org/publ/bcbs164.pdf. Accessed July 2013.

———. 2011. *Assessment of the Macroeconomic Impact of Higher Loss Absorbency for Global Systemically Important Banks*. October 10. http://www.bis.org/publ/bcbs202.pdf. Accessed July 2013.

———. 2013. *Results of the Basel III Monitoring Exercise as of 30 June 2012*. March. http://www.bis.org/publ/bcbs243.pdf. Accessed July 2013.

Beattie, Alan. 2012. *Who's in Charge Here?* New York: Penguin.

Beckley, Michael. 2011/12. "China's Century? Why America's Edge Will Endure." *International Security* 36, no. 1: 41–78.

Beeson, Mark. 2013. "Can China Lead?" *Third World Quarterly* 34, no. 2: 233–50.

Beeson, Mark, and Stephen Bell. 2009. "The G-20 and International Economic Governance: Hegemony, Collectivism, or Both?" *Global Governance* 15, no. 1: 67–86.

Bergheim, Stefan. 2005. "Global Growth Centres 2020." Deutsche Bank Research Current Issues, March.

Bernanke, Benjamin. 2005. "The Global Saving Glut and the U.S. Current Account Deficit." Sandridge Lecture, Virginia Association of Economists, Richmond, VA, March 10.

Bhagwati, Jagdish. 1988. *Protectionism*. Cambridge, MA: MIT Press.

———. 2004. *In Defense of Globalization*. New York: Oxford University Press.

Blinder, Alan. 2013. *After the Music Stopped*. New York: Penguin.

Blinder, Alan, and Mark Zandi. 2010. *How the Great Recession Was Brought to an End*. New York: Moody's Analytics.

Blundell-Wignall, Adrian, and Paul Atkinson. 2010. "Thinking Beyond Basel III: Necessary Solutions for Capital and Liquidity," *OECD Journal: Financial Market Trends* 1 (2010).

Blyth, Mark. 2002. *Great Transformations: Economic Ideas and Institutional Change in the Twentieth Century*. New York: Cambridge University Press.

———. 2013. *Austerity: The History of a Dangerous Idea*. New York: Oxford University Press.

Bolt, J., and J. L. van Zanden. 2013. "The First Update of the Maddison Project; Re-Estimating Growth Before 1820." Maddison Project Working Paper 4, http://www.ggdc.net/maddison/maddison-project/data.htm.

Bolton, John. 2007. *Surrender Is Not an Option*. New York: Threshold Editions.

Bowman, Karlyn, and Andrew Rugg. 2010. "TARP, the Auto Bailout, and the Stimulus: Attitudes about the Economic Crisis." *AEI Public Opinion Studies*. May.

Bown, Chad. 2010. "Antidumping, Safeguards, and Protectionism during the Crisis: Two New Insights from 4th Quarter 2009." VoxEU.org, February 18. http://www.voxeu.org/index.php?q=node/4635. Accessed July 3, 2012.

———. 2012. "Import Protection Update: Antidumping, Safeguards, and Temporary Trade Barriers through 2011." VoxEU.org, August 18. http://voxeu.org/article/import-protection-update-antidumping-safeguards-and-temporary-trade-barriers-through-2011. Accessed August 10, 2012.

Bown, Chad, and Meredith Crowley. 2013. "Import Protection, Business Cycles, and Exchange Rates: Evidence from the Great Recession." *Journal of International Economics* 90, no. 1: 50–64.

Bracke, Thierry, and Irina Bunda. 2011. "Exchange Rate Anchoring: Is There Still a De Facto US Dollar Standard?" European Central Bank Working Paper Series No. 1353. Frankfurt, Germany. June.

Brandt, Loren, and Zhu Xiaodong. 2010. "Accounting for China's Growth." IZA Discussion Paper No. 4764, Bonn, Germany. February.

Bremmer, Ian. 2009. *The End of the Free Market: Who Wins the War between States and Corporations?* New York: Portfolio.

———. 2012. *Every Nation for Itself: Winners and Losers in a G-Zero World*. New York: Portfolio.

Bremmer, Ian, and Nouriel Roubini. 2011. "A G-Zero World." *Foreign Affairs* 90, no. 2: 2–7.

Breslin, Shaun. 2013. "China and the Global Order: Signalling Threat or Friendship?" *International Affairs* 89, no. 3: 615–34.

Briand, Remy, Jennifer Bender, Juliana Bambaci, William Mok, and Raman Aylur Subramanian. 2012. Global Equity Allocation. MSCI Research. April.

Brooks, Stephen, and William C. Wohlforth. 2008. *World Out of Balance*. Princeton, NJ: Princeton University Press.

Brooks, Stephen, G. John Ikenberry, and William C. Wohlforth. 2012/13. "Don't Come Home, America: The Case against Retrenchment." *International Security* 37, no. 3: 7–51.

Brown, Meta, Andrew Haughwout, Donghoon Lee, and Wilbert van der Klaauw. 2013. "The Financial Crisis at the Kitchen Table: Trends in Household Debt and Credit." *Current Issues in Economics and Finance* 19, no. 2: 1–9.

Broz, J. Lawrence. 2010. "Exchange Rates and Protectionism." Unpublished manuscript, University of California, San Diego.

Brubaker, Rogers. 2011. "Economic Crisis, Nationalism, and Politicized Ethnicity." In Craig Calhoun and Georgi Derlugian, eds., *The Deepening Crisis: Governance Challenges after Neoliberalism*, 93–108. New York: New York University Press.

Buiter, Willem H., and Ebrahim Rahbari. 2011. "Global Growth Generators; Moving beyond 'Emerging Markets' and 'BRIC.'" http://www.cepr.org/sites/default/files/policy_insights/PolicyInsight55.pdf, Citi Global Economics. February.

Butler, Creon. 2012. "The G-20 Framework for Strong, Sustainable, and Balanced Growth: Glass Half Empty or Half Full?" *Oxford Review of Economic Policy* 28, no. 3: 469–92.

Burgin, Angus. 2012. *The Great Persuasion: Reinventing Free Markets since the Great Depression*. Cambridge, MA: Harvard University Press.

Burrows, Mathew, and Jennifer Harris. 2009. "Revisiting the Future: Geopolitical Effects of the Financial Crisis." *Washington Quarterly* 32, no. 2: 27–38.

Bussière, Matthieu, Emilia Pérez-Barreiro, Roland Straub, and Daria Taglioni. 2011. "Protectionist Responses to the Crisis: Global Trends and Implications." *World Economy* 34, no. 5: 826–52.

Callen, Tim. 2007. "PPP versus the Market: Which Weight Matters?" *Finance and Development* 44, no. 1.

Cammack, Paul. 2012. "The G20, the Crisis, and the Rise of Global Developmental Liberalism." *Third World Quarterly* 33, no. 1: 1–16.

Cao, Xun. 2012. "Global Networks and Domestic Policy Convergence: A Network Explanation of Policy Changes." *World Politics* 64, no. 3: 375–425.

Carvalho, Carlos, Stefano Eusepi, and Christian Grisse. 2012. "Policy Initiatives in the Global Recession: What Did Forecasters Expect?" *Current Issues in Economics and Finance* 18, no. 1: 1–11.

Chalk, Peter. 2012. "Assessing the Utility of Current Counterpiracy Initiatives Off the Horn of Africa." *Studies in Conflict and Terrorism* 35, no. 7–8: 553–61.

Chanley, Virginia, Thomas Rudolph, and Wendy Rahm. 2000. "The Origins and Consequences of Public Trust in Government: A Time-Series Analysis." *Public Opinion Quarterly* 64, no. 3: 239–56.

Chinn, Menzie, and Jeffrey Frankel. 2007. "Will the Euro Eventually Surpass the Dollar as Leading International Reserve Currency?" In Richard Clarida, ed., *G7 Current Account Imbalances: Sustainability and Adjustment*, 283–337. Chicago: University of Chicago Press.

Chinn, Menzie, and Jeffry Frieden. 2011. *Lost Decades: The Making of America's Debt Crisis and the Long Recovery*. New York: W. W. Norton.

Chwieroth, Jeffrey M. 2009. *Capital Ideas: The IMF and the Rise of Financial Liberalization*. Princeton, NJ: Princeton University Press.

Claessens, Stijn, M. Ayhan Kose, and Marco Terrones. 2011. "Financial Cycles: What? How? When?" IMF Working Paper WP/11/76. Washington, DC. April.

Coenen, Günter, Christopher Erceg, Charles Freedman, Davide Furceri, Michael Kumhof, René Lalonde, Douglas Laxton, Jesper Lindé, Annabelle Mourougane, Dirk Muir, Susanna Mursula, Carlos de Resende, John Roberts, Werner Roeger, Stephen Snudden, Mathias Trabandt, and Jan in't Veld. 2010. "Effects of Fiscal Stimulus in Structural Models." IMF Working Paper WP/10/73. Washington, DC. March.

Cohen, Benjamin J. 2008. "The International Monetary System: Diffusion and Ambiguity." *International Affairs* 84, no. 3: 455–70.

Cohen, Benjamin J., and Tabitha M. Benney. 2014. "What Does the International Currency System Really Look Like?" *Review of International Political Economy*: forthcoming.

Cohen, Stephen, and J. Bradford DeLong. 2009. *The End of Influence*. New York: Basic Books.

Cohen, Benjamin H. 2013. "How Have Banks Adjusted to Higher Capital Requirements?" *BIS Quarterly Review* (September 15): 25–41.

Cole, Christopher. 2012. "Volatility of an Impossible Object: Risk, Fear and Safety in Games of Perception." Artemis Capital Management letter to investors, September 30. Santa Monica, CA. http://www.artemiscm.com/wp-content/uploads/2012/10/ArtemisVegaQ32012_Volatility_of_an_Impossible-Object.pdf.

Congressional Budget Office. 2013. "Updated Budget Projections: Fiscal Years 2013 to 2023." http://www.cbo.gov/sites/default/files/cbofiles/attachments/44172-Baseline2.pdf, May 14, 2013.

Cooper, Andrew. 2010. "The G20 as an Improvised Crisis Committee and/or a Contested 'Steering Committee' for the World." *International Affairs* 86, no. 3: 741–57.

Corsetti, Giancarlo, and Gernot J. Müller. 2011. "Multilateral Economic Cooperation and the International Transmission of Fiscal Policy." National Bureau of Economic Research Working Paper No. 17708. December.

Cortell, Andrew P., and James W. Davis Jr. 1996. "How Do International Institutions Matter? The Domestic Impact of International Rules and Norms." *International Studies Quarterly* 40, no. 4: 451–78.

Cowen, Tyler. 2011. *The Great Stagnation*. New York: Dutton.

Cox, Robert. 1979. "Ideologies and the New International Economic Order: Reflections on Some Recent Literature." *International Organization* 33, no. 2: 257–302.

Crotty, James. 2009. "Structural Causes of the Global Financial
Crisis: A Critical Assessment of the 'New Financial Architecture.'"
Cambridge Journal of Economics 33, no. 4: 563–80.

Crouch, Colin. 2011. *The Strange Non-Death of Neoliberalism.* Cambridge,
UK: Polity Press.

Culpepper, Pepper. 2010. *Quiet Politics and Business Power: Corporate Control in
Europe and Japan.* Cambridge: Cambridge University Press.

Dadush, Uri, Shimelse Ali, and Rachel Esplin Odell. 2011. "Is Protectionism
Dying?" Carnegie Papers in International Economics, May 26. http://
carnegieendowment.org/files/is_protectionism_dying.pdf. Accessed June
20, 2012.

Dadush, Uri, and Vera Eidelman, eds. 2011. *Currency Wars.* Washington,
DC: Carnegie Endowment for International Peace.

Dadush, Uri, and Bennett Stancil. 2010. "The World Order in 2050." Carnegie
Policy Outlook. http://carnegieendowment.org/files/World_Order_in_2050.
pdf. Accessed July 2013.

Dahl, Robert A. 1957. "The Concept of Power." *Behavioral Science* 2, no.
3: 201–15.

Darling, Alistair. 2011. *Back from the Brink: 1000 Days at Number 11.*
London: Atlantic Books.

Das, Dilip K. 2009. "Sovereign Wealth Funds: The Institutional Dimension."
International Review of Economics 56, no. 1: 85–104.

Davies, James, Susanna Sandström, Anthony Shorrocks, and Edward Wolff.
2011. "The Level and Distribution of Global Household Wealth." *Economic
Journal* 121, no. 551: 223–54.

Davies, Michael, and Tim Ng. 2011. "The Rise of Sovereign Credit
Risk: Implications for Financial Stability." *BIS Quarterly Review*,
September: 59–70.

Davis, Christina, and Krzysztof Pelc. 2013. "Cooperation in Hard
Times: Self-Restraint of Trade Protection." Paper presented at the American
Political Science Association annual meeting, Chicago, IL, August.

De Grauwe, Paul, and Yuemei Li. 2013. "Panic-Driven Austerity in the
Eurozone and Its Implications." VoxEU.org, February 21. http://www.voxeu.
org/article/panic-driven-austerity-eurozone-and-its-implications. Accessed
July 2013.

Deibert, Ronald J. 2013. *Black Code: Inside the Battle for Cyberspace.*
Toronto: Signal.

Development Research Center of the State Council, and the World Bank.
2013. *China 2030: Building a Modern, Harmonious, and Creative Society.*
Washington, DC: World Bank Publications.

Dobbs, Richard, Susan Lund, Charles Roxburgh, James Manyika, Alex Kim,
Andreas Schreiner, Riccardo Boin, Rohit Chopra, Sebastian Jauch, Hyun
Kim, Megan McDonald, and John Piotrowski 2010. *Farewell to Cheap*

Capital? The Implications of Long-term Shifts in Global Investment and Saving. Washington, DC: McKinsey Global Institute.

Dominguez, Kathryn. 2006. "The European Central Bank, the Euro, and Global Financial Markets." *Journal of Economic Perspectives* 20, no. 4: 67–88.

Downs, George, David Rocke, and Peter Barsoom. 1996. "Is the Good News about Compliance Good News about Cooperation?" *International Organization* 50, no. 3: 379–406.

Doyle, Peter. 2012. Resignation letter to the IMF Executive Board, June 18. http://cnnibusiness.files.wordpress.com/2012/07/doyle.pdf. Accessed July 12, 2012.

Dreher, Axel. 2006. "Does Globalization Affect Growth? Evidence from a New Index of Globalization." *Applied Economics* 38, no. 10: 1091–110.

Dreher, Axel, Noel Gaston, and Pim Martens. 2008. *Measuring Globalisation: Gauging Its Consequences.* London: Springer.

Drezner, Daniel W. 1999. *The Sanctions Paradox: Economic Statecraft and International Relations.* Cambridge: Cambridge University Press.

——, ed. 2003. *Locating the Proper Authorities.* Ann Arbor: Michigan University Press.

——. 2006. *U.S. Trade Strategy: Free Versus Fair.* New York: Council on Foreign Relations Press.

——. 2007a. "The New New World Order." *Foreign Affairs* 86, no. 2: 34–46.

——. 2007b. *All Politics Is Global: Explaining International Regulatory Regimes.* Princeton, NJ: Princeton University Press.

——. 2009. "Bad Debts: Assessing China's Financial Influence in Great Power Politics." *International Security* 34, no. 1: 7–45.

——. 2010. "Will Currency Follow the Flag?" *International Relations of the Asia-Pacific* 10, no. 3: 389–414.

——. 2013a. "The Tragedy of the Global Institutional Commons." In Martha Finnemore and Judith Goldstein, eds., *Back to Basics: State Power in a Contemporary World.* New York: Oxford University Press.

——. 2013b. "Military Primacy Doesn't Pay (Nearly as Much as You Think)." *International Security* 38, no. 1: 52–79.

Drezner, Daniel W., and Kathleen R. McNamara. 2013. "International Political Economy, Global Financial Orders and the 2008 Financial Crisis." *Perspectives on Politics* 11, no. 1: 155–66.

Eberstadt, Nicholas. 2012. "Japan Shrinks." *Wilson Quarterly*: 30–37.

Economy, Elizabeth. 2010. *The River Runs Black: The Environmental Challenge to China's Future.* Ithaca, NY: Cornell University Press.

Edwards, Martin, and Stephanie Senger. 2014. "Listening to Advice: Assessing the External Impact of IMF Article IV Consultations of the United States, 2010–2011." *International Studies Perspectives*: forthcoming.

Eichengreen, Barry. 1989. "Hegemonic Stability Theories of the International Monetary System." NBER Working Paper No. 2193. Cambridge, MA. September.

———. 2008. *Globalizing Capital: A History of the International Monetary System*. 2nd ed. Princeton, NJ: Princeton University Press.

———. 2009. "The Last Temptation of Risk." *National Interest*, no. 30: 8–14.

———. 2011a. "Mr. Bernanke Goes to War," *National Interest*, no. 111: 6–14.

———. 2011b. *Exorbitant Privilege: The Rise and Fall of the Dollar and the Future of the International Monetary System*. New York: Oxford University Press.

———. 2011c. "Crisis and Growth in the Advanced Economies: What We Know, What We Don't Know, and What We Can Learn from the 1930s." *Comparative Economic Studies* 53, no. 3: 383–406.

———. 2013a. "Currency War or International Policy Coordination?" Unpublished manuscript, University of California, Berkeley, January.

———. 2013b. "Number One Currency, Number One Country?" *World Economy* 36, no. 4: 363–74.

Eichengreen, Barry, and Kevin O'Rourke. 2010. "A Tale of Two Depressions," VoxEU.org, March 8. http://www.voxeu.org/index.php?q=node/3421. Accessed July 3, 2012.

———. 2012. "A Tale of Two Depressions Redux," VoxEU.org, March 6. http://www.voxeu.org/article/tale-two-depressions-redux. Accessed August 2, 2012.

Eichengreen, Barry, Donghyun Park, and Kwanho Shin. 2011. "When Fast Growing Economies Slow Down: International Evidence and Implications for China." NBER Working Paper No. 16919, Cambridge, MA. March.

Elliott, Douglas. 2010. "Basel III, the Banks, and the Economy." Unpublished manuscript. Brookings Institution, Washington, DC.

Erixon, Fredrik, and Razeen Sally. 2010. "Trade, Globalization and Emerging Protectionism Since the Crisis." ECIPE Working Paper no. 02/2010. Brussels.

Eurasia Group. 2011. China's Great Rebalancing Act. August.

European Banking Authority. 2013. Basel III monitoring exercise. March. http://www.eba.europa.eu/documents/10180/16145/ISG-Basel-III-monitoring-exercise---Public-Report--Final-.pdf/032c18a8-979f-4 3b7-96ed-2d279b93c5a2. Accessed July 2013.

European Central Bank. 2013. "Is There a Risk of a Creeping Rise in Trade Protectionism?" *ECB Monthly Bulletin* (July): 87–97.

Evenett, Simon. 2013. "Protectionism's Quiet Return: The GTA's Pre-G8 Summit Report." VoxEU.org, June 13. http://www.voxeu.org/article/protectionism-s-quiet-return-gta-s-pre-g8-summit-report. Accessed June 15, 2013.

Farrell, Henry, and Abraham Newman. 2010. "Making Global Markets: Historical Institutionalism in International Political Economy." *Review of International Political Economy* 17, no. 4: 609–38.

Farrell, Henry, and John Quiggin. 2013. "Consensus, Dissensus and Economic Ideas: The Rise and Fall of Keynesianism During the Economic Crisis." Unpublished manuscript, George Washington University.

Feis, Herbert. 1966. *1933: Characters in Crisis*. Boston: Little Brown and Company.

Ferchen, Matt. 2013. "Whose China Model Is It Anyway? The Contentious Search for Consensus." *Review of International Political Economy* 20, no. 2: 390–420.

Ferguson, Niall. 2004. "A World without Power." *Foreign Policy*, no. 143: 32–39.

———. 2010. "Complexity and Collapse." *Foreign Affairs* 89, no. 2: 18–32.

Financial Stability Forum. 2008. "Report of the Financial Stability Forum on Enhancing Market and Institutional Resilience." April 7. http://www. financialstabilityboard.org/publications/r_0804.pdf. Accessed July 2013.

Finnemore, Martha, and Kathryn Sikkink. 1998. "International Norm Dynamics and Political Change." *International Organization* 52, no. 4: 887–917.

Flandreau, Marc, Jacques Le Cacheux, Frédéric Zumer, Rudi Dornbusch, and Patrick Honohan. 1998. "Stability without a Pact? Lessons from the European Gold Standard, 1880-1914." *Economic Policy* 13, no. 26: 115–62.

Fogel, Robert. 2010. "123,000,000,000,000.*" *Foreign Policy* no. 177: 70–75.

Foot, Rosemary, and Andrew Walter. 2011. *China, the United States, and Global Order.* Cambridge: Cambridge University Press.

Forster, John. 2006. "Global Sports Organisations and Their Governance." *Corporate Governance* 6, no. 1: 72–83.

Fourcade, Marion. 2006. "The Construction of a Global Profession: The Transnationalization of Economics." *American Journal of Sociology* 112, no. 1: 145–94.

Fox, Justin. 2009. *The Myth of the Rational Market.* New York: HarperCollins.

Freeland, Chrystia. 2012. *Plutocrats.* New York: Penguin.

Frieden, Jeffry. 2006. *Global Capitalism.* New York: W. W. Norton.

Frieden, Jeffry, Michael Pettis, Dani Rodrik, and Ernesto Zedillo. 2012. *After the Fall: The Future of Global Cooperation.* Geneva: International Center for Monetary and Banking Studies.

Friedman, Thomas, and Michael Mandelbaum. 2011. *That Used to Be Us: How America Fell Behind in the World It Invented and How We Can Come Back.* New York: Farrar, Straus and Giroux.

Fukuyama, Francis. 1992. *The End of History and the Last Man.* New York: Free Press.

G20 Information Centre. 2012. *2012 Los Cabos G20 Summit Final Compliance Report.* September 4. http://www.g20.utoronto.ca/ compliance/2012loscabos-final/index.html. Accessed October 3, 2013.

Gagnon, Joseph E. 2012. "Combating Widespread Currency Manipulation." Peterson Institute for International Economics Policy Brief PB12-19, July. http://www.iie.com/publications/pb/pb12-19.pdf.

———. 2013. "The Elephant Hiding in the Room: Currency Intervention and Trade Imbalances." Peterson Institute for International Economics working paper WP 13-2, http://www.iie.com/publications/wp/wp13-2.pdf. March.

Galbraith, John Kenneth. 1993. *A Short History of Financial Euphoria.* New York: Viking.

Gallagher, Kevin. 2014. *Countervailing Monetary Power: Emerging Markets, New Ideas, and the Re-regulation of Cross-border Finance.* Ithaca, NY: Cornell University Press.

Gamberoni, Elisa, and Richard Newfarmer. 2009. "Trade Protection: Incipient but Worrisome Trends," World Bank Trade Note #37, Washington, DC, March 2.

Garrett, Geoffrey. 2010. "G2 in G20: China, the United States, and the World after the Global Financial Crisis." *Global Policy* 1, no. 1: 29–39.

Gat, Azar. 2007. "The Return of the Authoritarian Great Powers." *Foreign Affairs* 86, no. 4: 59–69.

Gawande, Kishore, Bernard Hoekman, and Yue Cui. 2011. "Determinants of Trade Policy Responses to the 2008 Financial Crisis." World Bank Policy Research Working Paper No. 5862. October.

Geithner, Timothy. 2010. "Statement on the Report to Congress on International Economic and Exchange Rate Policies." April 3. http://www.ustreas.gov/press/releases/tg627.htm./. Accessed July 12, 2012.

Gelb, Leslie. 2009. *Power Rules*. New York: HarperCollins.

——. "GDP Now Matters More Than Force." *Foreign Affairs* 89, no. 6: 35–43

Gilpin, Robert. 1975. *US Power and the Multinational Corporation: The Political Economy of Foreign Direct Investment*. New York: Basic Books.

——. 1981. *War and Change in World Politics*. New York: Cambridge University Press.

Goldberg, Linda. 2010. "Is the International Role of the Dollar Changing?" *Current Issues in Economics and Finance* 16, no. 1: 1–7.

Goldsmith, Jack, and Eric Posner. 2005. *The Limits of International Law*. New York: Oxford University Press.

Goldstein, Joshua S. 2011. *Winning the War on War: The Decline of Armed Conflict Worldwide*. New York: Penguin.

Goldstein, Judith. 1996. "International Law and Domestic Institutions." *International Organization* 50, no. 4: 541–64.

Goldstein, Judith, and Robert Keohane, eds. 1993. *Ideas and Foreign Policy: Beliefs, Institutions, and Political Change*. Ithaca, NY: Cornell University Press.

Goldstein, Judith, and Lisa L. Martin. 2000. "Legalization, Trade Liberalization, and Domestic Politics: A Cautionary Note." *International Organization* 54, no. 3: 603–32.

Gordon, Robert J. 2012. "Is U.S. Economic Growth Over? Faltering Innovation Confronts the Six Headwinds." National Bureau of Economic Research working paper no. 18315. Cambridge, MA. August.

Gordon, Roger, and Gordon B. Dahl. 2013. "Views among Economists: Professional Consensus or Point-Counterpoint?" *American Economic Review* 103, no. 3: 629–35.

Gourevitch, Peter. 1986. *Politics in Hard Times: Comparative Responses to International Economic Crises*. Ithaca, NY: Cornell University Press.

Gowa, Joanne. 1984. *Closing the Gold Window: Domestic Politics and the End of Bretton Woods*. Ithaca, NY: Cornell University Press.

Gray, Julia, and Philip B. K. Potter. 2012. "Trade and Volatility at the Core and Periphery of the Global Economy." *International Studies Quarterly* 56, no. 4: 793–800.

Greenspan, Alan. 2007. *The Age of Turbulence*. New York: Penguin, 2007.

Grewal, David. 2008. *Network Power: The Social Dynamics of Globalization*. New Haven, CT: Yale University Press.

Grimes, William. 2009. *Currency and Contest in East Asia: The Great Power Politics of Financial Regionalism*. Ithaca, NY: Cornell University Press.

Grindle, Merilee S. 2004. "Good Enough Governance: Poverty Reduction and Reform in Developing Countries." *Governance* 17, no. 4: 525–48.

Gutner, Tamar, and Alexander Thompson. 2010. "The Politics of IO Performance: A Framework." *Review of International Organizations* 5, no. 3: 227–48.

Haas, Peter. 1992. "Banning Chlorofluorocarbons: Epistemic Community Efforts to Protect Stratospheric Ozone." *International Organization* 46, no. 1: 187–224.

Haass, Richard. 2008. "The Age of Nonpolarity." *Foreign Affairs* 87, no. 3: 44–56.

———. 2013. *Foreign Policy Begins at Home*. New York: Basic Books.

Haddow, Abigail, Chris Hare, John Hooley, and Tamarah Shakir. 2013. "Macroeconomic Uncertainty." *Bank of England Quarterly Bulletin*, no. 2: 100–109.

Hale, Thomas, David Held, and Kevin Young. 2013. *Gridlock: Why Global Cooperation Is Failing When We Need It Most*. London: Polity.

Hall, Peter. 1989. *The Political Power of Economic Ideas*. Princeton, NJ: Princeton University Press.

———. 1993. "Policy Paradigms, Social Learning, and the State: The Case of Economic Policymaking in Britain." *Comparative Politics* 25, no. 3: 275–96.

Halper, Stefan. 2010. *The Beijing Consensus*. New York: Basic Books.

Hathaway, Oona A. 1998. "Positive Feedback: The Impact of Trade Liberalization on Industry Demands for Protection." *International Organization* 52, no. 3: 575–612.

He, Ling-Ling, and Razeen Sappideen. 2009. "Reflections on China's WTO Accession Commitments and Their Observance." *Journal of World Trade* 43, no. 4: 847–71.

Helleiner, Eric, and Jonathan Kirshner, eds. 2009. *The Future of the Dollar*. Ithaca, NY: Cornell University Press.

Helleiner, Eric. 2010. "What Role for the New Financial Stability Board? The Politics of International Standards after the Crisis." *Global Policy* 1, no. 3: 282–90.

Helleiner, Eric, and Tony Porter. 2009. "Making Transnational Networks More Accountable." *Friedrich Ebert Foundation, Re-Defining the Global Economy: Dialogue on Globalization*. Occasional Papers 42: 14–24.

Henn, Christian, and Brad McDonald. 2011. "Protectionist Responses to the Crisis: Damage Observed in Product-Level Trade." IMF Working Paper WP/11/139. June.

Herndon, Thomas, Michael Ash, and Robert Pollin. 2013. "Does High Public Debt Consistently Stifle Economic Growth? A Critique of Reinhart and

Rogoff." *Political Economy Research Institute Working Paper No. 322.* University of Massachusetts Amherst. April.

Hills, Bob, and Glenn Hoggarth. 2013. "Cross-Border Bank Credit and Global Financial Stability." *Bank of England Quarterly Bulletin* (Q2): 126–36.

Hirschman, Albert. 1945. *National Power and the Structure of Foreign Trade.* Berkeley: University of California Press.

———. 1970. *Exit, Voice and Loyalty.* Cambridge, MA: Harvard University Press.

Hoffman, Michael. 2012. "The Political Economy of TARP: A Public Opinion Approach." Available at SSRN: http://ssrn.com/abstract=1998384.

Hoekman, Bernard. 2012. "Trade Policy: So Far So Good?" *Finance and Development* 49, no. 2: 17–19.

Hood, Michael. 2012. "The Volatility Conundrum." J. P. Morgan Institutional Market View. September 30.

Huang, Chin-Hao. 2013. "China's Soft Power in East Asia: A Quest for Status and Influence?" National Bureau of Asian Research Special Report No. 42. January.

Hufbauer, Gary Clyde, and Jared C. Woollacott. 2012. "Trade Disputes between China and the United States: Growing Pains So Far, Worse Ahead?" *European Yearbook of International Economic Law* 3, no. 1: 31–88.

Human Security Report Project. 2010. *Human Security Report 2009/2010: The Causes of Peace and the Shrinking Costs of War.* New York: Oxford University Press.

Hurd, Ian. 1999. "Legitimacy and Authority in International Politics." *International Organization* 53, no. 2: 379–408.

ICC International Maritime Bureau. 2013. "Piracy and Armed Robbery against Ships." London: October 17.

Ikenberry, G. John. 2000. *After Victory.* Princeton, NJ: Princeton University Press.

———. 2011. *Liberal Leviathan.* Princeton, NJ: Princeton University Press.

Independent Evaluation Office, IMF. 2011. IMF Performance in the Run-Up to the Financial and Economic Crisis. Washington, DC: IMF.

Inglehart, Ronald. 1997. *Modernization and Postmodernization: Cultural, Economic, and Political Change in 43 Societies.* Princeton, NJ: Princeton University Press.

Institute for Economics and Peace. 2012. Global Peace Index 2012. June.

———. 2013. Global Peace Index 2013. June.

Institute for International Finance. 2010. *Interim Report on the Cumulative Effect on the Global Economy of Proposed Changes to the Banking Regulatory Framework.* Washington, DC. June.

International Federation of the Red Cross and Red Crescent Societies. 2013. "Think Differently: Humanitarian Impacts of the Economic Crisis in Europe." IFRC economic crisis report. Geneva. Available at Ifrc.org., http://www.ifrc.org/PageFiles/134339/1260300-Economic%20crisis%20Report_EN_LR.pdf. Accessed October 30, 2013.

International Labour Organization. 2010. *Global Employment Trends: January 2010*. Geneva: International Labor Organization publications. January.

International Monetary Fund. 2009. *Global Financial Stability Report April 2009: Responding to the Financial Crisis and Measuring Systemic Risks*. World Economic and Financial Surveys. Washington, DC: IMF.

———. 2010. *World Economic Outlook: Recovery, Risk and Rebalancing*. Washington, DC.

———. 2012a. *Global Financial Stability Report: the Quest for Lasting Stability* April 2012.

———. 2012b. "The Liberalization and Management of Capital Flows: An Institutional View." November 14. http://www.imf.org/external/np/pp/eng/2012/111412.pdf. Accessed June 10, 2013.

———. 2012c. "People's Republic of China: Article IV Consultation." IMF Country Report No. 12/195, July. http://www.imf.org/external/pubs/ft/scr/2012/cr12195.pdf.

Ip, Greg. 2013. "Special Report: The Gated Globe." *Economist*, October 12.

Irwin, Neil. 2013. *The Alchemists: Three Central Bankers and a World on Fire*. New York: Penguin.

Islam, Iyanatul, and Anis Chowdhury. 2012. "Revisiting the Evidence on Expansionary Fiscal Austerity: Alesina's Hour?" VoxEU.org., February 28, http://www.voxeu.org/debates/commentaries/revisiting-evidence-expansionary-fiscal-austerity-alesina-s-hour. Accessed July 2013.

Jacobsen, John Kurt. 1995. "Much Ado about Ideas: The Cognitive Factor in Economic Policy." *World Politics* 47, no. 2: 283–310.

Jacques, Martin. 2009. *When China Rules the World: The End of the Western World and the Birth of a New Global Order*. New York: Penguin.

James, Harold. 2001. *The End of Globalization: Lessons from the Great Depression*. Cambridge, MA: Harvard University Press.

———. 2014. "Cosmos, Chaos: Finance, Power and Conflict." *International Affairs* 90, no. 1: 37–57.

Jentleson, Bruce. 2012. "Global Governance in a Copernican World." *Global Governance* 18, no. 2: 133–48.

Johnson, Simon, and James Kwak. 2010. *13 Bankers: The Wall Street Takeover and the Next Financial Meltdown*. New York: Pantheon.

Johnston, Adrian, and Michael Trebilcock. 2013. "Fragmentation in International Trade Law: Insights from the Global Investment Regime." *World Trade Review* 12, no. 4: 621–52.

Johnston, A. Iain. 2001. "Treating International Institutions as Social Environments." *International Studies Quarterly* 45, no. 4: 487–515.

———. 2013. "How New and Assertive Is China's New Assertiveness?" *International Security* 37, no. 4: 7–48.

Jones, Bruce. 2014. *Still Ours to Lead: America, the Rising Powers, and the Myths of the Coming Disorder*. Washington, DC: Brookings Institution Press.

Jorda, Oscar, Moritz Schularick, and Alan Taylor. 2012. "When Credit Bites
    Back: Leverage, Business Cycles, and Crises." NBER Working Paper No.
    17621. Cambridge, MA. October.
Joyce, Joseph. 2013. *The IMF and Global Financial Crises*. New York: Cambridge
    University Press.
Kagan, Robert. 2012. *The World America Made*. New York: Vintage.
Kahler, Miles, ed. 2009. *Networked Politics: Agency, Power and Governance*.
    Ithaca, NY: Cornell University Press.
———. 2010. "Asia and the Reform of Global Governance." *Asian Economic Policy
    Review* 5, no. 2: 178–93.
———. 2013. "Economic Crisis and Global Governance: The Stability of a
    Globalized World." In Miles Kahler and David Lake, eds., *Politics in the
    New Hard Times: The Great Recession in Comparative Perspective*. Ithaca,
    NY: Cornell University Press.
Kahler, Miles, and David Lake, eds. 2013. *Politics in the New Hard Times: The
    Great Recession in Comparative Perspective*. Ithaca, NY: Cornell University Press.
Katzenstein, Peter, and Stephen Nelson. 2013. "Reading the Right Signals and
    Reading the Signals Right: IPE and the Financial Crisis of 2008." *Review of
    International Political Economy* 20, no. 5: 1101–131.
Katzenstein, Peter, and Rudra Sil. 2010. *Beyond Paradigms: Analytical Eclecticism
    in the Study of World Politics*. New York: Palgrave Macmillan.
Kee, Hiau Looi, Cristina Neagu, and Alessandro Nicita. 2013. "Is Protectionism
    on the Rise? Assessing National Trade Policies during the Crisis of 2008."
    Review of Economics and Statistics 95, no. 1: 342–56.
Kennedy, Matthew. 2010. "China's Role in WTO Dispute Settlement." *World
    Trade Review* 11, no. 4: 555–89.
Kennedy, Scott. 2010. "The Myth of the Beijing Consensus." *Journal of
    Contemporary China* 19, no. 65: 461–77.
Keohane, Robert O. 1980. "Theory of Hegemonic Stability and Changes in
    International Economic Regimes, 1967–1977," in Ole Holsti, Randolph
    Siverson, and Alexander George, eds., *Change in the International System*,
    131–62. Boulder, CO: Westview Press.
———. 1984. *After Hegemony*. Princeton, NJ: Princeton University Press.
———. 2009. "The Old IPE and the New." *Review of International Political
    Economy* 16, no. 1: 34–46.
———. 2012. "Hegemony and After." *Foreign Affairs* 91, no. 4: 114–18.
Keohane, Robert O., and Lisa L. Martin. 1995. "The Promise of Institutionalist
    Theory." *International Security* 20, no. 1: 39–51.
Khanna, Parag. 2008. *The Second World: Empires and Influence in the New
    Global Order*. New York: Random House.
Kim, Soo Yoen. 2013. "Protectionism During Recessions: Is This Time
    Different?" *Political Economist* 9, no. 2: 6–8.
Kinderman, Daniel. 2008. "The Political Economy of Sectoral Exchange Rate
    Preferences and Lobbying: Germany from 1960–2008, and Beyond." *Review
    of International Political Economy* 15, no. 5: 851–80.

Kindleberger, Charles. 1973. *The World in Depression, 1929–1939*. Berkeley: University of California Press.

——. 1978. *Manias, Panics and Crashes: A History of Financial Crises*. New York: Basic Books.

——. 1988. *The International Economic Order: Essays on Financial Crisis and International Public Goods*. Cambridge, MA: MIT Press.

King, Gary, Robert Keohane, and Sidney Verba. 1994. *Designing Social Inquiry: Scientific Inference in Qualitative Research*. Princeton, NJ: Princeton University Press.

Kirshner, Jonathan. 2013. "Bringing Them All Back Home? Dollar Diminution and U.S. Power." *Washington Quarterly* 36, no. 3: 27–45.

——. 2014. *American Power after the Financial Crisis*. Ithaca, NY: Cornell University Press.

Kotios, Angelos, and George Galanos. 2012. "The International Economic Crisis and the Crisis of Economics." *World Economy* 35, no. 7: 869–85.

Kono, Daniel Y. 2006. "Optimal Obfuscation: Democracy and Trade Policy Transparency." *American Political Science Review* 100, no. 3: 369–84.

Koremenos, Barbara, Charles Lipson, and Duncan Snidal, eds. 2001. *The Rational Design of International Institutions*. New York: Cambridge University Press.

KPMG. 2010. Report. "Basel III: Pressure Is Building," December. http://www.kpmg.at/uploads/media/Basel_3-Pressure_is_building_2010.pdf. Accessed July 2013.

Krasner, Stephen D. 1976. "State Power and the Structure of International Trade." *World Politics* 28, no. 3: 317–47.

——, ed. 1983. *International Regimes*. Ithaca, NY: Cornell University Press.

——. 1991. "Global Communications and National Power." *World Politics* 43, no. 3: 336–66.

Kreps, David. 1990. "Corporate Culture and Economic Theory." In James Alt and Kenneth A. Shepsle, eds., *Perspectives on Positive Political Economy*, 221–75. Cambridge: Cambridge University Press.

Krugman, Paul. 2012. *End This Depression Now!* New York: W. W. Norton.

——. 2013. "How the Case for Austerity Has Crumbled." *New York Review of Books*. June 6.

Kupchan, Charles. 2002. *The End of the American Era*. New York: Knopf.

——. 2012. No *One's World*. New York: Oxford University Press.

Kurlantzick, Joshua. 2013. *Democracy in Retreat*. New Haven, CT: Yale University Press.

Lake, David A. 1983. "International Economic Structures and American Foreign Economic Policy, 1887–1934." *World Politics* 35, no. 4: 517–43.

——. 1993. "Leadership, Hegemony, and the International Economy: Naked Emperor or Tattered Monarch with Potential?" *International Studies Quarterly* 37, no. 4: 459–89.

———. 2009. "Open Economy Politics: A Critical Review." *Review of International Organizations* 4, no. 3: 219–44.

Lall, Ranjit. 2012. "From Failure to Failure: The Politics of International Banking Regulation." *Review of International Political Economy* 19, no. 4: 609–38.

Lanteigne, Marc. 2013. "Fire over Water: China's Strategic Engagement of Somalia and the Gulf of Aden Crisis." *Pacific Review* 26, no. 3: 289–312.

Lasswell, Harold D., and Abraham Kaplan. 1950. *Power and Society: A Framework for Political Inquiry.* New Haven, CT: Yale University Press.

Layne, Christopher. 2012. "This Time It's Real: The End of Unipolarity and the *Pax Americana.*" *International Studies Quarterly* 56, no. 1: 203–13.

Lazer, David. 1999. "The Free Trade Epidemic of the 1860s and Other Outbreaks of Economic Discrimination." *World Politics* 51, no. 4: 447–83.

Legro, Jeffrey. 2005. *Rethinking the World: Great Power Strategies and International Order.* Ithaca, NY: Cornell University Press.

Leonard, Mark. 2005. *Why Europe Will Run the 21st Century.* New York: PublicAffairs.

Levinson, Marc. 2010. "Faulty Basel." *Foreign Affairs* 89, no. 3: 76–88.

Lewis, Michael. 2010. *The Big Short: Inside the Doomsday Machine.* New York: W. W. Norton.

Lieber, Robert. 2011. "Staying Power and the American Future: Problems of Primacy, Policy and Grand Strategy." *Journal of Strategic Studies* 34, no. 4: 509–30.

Lo, Andrew W. 2012. "Reading about the Financial Crisis: A Twenty-One-Book Review." *Journal of Economic Literature* 50, no. 1: 151–78.

Loser, Claudio. 2009. "Global Financial Turmoil and Emerging Market Economies: Major Contagion and a Shocking Loss of Wealth?" *Global Journal of Emerging Market Economies* 1, no. 2: 137–58.

Lowery, Clay. 2007. "Remarks on Sovereign Wealth Funds and the International Financial System," San Francisco, June 21. US Department of the Treasury. http://www.ustreas.gov/press/releases/hp471.htm. Accessed August 2008.

Luce, Edward. 2012. *Time to Start Thinking.* New York: Atlantic Monthly Press.

Lukes, Steven. 1974. *Power: A Radical View.* New York: Macmillan.

Lund, Susan, Toos Daruvala, Richard Dobbs, Philipp Härle, Ju-Hon Kwek, and Ricardo Falcón. 2013. *Financial Globalization: Retreat or Reset?* Washington, DC: McKinsey Global Institute.

Lyngen, Narissa. 2012. "Basel III: Dynamics of State Implementation." *Harvard International Law Journal* 53, no. 2: 519–49.

MacMillan, Margaret. 2013. "The Rhyme of History: Lessons of the Great War." The Brookings Essay. http://www.brookings.edu/research/essays/2013/rhyme-of-history, December.

Macroeconomic Advisers. 2013. "The Cost of Crisis-Driven Fiscal Policy."
    Prepared for the Peter G. Peterson Foundation. http://pgpf.org/
    special-reports/the-cost-of-crisis-driven-fiscal-policy, October.
Madsen, Jakob. 2001. "Trade Barriers and the Collapse of World Trade During
    the Great Depression." *Southern Economic Journal* 67, no. 4: 848–68.
Mahbubani, Kishore. 2008. "The Case against the West." *Foreign Affairs* 87, no.
    3: 111–25.
———. 2013. *The Great Convergence: Asia, the West, and the Logic of One World.*
    New York: PublicAffairs.
Makkai, Toni, and John Braithwaite. 1992. "In and Out of the Revolving
    Door: Making Sense of Regulatory Capture." *Journal of Public Policy* 12, no.
    1: 61–78.
Maliniak, Daniel, Susan Peterson, and Michael Tierney. 2012. "TRIP
    around the World: Teaching, Research, and Policy Views of International
    Relations Faculty in 20 Countries." Teaching, Research and International
    Policy Project, College of William and Mary, Williamsburg,
    VA. May.
Maloney, Suzanne. 2010. "Sanctioning Iran: If Only It Were So Simple."
    Washington Quarterly 33, no. 1: 131–47.
Mann, Thomas, and Norman Ornstein. 2012. *It's Even Worse Than It
    Looks: How the American Constitutional System Collided with the New Politics
    of Extremism.* New York: Basic Books.
Mansfield, Edward. 1992. "The Concentration of Capabilities and International
    Trade." *International Organization* 46, no. 6: 731–64.
———. 1994. *Power, Trade and War.* Princeton, NJ: Princeton University Press.
Mansfield, Edward, and Helen V. Milner. 2013. "Preferential Trade Agreements
    in Hard Times." *Political Economist* 9, no. 2: 9–12.
Mansfield, Edward, and Diana C. Mutz. 2009. "Support for Free
    Trade: Self-Interest, Sociotropic Politics, and Out-Group Anxiety."
    International Organization 63, no. 3: 425–57.
Martin, Lisa L. 1992a. *Coercive Cooperation: Explaining Multilateral Economic
    Sanctions.* Princeton, NJ: Princeton University Press.
———. 1992b. "Interests, Power, and Multilateralism." *International Organization*
    46, no. 4: 765–92.
Martin, Paul. 2006. "A Global Answer to Global Problems: The Case for a New
    Leaders' Forum." *Foreign Affairs* 84, no. 3: 2–6.
———. 2008. *Hell or High Water: My Life In and Out of Politics.*
    Toronto: Emblem.
Mason, D. S., L. Thibault, and L. Misener. 2006. "An Agency Theory
    Perspective on Corruption in Sport: The Case of the International Olympic
    Committee." *Journal of Sport Management* 20, no. 1: 52–73.
Mastanduno, Michael. 2009. "System Maker and Privilege Taker: U.S. Power
    and the International Political Economy." *World Politics* 61, no. 1: 121–54.
Mazower, Mark. 2012. *Governing the World: The History of an Idea.*
    New York: Penguin.

McKeown, Timothy. 1985. "Hegemonic Stability Theory and 19th Century Tariff Levels in Europe." *International Organization* 37, no. 1: 73–91.

McNally, Christopher A. 2012. "Sino-Capitalism: China's Reemergence and the International Political Economy." *World Politics* 64, no. 4: 741–76.

McNamara, Kathleen. 2008. "A Rivalry in the Making? The Euro and International Monetary Power." *Review of International Political Economy* 15, no. 3: 439–59.

Mearsheimer, John. 2010. "The Gathering Storm: China's Challenge to US Power in Asia." *Chinese Journal of International Politics* 3, no. 4: 381–96.

Meunier, Sophie. 2013. "The Dog That Did Not Bark: Anti-Americanism and the 2008 Financial Crisis in Europe." *Review of International Political Economy* 20, no. 1: 1–25.

Miller, Manjari Chatterjee. 2013. "India's Feeble Foreign Policy." *Foreign Affairs* 92, no. 4: 14–19.

Milner, Helen V. 1997. *Interests, Institutions and Information: Domestic Politics and International Relations*. Princeton, NJ: Princeton University Press.

Minsky, Hyman. 1986. *Stabilizing an Unstable Economy*. New York: McGraw-Hill.

Mishkin, Frederic. 2010. "Over the Cliff: From the Subprime to the Global Financial Crisis." NBER Working Paper No. 16609. Cambridge, MA. December.

Moe, Timothy, Caesar Maasry, and Richard Tang. 2010. "EM Equity in Two Decades: A Changing Landscape." Goldman Sachs Global Economics Paper No. 204. September 8.

Moravcsik, Andrew. 2009. "Europe: The Quiet Superpower." *French Politics* 7, no. 3: 403–22.

Morrow, James D. 1994. "Modeling the Forms of International Cooperation: Distribution versus Information." *International Organization* 48, no. 3: 387–87.

Nadelmann, Ethan. 1990. "Global Prohibition Regimes: The Evolution of Norms in International Society." *International Organization* 44, no. 2: 479–526.

Naím, Moisés. 2013. *The End of Power*. New York: Basic Books.

Naoi, Megumi, and Ikuo Kume. 2011. "Explaining Mass Support for Agricultural Protectionism: Evidence from a Survey Experiment during the Global Recession." *International Organization* 65, no. 4: 771–95.

Nathan, Andrew, and Andrew Scobell. 2012. "How China Sees America." *Foreign Affairs* 91, no. 5: 32–47.

National Intelligence Council. 2008. *Global Trends 2025: A Transformed World*. Washington, DC: US Government Printing Office. November.

———. 2010. *Global Governance 2025*. Washington, DC: US Government Printing Office. September.

Naughton, Barry. 2010. "China's Distinctive System: Can It Be a Model for Others?" *Journal of Contemporary China* 19, no. 65: 437–60.

Nel, Philip. 2010. "Redistribution and Recognition: What Emerging Regional Powers Want." *Review of International Studies* 36, no. 4: 951–74.

Newman, Abraham, and Elliot Posner. 2011. "International Interdependence and Regulatory Power: Authority, Mobility, and Markets." *European Journal of International Relations* 17, no. 4: 589–610.

Nolan, Peter. 2012. *Is China Buying the World?* London: Polity.

Norrlof, Carla. 2010. *America's Global Advantage: U.S. Hegemony and International Cooperaion*. Cambridge: Cambridge University Press.

Norton Rose. 2008. "Sovereign Wealth Funds and the Global Private Equity Landscape." June. http://www.nortonrosefulbright.com/knowledge/ publications/15287/sovereign-wealth-funds-and-the-global-private-equity-land scape-survey. Accessed December 2013.

Nye, John. 2007. *War, Wine, and Taxes: The Political Economy of Anglo-French Trade, 1689–1900*. Princeton, NJ: Princeton University Press.

Nye, Joseph. 1990. "Soft Power." *Foreign Policy*, no. 80: 153–71.

———. 2004. *Soft Power: The Means to Success in World Politics*. New York: Public Affairs.

———. 2011. *The Future of Power*. New York: PublicAffairs.

Nyhan, Brendan, and Jason Reifler. 2010. "When Corrections Fail: The Persistence of Political Misperceptions." *Political Behavior* 32, no 2: 303–30.

Oatley, Thomas. 2011. "The Reductionist Gamble: Open Economy Politics in the Global Economy." *International Organization* 65, no. 2: 311–41.

Oatley, Thomas, and Robert Nabors. 1998. "Redistributive Cooperation: Market Failure, Wealth Transfers, and the Basel Accord." *International Organization* 52, no. 1: 35–54.

Oatley, Thomas, W. Kindred Winecoff, Andrew Pennock, and Sarah Bauerle Danzman. 2013. "The Political Economy of Global Finance: A Network Model." *Perspectives on Politics* 11, no. 1: 133–53.

Obstfeld, Maurice. 2012. "Financial Flows, Financial Crises, and Global Imbalances." *Journal of International Money and Finance* 31, no. 3: 469–80.

Organization for Economic Cooperation and Development. 2008. *Sovereign Wealth Funds and Recipient Country Policies*. Paris: OECD.

OECD and UNCTAD. 2012. "7th Report on G20 Investment Measures." http://www.wto.org/english/news_e/news12_e/igo_31may12_e.htm. Accessed July 10, 2012.

———. 2013. "9th Report on G20 Investment Measures." June 17. http://www.wto.org/english/news_e/news13_e/igo_17jun13_e.htm. Accessed June 24, 2013.

Ostry, Jonathan, Atish R. Ghosh, Karl Habermeier, Marcos Chamon, Mahvash S. Qureshi, and Dennis B. S. Reinhardt. 2010. "Capital Inflows: The Role of Controls." IMF Staff Position Note SPN/10/04. February 19.

Ozgercin, Kevin. 2012. "Seeing like the BIS on Capital Rules: Institutionalising Self-Regulation in Global Finance." *New Political Economy* 17, no. 1: 97–116.

Palmer, Donald, and Michael Maher. 2010. "The Mortgage Meltdown as Normal Accidental Wrongdoing." *Strategic Organization* 8, no. 1: 83–91.

Patrick, Stewart. 2010. "Irresponsible Stakeholders?" *Foreign Affairs* 89, no. 6: 44–53.

———. 2014. "The Unruled World: The Case for Good Enough Global Governance." *Foreign Affairs* 93, no. 1: 58–73.

Paulson, Henry. 2010. *On the Brink*. New York: Business Plus.

Pearson, Margaret M. 2001. "The Case of China's Accession to GATT/WTO." In David M. Lampton, ed., *The Making of Chinese Foreign and Security Policy in the Era of Reform, 1978–2000*. Palo Alto, CA: Stanford University Press.

Pepinsky, Thomas. 2012. "The Global Economic Crisis and the Politics on Non-Transitions," *Government and Opposition* 47, no. 2: 135–61.

Pettis, Michael. 2011. "China's Troubled Transition to a More Balanced Growth Model." New America Foundation. March 1. http://newamerica. net/publications/policy/china_s_troubled_transition_to_a_more_balanced_ growth_model. Accessed July 2013.

———. 2013. *The Great Rebalancing: Trade, Conflict, and the Perilous Road Ahead for the World Economy*. Princeton, NJ: Princeton University Press.

Philippon, Thomas, and Ariell Reshef. 2013. "An International Look at the Growth of Modern Finance." *Journal of Economic Perspectives* 27, no. 2: 73–96.

Pierson, Paul. 2004. *Politics in Time: History, Institutions, and Social Analysis*. Princeton, NJ: Princeton University Press, 2004.

Pinker, Steven. 2011. *The Better Angels of Our Nature: Why Violence Has Declined*. New York: Viking.

Ploch, Lauren, et al. 2011. "Piracy off the Horn of Africa." Congressional Research Service Report No. R40528. Washington, DC. April.

Ponticelli, Jacopo, and Hans-Joachim Voth. 2011. "Austerity and Anarchy: Budget Cuts and Social Unrest in Europe, 1919–2008." CEPR Discussion Paper 8513.

Porter, Michael, and Jan Rivkin. 2012. "Prosperity at Risk: Findings of Harvard Business School's Survey on U.S. Competitiveness." Harvard Business School US Competitiveness Project. Cambridge, MA. http://www.hbs.edu/ competitiveness/pdf/hbscompsurvey.pdf. Accessed July 2013.

Posner, Richard. 2009. *A Failure of Capitalism*. Cambridge, MA: Harvard University Press.

Prasad, Eswar. 2014. *The Dollar Trap: How the U.S. Dollar Tightened Its Grip on Global Finance*. Princeton, NJ: Princeton University Press.

Prasad, Eswar, and Isaac Sorkin. 2009. "Assessing the G-20 Stimulus Plans: A Deeper Look," Brookings Institution, Washington, DC. March.

Putnam, Robert, and Nicholas Bayne. 1987. *Hanging Together: Cooperation and Conflict in the Seven-Power Summits*. Cambridge, MA: Harvard University Press.

Quah, Danny. 2011. "The Global Economy's Shifting Centre of Gravity." *Global Policy* 2, no. 1: 3–9.

Quiggin, John. 2010. *Zombie Economics: How Dead Ideas Still Walk among Us*. Princeton, NJ: Princeton University Press.

Rachman, Gideon. 2011. *Zero-Sum Future: American Power in an Age of Anxiety*. New York: Simon and Schuster.

Rajan, Raghuram. 2010. *Fault Lines*. Princeton, NJ: Princeton University Press.

Ramo, Joshua Cooper. 2004. *The Beijing Consensus*. London: Foreign Policy Centre.

Reich, Simon, and Richard Ned Lebow. 2014. *Goodbye Hegemony! Power and Influence in the Global System*. Princeton, NJ: Princeton University Press.

Reilly, James. 2012. "China's Unilateral Sanctions." *Washington Quarterly* 35, no. 4: 121–33.

Reinhart, Carmen, and Vincent Reinhart. 2010. "After the Fall." National Bureau of Economic Research Working Paper No. 16334. Cambridge, MA. September.

Reinhart, Carmen, and Kenneth Rogoff. 2009. *This Time Is Different: Eight Centuries of Financial Folly*. Princeton, NJ: Princeton University Press.

———. 2010. "Growth in a Time of Debt." National Bureau of Economic Research Working Paper No. 15639. Cambridge, MA.

Rey, Hélène. 2013. "Dilemma Not Trilemma: The Global Financial Cycle and Monetary Policy Independence." Mimeo. London Business School. August.

Rickards, James. 2011. *Currency Wars: The Making of the Next Global Crisis*. New York: Portfolio.

RIPE editors. 2009. "RIPE Reading List on the Financial Crisis." *Review of International Political Economy* 16, No. 5: 743–45.

Roach, Stephen. 2009. "Manchurian Paradox." *National Interest*, no. 101: 59–65.

Rodrik, Dani. 2007. *One Economics, Many Recipes: Globalization, Institutions, and Economic Growth*. Princeton, NJ: Princeton University Press.

———. 2011a. *The Globalization Paradox*. New York: W. W. Norton.

———. 2011b. "The Future of Economic Convergence." National Bureau of Economic Research Working Paper No. 17400. Cambridge, MA. September.

———. 2014. "When Ideas Trump Interests: Preferences, Worldviews, and Policy Innovations." *Journal of Economic Perspectives* 28, no. 1: 189–208.

Rogers, Paul. 2008. "The Tipping Point?" Oxford Research Group Security Report. London. November. http://www.oxfordresearchgroup.org.uk/sites/default/files/thetippingpoint_0.pdf. Accessed July 3, 2012.

Rogowski, Ronald. 1989. *Commerce and Coalitions*. Princeton, NJ: Princeton University Press.

Rose, Andrew K. 2012. "Protectionism Isn't Counter-Cyclic (Anymore)." National Bureau of Economic Research Working Paper No. 18062. Cambridge, MA. May.

Roubini, Nouriel, and Steven Mihm. 2010. *Crisis Economics*. New York: Penguin Press.

Roxburgh, Charles, Susan Lund, and John Piotrowski. 2011. *Mapping Global Capital Markets 2011*. Washington, DC: McKinsey Global Institute.

Roxburgh, Charles, Susan Lund, Toos Daruvala, James Manyika, Richard Dobbs, Ramon Forn, and Karen Croxson. 2012. *Debt and Deleveraging: Uneven Progress on the Path to Growth*. Washington, DC: McKinsey Global Institute. January.

Ruddy, Brendan. 2010. "The Critical Success of the WTO: Trade Policies of the Current Economic Crisis." *Journal of International Economic Law* 13, no. 2: 475–95.

Ruggie, John Gerard. 1982. "International Regimes, Transactions, and Change: Embedded Liberalism in the Postwar Economic Order." *International Organization* 36, no. 2: 379–415.

Samans, Richard, Klaus Schwab, and Mark Malloch-Brown. 2011. "Running the World, After the Crash." *Foreign Policy*, no. 184: 80–83.

Sanderson, Henny, and Michael Forsythe. 2013. *China's Superbank: Debt, Oil and Influence: How China Development Bank Is Rewriting the Rules of Finance*. New York: Bloomberg Press.

Schirm, Stefan A. 2009. "Ideas and Interests in Global Financial Governance: Comparing German and US Preference Formation." *Cambridge Review of International Affairs* 22, no. 3: 501–21.

Schlieritz, Mark. 2013. "The Power of Ideas: Why Germany Is So Different and What It Means for the World." German Marshall Fund of the United States. Washington, DC. September.

Schwab, Susan. 2011. "After Doha." *Foreign Affairs* 90, no. 3: 104–17.

Schwartz, Herman. 2009. *Subprime Nation: American Power, Global Capital, and the Housing Bubble*. Ithaca, NY: Cornell University Press.

Schweller, Randal. 1998. *Deadly Imbalances*. New York: Columbia University Press.

———. 2011. "Emerging Powers in an Age of Disorder." *Global Governance* 17, no. 3: 285–97.

———. 2014. *Maxwell's Demon and the Golden Apple: Global Discord in the New Millennium*. Baltimore, MD: Johns Hopkins University Press.

Schweller, Randall, and Xiaoyu Pu. 2011. "After Unipolarity: China's Visions of International Order in an Era of U.S. Decline." *International Security* 36, no. 1: 41–72.

Scowcroft, Brent. 2012. "A World of Transformation." *National Interest*, no. 119: 8–11.

Seabrooke, Leonard, and Eleni Tsingou. 2009. "Revolving Doors and Linked Ecologies in the World Economy: Policy Locations and the Practice of International Financial Reform." Working Paper. University of Warwick. Centre for the Study of Globalisation and Regionalisation, Coventry, UK.

Shambaugh, David. 2013. *China Goes Global: The Partial Power*. New York: Oxford University Press.

Sharma, Ruchir. 2012. "Broken BRICs: Why the Rest Stopped Rising." *Foreign Affairs* 91, no. 6: 2–7.

Siles-Brügge, Gabriel. 2014. "Explaining the Resilience of Free Trade: The Smoot-Hawley Myth and the Crisis." *Review of International Political Economy*: forthcoming. (Online version available at http://dx.doi.org/10.1080/09692290.2013.830979.)

Simmons, Beth A. 1994. *Who Adjusts?* Princeton, NJ: Princeton University Press.

———. 2009. *Mobilizing for Human Rights: International Law in Domestic Politics.* New York: Cambridge University Press.

Singer, David Andrew. 2007. *Regulating Capital: Setting Standards for the International Financial System.* Ithaca, NY: Cornell University Press.

Skidelsky, Robert. 2009. "Where Do We Go from Here?" *Prospect.* January.

Slaughter, Anne-Marie. 2009. "America's Edge: Power in the Networked Century." *Foreign Affairs* 88, no. 1: 94–113.

Snidal, Duncan. 1985. "The Limits of Hegemonic Stability Theory." *International Organization* 39, no. 4: 579–97.

Snidal, Duncan, and Kenneth Abbott. 2000. "Hard and Soft Law in International Governance." *International Organization* 54, no. 3: 421–56.

Sobel, Mark, and Louellen Stedman. 2006. "The Evolution of the G-7 and Economic Policy Coordination." US Treasury Department Occasional Paper No. 3. Washington, DC. July.

Sohn, Injoo. 2013. "Between Confrontation and Assimilation: China and the Fragmentation of Global Financial Governance." *Journal of Contemporary China* 22, no. 82: 630–48.

Song, Guoyou, and Wei Jin Yuan. 2012. "China's Free Trade Agreement Strategies." *Washington Quarterly* 35, no. 3: 107–19.

Sorkin, Andrew Ross. 2009. *Too Big to Fail.* New York: Viking Press.

Soskice, David W., and Peter Hall, eds. 2001. *Varieties of Capitalism: The Institutional Foundations of Comparative Advantage.* Oxford: Oxford University Press.

Starrs, Sean. 2013. "American Economic Power Hasn't Declined—It Globalized! Summoning the Data and Taking Globalization Seriously." *International Studies Quarterly* 57, no. 4: 817–30.

Steffek, Jens. 2003. "The Legitimation of International Governance: A Discourse Approach." *European Journal of International Relations* 9, no. 2: 249–75.

Steil, Benn. 2010. "Debt and Systemic Risk: The Contribution of Fiscal and Monetary Policy." *Cato Journal* 30, no. 2: 391–96.

Stein, Arthur. 1984. "The Hegemon's Dilemma: Great Britain, the United States, and the International Economic Order." *International Organization* 38, no. 2: 355–86.

Steinfeld, Edward. 2010. *Playing Our Game: Why China's Rise Doesn't Threaten the West.* New York: Oxford University Press.

Stiglitz, Joseph. 2002. *Globalization and Its Discontents.* New York: W. W. Norton.

———. 2013. *The Price of Inequality.* New York: W. W. Norton.

Stokes, Doug. 2013. "Achilles' Deal: Dollar Decline and US Grand Strategy after the Crisis." *Review of International Political Economy:* forthcoming.

Strange, Susan. 1987. "The Persistent Myth of Lost Hegemony." *International Organization* 41, no. 4: 551–74.

Subramanian, Arvind. 2011. *Eclipse: Living in the Shadow of China's Economic Dominance.* Washington, DC: Peterson Institute for International Economics.

————. 2013. "Preserving the Open Global Economic System: A Strategic Blueprint for China and the United States." Peterson Institute for International Economics PB13-16. Washington, DC. June.

Subramanian, Arvind, and Martin Kessler. 2013. "The Hyperglobalization of Trade and Its Future." Peterson Institute for International Economics Working Paper 13-6, July. Washington, DC. http://www.iie.com/publications/wp/wp13-6.pdf.

Temin, Peter, and David Vines. 2013. *The Leaderless Economy: Why the World Economic System Fell Apart and How to Fix It.* Princeton, NJ: Princeton University Press.

Themnér, Lotta, and Peter Wallensteen. 2012. "Armed Conflicts, 1946–2011." *Journal of Peace Research* 49, no. 4: 565–75.

Thirkell-White, Ben. 2009. "Dealing with the Banks: Populism and the Public Interest in the Global Financial Crisis." *International Affairs* 85, no. 4: 689–711.

Trichet, Jean-Claude. 2010. "The Changing World of Global Governance." Keynote address to Institute of International Finance, Spring Membership Meeting. Vienna. June 10. http://www.bis.org/review/r100615b.pdf?frames=0. Accessed July 2013.

Truman, Ted. 2010. *Sovereign Wealth Funds: Threat or Salvation?* Washington, DC: Peterson Institute for International Economics.

Underhill, Geoffrey, and Xiaoke Zhang. 2008. "Setting the Rules: Private Power, Political Underpinnings, and Legitimacy in Global Monetary and Financial Governance." *International Affairs* 84, no. 3: 535–54.

United Nations Conference on Trade and Development. 2013. *Global Value Chains: Investment for Trade and Development.* World Investment Report. New York.

United Nations Development Programme. 2013. *2013 Human Development Report.* New York: UNDP.

U.S. Council of Economic Advisers. 2013. "Economic Activity during the Government Shutdown and Debt Limit Brinksmanship." Office of the President. White House.gov. October 25, 2013. http://www.whitehouse.gov/sites/default/files/docs/weekly_indicators_report_final.pdf.

U.S. Government Accountability Office. 2013. "U.S. and International Sanctions Have Adversely Affected the Iranian Economy." GAO-13-326. February 15. http://www.gao.gov/assets/660/652314.pdf. Accessed October 25, 2013.

van Rixtel, Adrian, and Nicholas Vause. 2012. "Highlights of the BIS International Statistics." *BIS Quarterly Review* (June): 11–24.

Véron, Nicolas. 2012. "Financial Reform after the Crisis: An Early Assessment." Peterson Institute for International Economics Working Paper 12-2. Washington, DC. January. http://www.iie.com/publications/wp/wp12-2.pdf.

Vitali, Stefania, James B. Glattfelder, and Stefano Battiston. 2011. "The Network of Global Corporate Control." PLOS One 6, no. 10: e25995.

Wallace, Jeremy. 2011. "Authoritarian Information Problems: Data Manipulation in China." Unpublished manuscipt, The Ohio State University.

Wang, Hongying, and Erik French. 2013. "China's Participation in Global Governance from a Comparative Perspective." *Asia Policy* 15, no. 1: 89–114.

Wang, Jisi. 2012. "Understanding Strategic Distrust: The Chinese Side." In Ken Leiberthal and Wang Jisi, *Assessing U.S.-China Strategic Distrust*. Washington, DC: Brookings Institution.

Webb, Michael. 1995. *The Political Economy of Policy Coordination: International Adjustment since 1945*. Ithaca, NY: Cornell University Press, 1995.

Weiss, Thomas, and Rorden Wilkinson. 2013. "Rethinking Global Governance? Complexity, Authority, Power, Change." *International Studies Quarterly*: forthcoming.

Wendt, Alexander. 1999. *Social Theory of International Politics*. Cambridge: Cambridge University Press.

Whitehead, Barbara Dafoe. 2008. "A Nation in Debt." *American Interest* 3, no. 6: 12–25.

Wilf, Meredith. 2013. "A Stake in the International: US Banks and Basel III Regulatory Announcements." Unpublished manuscript, Princeton University.

Willett, Thomas. 1999. "Developments in the Political Economy of Policy Coordination." *Open Economies Review* 10, no. 2: 221–53.

Williamson, John. 1990. "What Washington Means by Policy Reform." In John Williamson, ed., *Latin American Adjustment: How Much Has Happened?* Pp. 7–20. Washington, DC: Institute for International Economics.

———. 2012. "Is the 'Beijing Consensus' Now Dominant?" *Asia Policy* 13, no. 1: 1–16.

Wilson, Bruce. 2007. "Compliance by WTO Members with Adverse WTO Dispute Settlement Rulings: The Record to Date." *Journal of International Economic Law* 10, no. 2: 397–403.

Wilson, Dominic, and Roopa Purushothaman. 2003. "Dreaming with BRICs: The Path to 2050." Goldman Sachs Global Economics Paper No. 99, New York, October.

Woetzel, Jonathan, Janamitra Devan, Richard Dobbs, Adam Eichner, Stefano Negri, and Micah Rowland. 2009. *If You've Got It, Spend It: Unleashing the Chinese Consumer*. New York: McKinsey Global Institute.

Wohlforth, William C. 1999. "The Stability of a Unipolar World." *International Security* 24, no. 1: 5–41.

Wolf, Martin. 2004. *Why Globalization Works*. New Haven, CT: Yale University Press.

Wolfe, Robert. 2012. "Protectionism and Multilateral Accountability during the Great Recession: Inferences from Dogs Not Barking." *Journal of World Trade* 46, no. 4: 777–813.

Woolridge, Adrian. 2012. "The Visible Hand: Special Report on State Capitalism." *Economist*. January 21.

World Bank. 2010. "World Bank Group Reform: An Update." September 30. http://siteresources.worldbank.org/DEVCOMMINT/ Documentation/22723851/DC2010-0014(E)Reform.pdf. Accessed June 12, 2013.

———. 2011. *Multipolarity: The New Global Economy*. Global Development Horizons 2011. Washington, DC. http://siteresources.worldbank.org/ INTGDH/Resources/GDH_CompleteReport2011.pdf.

———. 2013. Migration and Development Brief 21, October 2. http://siteresources.worldbank.org/INTPROSPECTS/ Resources/334934-1288990760745/MigrationandDevelopmentBrief21.pdf. Accessed October 15, 2013.

World Economic Forum. 2012. "Global Agenda Council on Geopolitical Risk." Davos Klosters, Switzerland, January 29.

———. 2013. *Global Competitiveness Report 2012–2013*. Davos: WEF.

World Trade Organization. 2012. "Regional Trade Agreements Information System." http://rtais.wto.org/UI/PublicMaintainRTAHome.aspx. Accessed July 3, 2012.

———. 2013. "WTO Report on G-20 Trade Measures." June 17. http://www.wto. org/english/news_e/news13_e/igo_17jun13_e.htm. Accessed June 20, 2013.

Xing, Yuqing, and Neal C. Detert. 2010. "How the iPhone Widens the United States Trade Deficit with the People's Republic of China." Asian Development Bank Institute Working Paper No. 257. Tokyo, Japan. December.

Yergin, Daniel, and Joseph Stanislaw. 1997. *The Commanding Heights*. New York: Simon and Schuster.

Young, Kevin L. 2012. "Transnational Regulatory Capture? An Empirical Examination of the Transnational Lobbying of the Basel Committee on Banking Supervision." *Review of International Political Economy* 19, no. 4: 663–88.

———. 2013. "Financial Industry Groups' Adaptation to the Post-Crisis Regulatory Environment: Changing Approaches to the Policy Cycle." *Regulation & Governance* 7, no. 4: 460–80.

Yu, Hong. 2014. The Ascendancy of State-Owned Enterprises in China: Development, Controversy and Problems. *Journal of Contemporary China* 23, no. 85: 161–82.

Zakaria, Fareed. 2008. *The Post-American World*. New York: W. W. Norton.

Zaring, David. 2009/10. "International Institutional Performance in Crisis." *Chicago Journal of International Law* 10, no. 2: 475–504.

Zhang, Xiaowen, and Xiaoling Li. 2014. "The Politics of Compliance with Adverse WTO Dispute Settlement Rulings in China." *Journal of Contemporary China* 23, no. 85: 143–60.

Zhu, Wenli. 2001. "International Political Economy from a Chinese Angle."
     Journal of Contemporary China 10, no. 1: 45–54.
Zoellick, Robert. 2005. "Whither China: From Membership to Responsibility?"
     Remarks to the National Committee on U.S.-China Relations, New York
     City, September 21. http://2001-2009.state.gov/s/d/former/zoellick/
     rem/53682.htm. Accessed July 3, 2013.

INDEX